Calling Back Your Power

To Andre –
Here's to joy & the "All"
living from the
that you are!

Susette Faith Foster

Calling Back Your Power

Suzette Faith Foster

Meet Suzette Online
Blog: CallingBackYourPower.com

Front cover: Lee Aldridge photographed Suzette in Duke Forest, Durham, North Carolina (2010). Lee also contributed to the cover design. www.LeeAldridge.com
Cover design created by Katie Baker of Baker Ad Design.
Charlotte, North Carolina 704-846-4307

First Printing November, 2011
Published by Choose 2 Thrive Publishing

ISBN: 978-0-9848421-0-0 (Paperback)

Author's note

I am sharing information that I have learned and/or experienced personally or with clients to help you make informed decisions. I am offering safe, non-invasive options to help you achieve optimal health.

I am not a doctor and I am not practicing medicine. I am a holistic wellness practitioner who understands how the body works energetically and offers energetic rebalancing.

My work is not intended to be a substitute for the diagnosis or advice from your doctor or other qualified licensed professionals. A conscious effort has been made to present information that is both accurate and truthful.

To you, dear reader and
to the three most important women in my life: my mother
Marie, thanks for your unwavering love and to my daughters,
Brianna and Brittany, thanks for adding such richness and
depth to the fabric of my life.

Acknowledgements

First and foremost, I am grateful for the oneness I AM with the infinite, intelligent field of consciousness that I call God, Spirit, which orchestrated the quality of support I have received in getting this book to print. I extend my deep appreciation and gratitude to the following folks.

My editor, Cassandra Khan, has heard me say "Thanks so much!" so many times and, yet, it is still not enough for all that she is and all that she has brought to me and this book. Her knowledge of writing and love for these teachings has made the editing process a joy.

Thanks to Amy Simpson and Shakiria Howie for their positive comments and suggestions in reviewing and editing several chapters.

To Lee Aldridge, photographer extraordinaire, for her photography and original cover design; to Katie Baker, of Baker Ad Design, whose creativity always delivers—giving the cover more graphic elements; and to Callee Maher whose breadth of numerology expertise helped me choose the book title and the chapter titles. And thanks to George Salmi for creating my book video trailer.

Friends contributed valuable time and feedback. Thanks to Robin Joy Bickford, Lu Hillman, Joseph Asterita, Worth Durgin and Michael Bannan. And to Sandi Baron who gave me invaluable guidance on raising the quality of my writing. She also encouraged me to attend the Mid West

Writer's Workshop in Indiana. What a high-quality, passion-driven conference.

Thanks to my virtual assistant, Andrea Armstrong, for her caring support and continual technological expertise.

Kudos to Christine Kloser's Transformational Authors Program for easing the writing and publishing process and enlightening transformational authors.

Sharon Wood, an exceptional writing teacher, fanned the flames of my desire to take my writing to the next level.

Much love and gratitude to my daughter Brittany who allowed me to share our challenges with the hope others could learn from our experiences. And thank you to my clients who allowed me to enlighten others with their stories.   A "delicious" thank you to Kelly Marra, my raw food chef. She maximized my time at the keyboard and prepared me with a variety of tasty and nutritious food.

Big thanks to Unity Church of Raleigh and my Grace Circle of friends for keeping me in their prayers and providing me with such loving support.

Again, thanks to those mentioned above and those not mentioned who, in some way, encouraged me in the writing of this book. I am blessed to be touched by your Light.

Contact information:

Editor, Cassandra	713-382-4342
Photography, Lee	LeeAldridge.com
Baker Ad Design, Katie	704-846-4307
Virtual Assistant, Andrea	setms.com
Numerology, Callee	707-779-9865
Raw Food Chef, Kelly	RawLifeCoaching.com

Calling Back Your Power

Suzette Faith Foster

Table of Contents

Chapter 9
The Creative Genius of Spirit (Cont.)
>   Spiritual Guidance—On Short Notice
>   Spiritual Guidance—Connecting with Others
>   Spiritual Guidance—Some Are Not Ready to Receive
>   It.

How Spirit Comforts You
>   Using Red Cardinals as a Sign
>   Using a Martini as a Sign
>   Your Pets Will Connect with You from Spirit
>   Spiritual Guidance—May Seem to Change Its Mind

Diamonds In the Rough
>   Learning and Growing Through Relationships
>   Changing Your Perspective
>   You are a Masterpiece in the Making
>   Honoring Other People's Journeys

Good, Good Vibrations
>   Letting Go of Controlling the Outcome
>   Befriend Your Feelings
>   Today's To-Do List: Feel Good

LAFTER as Medicine

The Alchemy of Change
>   Layer by Layer You Clear… Getting to Your Next Best
>   Level
>   Dealing with Hurt
>   The "Journey" Rewarded my Clients with Inner Peace

Introduction

Promise me that you'll give faith a fighting chance
And when you get the choice to sit it out or dance
I hope you dance...I hope you dance.

Inspired by Lee Ann Womack's song, Mark Sanders and Tia Sillers wrote the book *I Hope You Dance*. My friend Andrea gave me this little treasure in November of 2005 and wrote inside its cover, "To celebrate the day you dance again. I hope you heal quickly."

I have always loved to dance. I find it a form of celebration. My kitchen floor often becomes the dance space on which I glide and turn as high energy songs inspire me to express my joy. I love the freedom of dancing at home, totally oblivious to style or grace, simply engaging in the bliss of the moment.

Dancing is also the balm that soothes the pain of challenging life experiences. Dancing helped me feel better as I faced heartache and feelings of failure while my marriage was dissolving. Dancing lessened my gut-wrenching pain when my daughter chose a destructive path of depression, drugs and suicide attempts. Dancing shifted my mood through those difficult times and, even now, when life feels so good, I dance. I choose to dance.

1

My friends are used to my dancing even when there isn't a dance floor. I allow the rhythm to move through me; all I need is space and music. I even danced this morning at the local organic farmers' market. I expected to pick up a few veggies and return to write when I found my neighbors Karl and Matt playing guitars and singing "Margaritaville." What a great touch, music at a farmer's market. So, at 10 o'clock on a Saturday morning, I stayed for several songs and every fiber of my being just had to dance! Thanks, guys.

I appreciate dancing even more since my life-altering injury on November 3, 2005. I had a crucial choice to *sit it out or dance*. I was instantly paralyzed from a mountain biking accident. Moments later, I stopped breathing. I had the same injury as Christopher Reeve.

I gave faith a fighting chance. I chose to dance.

My doctor, Robert E. Isaacs, Director of Spine Surgery at Duke University Medical Center, said that my injury "was pretty graphic—historically, it is one people do not survive." And, with the severity of my spinal cord injury, my prognosis for mobility was terrible.

I created a very different outcome. I embraced the full capacity of who I believe we really are limitless spiritual and energetic beings. My results surpassed my doctor's expectations with what many would call two medical miracles: regaining my breath and becoming fully functioning. I am an example that miracles can occur or, when we change our perspective, be created and are available to each of us more than we realize.

Five years before I broke my neck, I was guided to my passion and path of service as a holistic wellness facilitator, teacher and speaker. I give credit for my phenomenal recovery to my belief in the teachings and processes I share in this book. The time I devoted to my spiritual expansion ended up providing the wisdom and inner conviction that saved my life.

At that critical juncture between life and death, I stayed in the moment, tapped into my infinite, ever-present inner wisdom and Higher Power, and held tight to my trust that *everything* is in divine order. The teachings and beliefs within these pages explain why I was able to create such an unexpected outcome and how I learned to emotionally and physically "dance" through many of life's challenges.

Come dance with me. These "dance steps" helped me choose calm over chaos and helped me turn my life around. I'll show you how I released limitations and refused to accept the status quo. I believe we are all here on a special spiritual journey to attain our highest potential.

My clients dramatically improve their life situations when they relate to them from a spiritual and energetic perspective. They learn to view their bodies, thoughts, situations and even the universe as subtle energy fields moldable by their minds, intentions and feelings.

Stress, anger and resentment in fact, all negative emotions—block the flow of life-enhancing energy. Our sessions balance these subtle energy fields. Emotional pain and physical symptoms go away as the healthy energy flow returns.

Life coaching, energy and sound healing sessions help clients cancel scheduled surgery; avoid exhaustive and expensive medical treatment; get off prescription medicine; release pain, depression and addiction; and feel more peace and joy in their daily lives. One client healed her cancer in five sessions. My clients were ready for the personal freedom that they wanted and deserved. They were willing to see life from a different perspective.

If you are already aligned with mind, body and spirit awareness, you have an opportunity to move into a deeper knowing and deeper owning of these teachings. If you find these results surprising, that is okay. Consider that we have learned throughout life to look for answers to health problems outside of ourselves in surgery and medication. *Calling Back Your Power* offers a fresh perspective.

If you look at the world from a purely scientific view, I invite you to research the teachings of quantum physics that I mention in chapter 3. You will find information from world-renowned researchers at prestigious universities who have uncovered evidence supporting the spiritual and energetic truths that have been practiced for millennia. Western medicine is perplexed at my remarkable results, though they are explained by and align with ancient spiritual teachings and the 80-year-old science of quantum physics.

If you come from a biblically-based background, you will recognize many of these truths. For example, "Let God transform you into a new person by changing the way you think" (Romans 12:2); or "Whatsoever ye shall ask in prayer *believing*, ye shall receive" (Matthew 21:22); and "Therefore I tell you, whatever you ask for in prayer, believe that you have received it, and it will be yours" (Mark 11:24).

If you believe God has failed you and you question any Higher Power, I invite you to read this book with an open mind. And while doing so, affirm that you will *feel and know* the Truth of *your* Being.

There are as many spiritual beliefs offering avenues to explore as there are names representing the one Higher Power. While reading this book, be open to pondering and then deepening your faith in this energetic Universe and in your innate power. Nothing has to be forced. Relax and be open to the Divine working through you, for you.

In life, spiritual evolution is a given, although the amount of pain, disease and difficulty is optional. Yes, I said optional. You deserve to find the options and answers—the freedom— that is divinely yours.

I had embarked on this journey before I needed these principles for my ultimate ordeal—my biking incident. Was I perfect in my work with these principles? No. I had, and still have, plenty of life trials with which to *practice* these principles. But, these teachings resonate with me and I am consistent in my efforts. I learned the value of being present in the moment and of reacting from empowerment, not fear. My preparation gave me the awareness and spiritual strength I needed at the pivotal moment I stopped breathing and throughout my recovery.

Inviting You to Dance

I invite you to take the incremental or giant steps that create your own personal dance as you journey through life. Hear the songs that are calling you to move at your right and perfect tempo. Let no one step on your toes! Practice your dance steps over and over as you move through life's struggles, deepen your beliefs and grow your confidence. Your own positive results will multiply. Your life will transform right before your eyes.

I'm writing this book from my heart, hoping to help you know who you really are and what you came here to be. This book offers you a shift in consciousness which leads to better life experiences. It will help you "remember" more fully your essence. I offer *Calling Back Your Power* to you, dear reader.

Spirit is using this book as a portal to higher awareness. The consciousness, energetically imbued within its pages, will quicken the dissolution of your fears, programming and limited beliefs, while awakening you to your next level of spiritual expansion.

How I Became Interested in the Mind, Body, and Spirit Connection

I often get asked how I started down this path. The short answer is we are always guided for our destiny path's highest good. The longer answer follows.

In the mid 1990s, my former husband's job transfer moved our family from Maine to North Carolina. I brought with me the book *Women's Bodies, Women's Wisdom,* written by Christiane Northrup, MD. She is highly recognized and respected for her holistic medical knowledge. I aligned with her teachings and over the years my respect and appreciation for this pioneer and visionary has deepened. Over the last thirty years, she has persevered with integrity in leading women to a deeper understanding of holistic medicine and their own innate wisdom.

People align to different books and teachings as they move through life. As you read this book, you may resonate with some thoughts, not others. My words may clarify feelings and ideas that you have, or at other times you may feel resistance to them. Please set aside the ones that bring up resistance and focus on what feels right to you. You align more to your spiritual essence by not seeing ideas as right or wrong but rather as not being for you at this time.

I did that while reading *Women's Bodies, Women's Wisdom.* I skipped over the chapter on the chakras. Chakras are energy centers within our bodies that receive, assimilate and express life-force energy. This seemed too *out there* for me so I skipped over it and enjoyed everything else that did resonate. My reaction to the concept of chakras seems rather comical to me, considering that a mere five years later I was drawn to Reiki, an ancient, Japanese healing modality that balances the chakras. Oh, the joyous path of evolving!

My introduction to Reiki in the winter of 1998 was my first exposure to metaphysics. I was nearly 40 years old and my marriage of 18 years—actually a 26-year relationship with my high school sweetheart—was dissolving. Reiki helped me awaken more to my untapped inner strength while experiencing such a dramatic life change.

I remember the day I was invited to attend a Reiki healing group. Bill Alford, a retired neighbor with whom I often road biked, asked me to join him. I knew nothing about Reiki, but I did know Bill. I wondered if this was another of his crazy ideas. Bill is young at heart and physically fit for his age. He sports a gray ponytail and is very liberal in his thinking. I lovingly refer to him as my retired hippie friend. Luckily, we were bike riding when he invited me to the Reiki class so he didn't see me roll my eyes.

Something drew me there though and I was intrigued. Instead of eating my words, I had to unroll my eyes. Bill, his wife, Gunilla, and I still laugh over this story because today, 13 years later, I am fully engaged in my life's calling and passionately sharing energy healing modalities and universal truths. Thanks, Bill!

I grew up Catholic, but I just couldn't wrap my mind around God being "a man in the sky." My greater spiritual awareness awakened in 1998.

My experience of Reiki, spiritual books and workshops led me to a new awareness of spirituality. I resonate with the truths that I am one with a Higher Power and not separate from it. I am deepening an understanding of the wonderful connection of mind, body and spirit. I am getting in touch with the fullness of who I Am. And, I am being steered along my destiny path.

You, too, are being steered along your destiny path.

I am honored to be part of your journey.

Let's dance!

Chapter 1
Choosing to Dance

You must meet the outer world with the inner world or existence will crush you. -Mark Nepo

We all hold, whether tapped or untapped, the healing and manifesting potential of the mind, body and spirit. It took one experience for me to validate the depth and power of this potential.

I met up with my friends Charlie and Andy for our weekly bike ride at Lake Crabtree, a county park bordering Raleigh, North Carolina. Our single-track mountain biking excursions involved leaning into curves, riding over roots and obstacles, and jumping piles of logs.

We approached a trail, one with an expansive view of Lake Crabtree surrounded by her forested shoreline. Tall office buildings poked above the tree tops. We breathed in the beauty of this mild autumn day, a palette in shades of green sprinkled with maple tree leaves bursting into their seasonal glory of orange and red. Sunlight shimmered on the water and reflected a scattering of billowy clouds against a Carolina blue sky. Nature drew us into the woods—the fresh fragrance of the pines, the sunlight dappling the trees and the dead leaves crackling like fire beneath our tires. The forest came alive.

The bike trails were miles of roughly cleared paths worn smooth by riders over the years, yet enough bulging roots remained to force our focus. We rode into and out of gullies, up and over piles of logs and across a 20-foot-long narrow wooden plank system. These planks stood about 18 inches off the ground and were no wider than a cereal box. If we lost our balance, we'd bounce onto the ground and continue riding the path or try again. The challenge was to stay on the entire length of wooden planks.

We reached a familiar teeter-totter, one we had mastered many times, riding up one side and down the other. Then we stopped and contemplated a much bigger and heavier teeter-totter that was new to the trail. I wanted to try it. The challenge excited me. Charlie and Andy rode on by, stopped, and turned around to watch me.

In mountain biking, speed is your friend. I pressed forward.

My front tire made contact with the teeter-totter and climbed to the top. But, my bike never came down the other side. It stood upright at the top of the teeter totter for several seconds, without me; I had gone flying over my handle bars. Then the bike fell to the ground. My only memory is of sailing through the air. A flood of thoughts
rushed through me. I knew I was barreling head-first into the ground.

I heard my neck snap.

I tried to move my arms, my legs, my body—nothing moved. I waited for the pain—there was no pain. I was just lying there. Charlie had rushed to my side. I looked in his eyes; he was shocked and wanted answers. I wanted to talk—I really did, but no sound would come out. I mouthed 911 three times before he understood.

Then I stopped breathing—the imminent death sentence.

I had no movement, no voice, no breath.

I had taken a fall; taking falls is part of mountain biking. Before, I always got back up, bruised, cut, a little blood, but nothing serious. But on this day, November 3, 2005, I was paralyzed from head to toe.

Caught between life and death, my instincts propelled me to my inner power. I daily practiced spiritual and holistic healing principles. I embraced the interconnectedness of my mind, body and spirit, including the law of attraction, which states we attract into our experiences what we focus on. I had strong faith in my body's healing potential. And, I still had access to my mind.

I do what I encourage my clients to do. I memorize a short, powerful mantra and use it daily to call back my power. My mantra rushed forth.

Still on the ground, motionless, breathless, I willed my body, emphatically. *"I refuse to accept this limitation, God is my Source!"*

Boom! What felt like a huge lightning bolt without the pain coursed through me. I was on to something. My beliefs— my thoughts—continued to spill from my mind to every cell in my body.

"I refuse to accept this limitation, God is my Source!"

A second bolt instantly went through me. My left arm flopped at my side.

Moments later I regained my breath! My lifeless form had accepted the dance of my mind, body and spirit.

The ambulance arrived in 17 minutes and took me to Duke University Medical Center. I was in a large examination room, more like a private room than a curtained area. There was a flurry of activity, much of which I don't remember. An ER doctor told me that my full paralysis was the result of my C 1 and C 2 neck vertebrae fractures and a profound spinal cord injury. He said my C 2 vertebra was broken into two separate pieces.

My first thought was "That sounds like it could be serious."

The emergency room filled with friends and family. I told them, "This is temporary. See me dancing."

My doctor, Robert E. Isaacs, Director of Spine Surgery at Duke Medical Center, told me that most people with severe spinal cord injury don't even make it to the emergency room. They die at the scene because they stop breathing. He said the surviving few who don't stop breathing are left quadriplegic. "People like you don't exist," he said.

But I do exist.

He may have had more questions than answers to why I had lived. And, though he didn't seem to resonate with my "out-there" mind power, he did respect my beliefs. My first and only surgery took place late that night. He said right before surgery, "Reconnecting your C 2 is my responsibility, and using your mind to your full advantage is yours."

Going into surgery, my head was not connected to my body by bone. The C 2 was broken in half. Dr. Isaacs entered through the front of my neck and reconnected my vertebra to the spinal column with a one-inch plus screw. He verified the position of the screw every quarter turn with x-rays. The surgery was a success. But I was still left a quadriplegic—a condition that I, in stark contrast to Western medical thinking, vehemently considered impermanent.

I used the teachings I learned along my spiritual journey and shared as a holistic life coach to influence my outcome. Our bodies do not know the difference between what *is* and what we affirm and expect—the nervous system creates pathways from the thought—whether the thought is real, remembered or made up. That's why I ignored what was so obvious, and I gave little attention to my paralyzed body. I refused to spend energy asking "why me" or rehashing "what ifs."

Instead, I directed my mind, time and energy into my healing. I more than desired — I expected — to ride a bike and dance again. In my mind I felt the excitement of high energy dance music and saw myself dancing with my friends on a crowded floor. I visualized riding my bike and saw in detail the greenway trails, the woods and a pond with a water fountain in it.

The visualizations helped me create feelings of excitement, gratitude and expectation — energetically imprinting into my body that I was already healed. These all magnified my momentum, strongly drawing my healing to me.

I combined my expectations and visualizations with my physical therapy which started within 18 hours of the surgery. Trusting that my body would respond, I prepared my mind before taking my first step. I visualized myself walking the full length of the long corridor, much further than what the therapist asked me to do. And I did walk the length of the corridor. My arms felt as if they were encased in cement. I ignored that feeling and when I had to lift my arms, I first saw myself doing it with ease.

I attribute a great deal of my recovery to first visualizing my success; whether I was opening a flip-top yogurt container or bringing the spoon to my mouth, before I moved I visualized it done. Each day in the hospital I developed more dexterity. This was promising; the earlier a quadriplegic has movement, the better her prognosis.

Everything was physical therapy at this point. But not all of it was serious. The day I left ICU, my daughter Brittany and my ex-husband were visiting during dinner. They knew me as a physically active, independent and healthy woman. And now they saw me paralyzed and painstakingly attempting to put some food in my mouth.

My spoon's handle was modified with a fat red rubber piece to assist my grasp. Even then, my paralysis made it hard to get food to my mouth. What my daughter saw was me playing "airplane," like I had when she was a baby during feeding time. Brittany broke out in laughter and the laughter was contagious. As is often said, laughter is good medicine.

I loved having family and friends with me but I also relished the quiet time. I knew the profound healing I desired was my responsibility from the inside out. When I was alone I focused on rebalancing my energy field. I did affirmations, visualizations and meditation. I also bathed my body in the healing sound frequencies of Tom Kenyon's nearly four-octave voice.

By rebalancing my energy, I was able to do miraculous things. When I awoke from surgery I refused pain medicine. And I still expected to heal in comfort. I did, experiencing no pain. They said I would be in ICU for seven to 10 days. I said I would be out in two; I walked out of ICU two days later. They predicted my hospital stay would be three weeks, minimum. I said I would be released in a week; I was released in one week.

Dr. Isaacs told me that I had the same injury as the late Christopher Reeve, who had received immediate medical attention of the highest quality after being thrown from his horse in an equestrian competition in 1995. He was still left a quadriplegic with a breathing apparatus. It took 17 minutes for EMS to reach me. But I had everything I needed. I had my mind and my connection to the Higher Power that many of us call God or Spirit.

Dr. Isaacs said, "Considering Suzette's spinal cord damage, her results surpassed medical expectations. The rapidity and completeness of her improvement were truly remarkable."

I am a testament to the amazing healing capacity of our bodies. We can accomplish more than most of us realize as we stretch our thinking beyond traditional medicine which focuses only on matter and *sees the mind separate from the body.*

My Recovery Continues

The first two weeks at home I spent most of my time in bed. I got up for short spells to eat, go to the john, be showered, do my physical therapy and walk. I had to budget my energy, choosing between a friend's visits or taking a shower.

Sixteen days after my injury, Charlie took me for an unassisted half-mile walk on my street. We walked further each day. Three weeks after my injury, I felt a shift in strength and function; it was Thanksgiving Day and I walked one and one-half miles.

I became more and more able to do the things we take for granted; unscrew my supplement bottles, button and zip my clothing and move my plate from the table to the sink without dropping it.

My affirmations, "This is temporary, see me dancing," became reality one month after my injury. I went to the Raleigh Ski and Outing Club's annual Christmas event. This club is where Charlie, Andy and I met and I knew I would see many friends there.

Before driving us, my friend Amy showered me, dried and curled my hair and put my make-up on. I felt nurtured and loved. When we arrived I felt more love; my friends' hugs and words of encouragement expanded my heart.

The jovial atmosphere was palpable, teasing me to dance—not that I needed much teasing. So, I did. I danced twice. My legs and feet felt so heavy, almost as if glued to the floor. My dance partner and I locked arms, our hands resting on each other's elbows for balance and safety. I wasn't graceful but I was dancing. I was, very sl-ow-ly dancing, every part of me thankful to God and to my body.

After an hour I felt as if I could fall asleep sitting up. It took all my remaining energy to say goodbye to friends and walk to the car with Amy. I carried with me the warmth of the evening.

This was a major accomplishment for me, and more evidence that we are so much more than we have been taught to realize.

Support of Loved Ones

I was single and lived alone, but I was not left alone. My mother and siblings live in Maine and I live in North Carolina. Mom flew down immediately and stayed three weeks. Sometimes it took everything she had to see me so disabled. She stayed at my side tending to my every need: getting me water, helping me in and out of bed, dressing me and answering my phone. She also took care of the household duties of cooking, cleaning and laundry. Her love and support were immeasurable; I will never be too old for the powerful healing force of my mother's love.

My daughters Brittany, a senior in high school, and Bri, two hours away at the University of North Carolina, Wilmington, visited when they could.

I had once told Britt that *if* I ever got a tattoo it would be of a heart with wings on each side. She must have channeled her feelings of pain into love, for at two o'clock in the morning, when I returned from surgery to the ICU, she was waiting with a painting—the acrylics had yet to dry on the wings.

My ex-husband Rick was there for me, too. He came to the emergency room and then to the hospital each evening after work. He made sure I had the best doctors and he encouraged me. But it was his presence more than his actions that strengthened me. We had moved in different life directions and had divorced seven years earlier, and still, a depth of caring remained between us. My older daughter Bri recently shared, nearly six years after my injury, how watching her father's attentiveness toward her mother mended something in her that had broken. Her heart feels it more than she can articulate it. It's as though her sense of family has been restored, not through a physical reunion of her parents, but something special—a reunion of the hearts of the two adults she loves most.

My sister Bea, who loathes flying, felt compelled to fly here anyway, saying the power of her love for me surpassed her gripping fear. With the help of a Kahlua Sombrero en route, she was here to surprise me when I returned home from the hospital. The fact that she got on a plane on short notice assured me that when push comes to shove, she, too, would be there for me.

My sister Ramona, my brother Doug and other family members checked in with me often and kept me in their positive thoughts.

My friends Jodi and Amy nurtured my spirit in the emergency room and beyond. Amy and I had each purchased a Staple's "Easy Button" a few weeks earlier for our law of attraction work. It's that three-inches round, red button which when pushed says, "That was easy." Quick-thinking Amy grabbed her Easy Button on her rush out the door to come to the emergency room. Just like in our law of attraction work, she pushed the button and it said, "That was easy." We all laughed. This was an affirmation that lightened and eased my recovery.

Jodi and Amy visited me daily in the hospital and stayed either with me or in the reception room for hours at a time. They shared bedside duty with my Mom, tending to my needs and keeping the mood positive. Jodi even helped me feel "put together" with a little make-up, a dab of lipstick.

They wrote positive thoughts—"I Am Love" and "I Am Whole"—in black magic marker on the intravenous bags which raised the energetic vibration of the nutrients. Jodi brought meals and Amy handled all the logistics of my emails, bills, business calls, doctor's appointments, grocery shopping and my in-home physical therapy. She created a calendar on the internet so friends could sign up to drive me to doctor appointments, bring meals in, and take turns visiting. They were my Earth angels.

Charlie walked daily with me. My guy friends from my Rotary Club signed up to give me my showers. No, just kidding! Though they did, with the help of their wives, bring me meals. I was honored by the care and concern of so many people.

Becoming More Mobile

I continued healing. Even though I had a stiff neck, I drove my own car four months post surgery. I remember the first time. It was March in North Carolina, a balmy 75°. I planned to drive just through my neighborhood in my red convertible with the top down. Instead, I drove all the way to Jodi's house to surprise her. I passed at least a hundred Bradford pear trees with white flowers fully opened, ushering in spring. Each spring I love driving down that road just to feast my eyes on them for the three weeks they are in bloom. This day, an intense appreciation for all I was experiencing welled up within me.

Shortly thereafter, my friends Charlie, Lyle, Amy and Sue joined me at the Cary YMCA for a cycling class—on stationary bikes—and a celebratory dinner nearby at Connolly's Irish Pub.

At eight months post surgery, on the eve of my 48th birthday, Charlie, Andy and several other friends from the Raleigh Ski and Outing Club joined me for my first outdoor bike ride along the flat, paved trail around Lake Pine.

Today, I deal with subtle reminders: neuropathy in my fingers and body and heaviness in my legs—I'm still claiming that this too is temporary. I hike, weight train, bike and do yoga. Charlie and I continue our weekly bike rides, minus the obstacles. We are riding part of the American Tobacco Trail, spanning three counties; we share the trail with walkers, runners, cyclists and horseback riders.

18

My Beliefs

I credit my beliefs and daily spiritual practice for my ability to stay calm and regain my breath and the full functioning of my body. I believe that I am pure energy and one with a Higher Power, that everything happens for a higher purpose and that my body responds to my thoughts. I am living the emotional and physical freedom that the mind, body and spirit principles allow.

Earlier on in my spiritual practice I thought that being immersed in this consciousness protected me from life's challenges. I realize now that it doesn't always. It does offer me the awareness to trust in my soul's bigger plan, stay in control of my reactions and adjust my beliefs, thoughts and expectations to improve my outcomes. That is the dance of life.

I invite you to come along with me as we build the momentum for living with more joy, freedom and soul expression.

Chapter 2
Living Heaven on Earth

"A new heaven" is the emergence of a transformed state of human consciousness, and "a new earth" is its reflection in the physical realm. - Ekhart Tolle

This book is for you. Know that I honor you and where you are on your life journey. There is neither one right path nor any need to judge one path better than another.

Calling Back Your Power represents my deepest truths and the teachings I embrace—the ones that were responsible for my healing. And I am here to share them with you. Part of growing and stretching spiritually is pondering ideas, some about which you may rarely think or even ones with which you disagree; embrace what feels good and set the rest aside.

I invite you to engage with me in discovering, exploring and deepening the truth of your own understanding. Intentions and expectations create a higher vibration that amplifies your likelihood of getting what you want or need. Please join me in intending that while reading this book you receive the inspiration and wisdom meant just for you. Affirm what you want. For example, you may want to allow in the energetic and emotional shifts that will assist your spiritual journey, deepen your connection to Spirit and strengthen your resolve for a daily practice to achieve more peace, joy and fulfillment.

I believe you are on this earth plane to experience joy and freedom. And you are here as a life learner—both student and teacher to family, friends, co-workers and even strangers. You are here to grow your soul. Spiritually, even though you may not be aware of it, you attract each person and experience for that purpose—soul expansion.

The road to heaven on earth can be a little bumpy at times. Hang on. You are forever a student in the game of life. Gaining spiritual awareness, including self-reflection, leads to understanding the intrinsic value of the challenges—that there is higher meaning and purpose in them. Think of them as your lessons for this lifetime.

Your daily life is an experiential workshop. Many people have learned that by taking a proactive role their lives become easier and more fun. They create for themselves more energy and vibrant health, their interactions with family and peers are more satisfying and their present spiritual practices are deepened and made more meaningful. When challenges do come along, they have the tools to handle them.

Thoughts, attitudes and perspectives are the energetic paintbrushes that create the landscape of life—happy, colorful and expansive, or dark, limited and messy. I encourage you to use the light of your divine essence to live as the creative artist you truly are. A wondrous turnaround is available, no matter what you are experiencing today. Just as a painter reuses a canvas for a new painting, you can re-create your life—your masterpiece.

There is an inner power available to help you create this masterpiece. As you tap into your power, each day becomes an opportunity to build the life you desire. Creating life on your terms requires accepting your situation, surrendering to it and choosing the best attitude you can muster. Your inner power will help you do that.

Each day, to ease your challenges and celebrate your triumphs, remember to "dance." On some days, you will feel connected to your personal power and the dance steps will come easily. On other days, as if dancing with two left feet, you may wallow in self-pity. That's okay. Accept it as part of learning the dance. If you gave it your personal best, accept that as enough. Keep trying; keep practicing your dance steps.

Dance. It makes living on earth easier.

It Is Your Nature to Evolve Spiritually

You are a spiritual being having a human experience to grow your soul. The challenges of life offer you experiences to do so—to discover and transform your limiting beliefs and old, debilitating programming. Time and experiences fine tune your ability to recognize and let go of unhealthy thoughts, habits and reactions.

The principles you find within these pages will guide you to see life from a deeper or different perspective and navigate you through chaos and emotional challenges toward inner peace and prosperity.

As you practice these principles, your results will help you increase your belief in their power. As you align to these principles, understand that your degree of belief in them is a critical component—the magic key—to reap the life you desire. People grow into belief and their varying degrees of belief in these principles create varying degrees of success.

Even if you are a person of integrity who is fully aligned with a spiritual discipline, you will still attract challenging situations, seemingly out of nowhere. You may say, "How could my positive attitude and faith attract this experience?" On an inner level, you attract them because you are ready to expand beyond your present awareness.

The trials you experience often may not make sense from the perspective of your human-mind thinking. For example, many of you live within your means and invest in a diversified portfolio and you still have had to deal with financial setbacks due to rising living expenses, or the stock market crashing and your nest egg plummeting. Or you are a critical thinker and a team player who often works overtime and you still got fired. Or you faithfully practice spiritual principles and wonder why your results are not consistent. In any of these situations, you may feel like throwing your arms up and shouting, "How come?" "Why me?" "Do these principles really work?" "Have I not proved my faith in these principles enough already?"

If you feel you have done everything "right" and still find yourself caught up in an unexplainable, perhaps even horrific, experience or two, you are not alone. Show yourself some compassion; remind yourself that you are here on the earth plane for a higher purpose and you've just been given another opportunity to evolve your soul even further. You may be saying, "I don't want to evolve spiritually if this is what it takes."

Stay with me. The good news is you do have transformative power. Take a few deep breaths and realize that when you see your trials, even the very challenging ones, from the perspective of heightened spiritual awareness, you will see the gift your trials offer you. And, yes, you read that correctly. I did say gift.

This gift is the soul growth that challenges offer. And, ultimately, we are here for soul growth. Acceptance of the problem, even without understanding it, is a spiritual lesson we are here to learn. Acceptance shifts the energy field, creating inner peace. Inner peace allows intuitive guidance, solutions and blessings to flow easily and your situations improve. Basically, inner peace equates to outer blessings.

Spirit—that powerful organizing intelligence—will orchestrate great outcomes when you get to the place of acceptance and inner peace.

We are awakening, collectively, to a much deeper awareness of our innate potential in this multidimensional universe. Spiritual masters around the world agree that humanity is now experiencing, at an accelerated rate, a monumental shift in consciousness. This shift is helping us remember the All that we are. It can stimulate pain and be disruptive. Even so, your soul very courageously chose to be part of this personal and planetary evolution. Make the best of this shift. Let it be the impetus to adjust your perspective, improve your life and experience more inner peace.

Computers weren't invented a hundred years ago because collective consciousness—humanity—was not ready for such advanced technology. Humanity, as a whole, has not been ready for this advanced spiritual awareness, until now. This shift is helping us leap to a higher knowing of spiritual truth and a willingness to move outside the comfort zone of our third-dimensional world.

This book is in your hands because, at some level, you are willing to expand to a higher awareness; you will own these teachings at a deeper level or, for those newer to this journey, awaken to them. All of us are at a critical juncture—one offering challenges that require us to deepen our knowing and faith and develop more consistently this higher perspective.

Reach for the higher aspects of yourself—to those realms of consciousness that are beyond Earth's material world and transform your challenges with more ease and grace.

The transformation is eased by seeing your life from two viewpoints.

First viewpoint: Your inner peace and success increase with your willingness to simply *observe* your challenges with relationships, jobs and finances. Make a conscious effort not to react to or worry about them, nor to engage negatively with them in any way. This involves a learning curve and is not always easy to do, but that, my friend, is the journey of evolving.

Write some post-it notes to yourself and stick them up around your home: *Observe, Just Observe What Is,* and *React With Love.* Keep trying, no matter how many times you overreact. Catching yourself when you overreact is progress. Accept the baby steps and hang in there.

Second viewpoint: You've been taught all your life to view your world only from your human-mind, seeing it from a material perspective. You will power your growth as you retrain your brain from human-mind to spirit-mind awareness. The challenge for beginners and seasoned spiritual practitioners alike is to remember who you really are—pure Spirit, pure potential. Stepping forward and learning to walk with a foot in both worlds takes a conscious effort and patience.

Think about how your body and mind play with each other in the three-dimensional realm of this earth plane. Your human mind naturally looks for tangible solutions to your problems; it looks for more money, toned abs, the better job or a different mate.

This spiritual evolutionary shift offers you an opportunity to create solutions by propelling you not toward material solutions but toward your oneness with Spirit. You are multi-dimensional, and when you awaken to the consciousness of *already* being Spirit—*you* become the power that naturally transcends problems.

You will attract the material solutions by first changing your perspective. Focus less on the problems you observe in the third dimension and focus more on the transformational power of who you really are. You are so much more than you realize. You are a profound spiritual being. You are infinite Spirit.

Every religion and spiritual tradition recognizes an invisible Higher Power that is infinite, all knowing and all powerful. This is the essence of who you are. Yet because we live in a world where we mostly focus only on what is visible, finite and material, it may be difficult for some to accept that their real essence is so powerful and so invisible.

You have been surrounded by and working with invisible phenomena all your life. You can't see oxygen; you just take a breath and you know and trust oxygen is there. You can't see the radio waves that carry signals for your cell phone; you just call a friend and you know the waves are there. You can't see gravity; but you are definitely aware of it when you trip and fall to the ground. I invite you to embrace more fully the invisible, non-physical aspects of yourself as Spirit. The Universe's evolution is encouraging us—sometimes it feels like it's forcing us—to release our grip on the material world and tap into the infinite, all-powerful wisdom of Spirit.

Paul Gorman shares in his book *The Giving* Self (Ordering information can be found on my site at www.CallingBackYourPower.com/URL), "It is only our finite human-mind that sees the problem and cannot solve it. Spirit sees no problem because Spirit has no problem and in your pure state—when your mind is silent, empty, and receptive—you are that Spirit in full awareness." Wow! I find that powerful and love to read it over and over.

Meditation creates a space for that silent, empty and receptive mind. Silent meditation allows infinite wisdom to dissolve limiting beliefs, old programming and worry. As your inner environment improves, your outer situations also improve—it is the nature of Spirit. It's Divine law.

Most people who recognize a Higher Power believe that God, or Spirit, is everywhere. Gorman says, "If Spirit is everywhere, then you and your entire world are Spirit. Not Spirit *and* a human body. Not Spirit *and* money, just Spirit. There is only Spirit."

You are the infinite aspect of Spirit right here, right now. Your bank account and your body are the infinite aspects of Spirit right here, right now. You may be saying, "I don't think so. My savings account is non-existent." Again, you've been conditioned, living from your human mind, to give power and focus only to what you can see and feel; for example, your depleted bank account or a sore back. Your human mind doesn't recognize bank accounts or bodies as the invisible prosperity or wholeness of Spirit they actually are. So, yes, from the human-mind perspective, your savings account is depleted. It's as if the human mind sees only through distorted glasses and focuses on a distorted image—the image of a depleted savings account—thus convincing itself of its limitation and lack.

One of my clients said these ideas felt right but her mind had a hard time holding on to them. I suggested she just keep reminding herself that she is more than her limited bank account or diseased body.

Paul Gorman reminds us that there is no such limitation, lack, illness or discord because there is no lack of Spirit. Spirit fills all space. There is no space vacant of the fullness of Spirit.

Let lack or worry of any kind be a clue that you are viewing life through the limited human-mind perspective. When you catch yourself feeling anxious about an unfulfilling job or relationship, or the lack of money, go into meditation or sit quietly and let Spirit dissolve that limited thinking or worry. Sit in the silence daily and feel the light of Spirit within you. Let Spirit reveal to you the peace and prosperity available through the spirit-mind perspective. Change is created when you embrace your spiritual all-ness. And as your inner environment improves, your outer situations also improve—it is the nature of Spirit. It's divine law.

It's a lifelong journey to deepen your knowing and move through the phases of accepting your experiences and believing in your inner power. The challenge is to stay at a level of higher consciousness and accept whatever problem you experience as temporary until you can allow in enough spiritual wisdom to create change.

When you reach the point of consistently owning your spiritual essence, miracles will be everyday occurrences. For now, most of us still vacillate between human-mind perspective and spirit-mind perspective. Again, that is the journey of evolving. Depending on your soul lessons, you will have areas where it is easier to call back your power and own your spiritual essence and areas in which are more difficult to do so.

Having honed my role as a spiritual being having a human experience proved valuable when my body stopped breathing; my spirit-mind perspective naturally took over. My job was to ignore what was obvious to my human mind, allowing myself to be who I really am—infinite wholeness, one with God. That area proved easy for me to call back my power, other areas of my life require more growth. It is the nature of evolving.

The nature of a spiritual journey is to evolve to an awareness that reveals spiritual wholeness and allows acceptance of readily available blessings. Start to recognize the distorted human-mind images—insufficient bank account balances, diseased bodies and physical exhaustion.

To improve these situations, begin to evolve from human-mind thinking to spirit-mind thinking. Consider stepping outside of the box that always identifies everything as physical. Evolve from focusing mostly on the visible, material realm to accepting and working more with the invisible, non-physical realm of Spirit. This will help dissolve the mental programs and beliefs that create lack mentality, worry and disease.

There is a learning curve to living the truth of your Being; allow the journey to unfold. Every moment is an opportunity to leap from knowing truth to living truth. Many people recognize the truth of these principles but haven't created the habit of living from them.

The situations in your life are great feedback as to how aligned you are with being the creator you came here to be. Pay attention to any unhealthy relationships, health challenges, financial insecurity or an unfulfilling job — reminders that there is much to gain by viewing these areas more from the spirit-mind perspective. Wherever you are on the continuum of knowing and practicing spiritual awareness is neither right or wrong nor good or bad. It is all just valuable feedback for the soul journey you incarnated to participate in.

Are you ready to enjoy life's possibilities? Are you ready for Heaven on Earth?

Chapter 3
Your Energetic World

It is when we go beyond our edge that we discover the next layer of potential and experience ourselves and our relationship to the world in a new way. - Alan Seale

I owe my recovery and many other personal successes to embracing my body, my thoughts and, in fact, everything around me as energy. Infinite wisdom, abundance, health, wealth and joy are also malleable energies. This energy is molded by our thoughts—the thoughts we entertain every moment of our lives. New experiences can be just a belief and a thought away. We create it all—what we want and what we don't want.

Dr. Isaacs said, historically, people with my spinal cord injury are dead at the scene because they stop breathing. I regained my breath because I used the power of my thoughts to tap into the ever-present, divine, intelligent energy field.

What *field of energy* was I accessing?

What spiritual and scientific truth was I tapping into?

Why aren't more people taking advantage of this *field of intelligence*?

The answers to these questions are the reason I am so excited to be sharing this book. The answers are revealed within these pages.

Evidence that Challenges Our Traditional Beliefs

Everything traditional science and medicine teach us about the relationship of our bodies to our world is based on Isaac Newton's work from the 17th century. His world was the world of matter and gravity, the only world that most of us have been taught to embrace. It does not recognize the power of the mind and there is no room here for results like mine. I snapped my neck in two. I could not talk. I could not move. I could not breathe. I had access only to my mind.

Quantum physics, an 80-year-old realm of scientific study, takes into account mind power, the interconnected relationship of thoughts *with* matter. It *does* allow for my remarkable results. Worldwide research has demonstrated that our thoughts and intentions affect our bodies by *communicating* with fields of invisible energy. Quantum physics offers us a new way of understanding our body's healing potential and the universe we live in.

Objects larger than 1/1000 of an inch obey the laws of Newtonian physics; they have enough mass to have a gravitational field. Objects less then 1/1000 of an inch obey laws of quantum physics; their mass is too small to have a gravitational field of any consequence. The space between the neurons and synapses in our brains is 1/1000 of an inch. The neurological events responsible for thought, the jumping of neurotransmitters across a synapse, are clearly in the quantum world. This neurological design allows for our thoughts to affect our experiences.

Physicist Fred Allen Wolf, PhD, said, "quantum physics points to, you can't have a universe without mind entering into it, mind shaping the very thing being perceived."

Lynn McTaggart, in her book *The Field*, shares the following about quantum physics research: "The scientists, all from credible top ranking institutions—Princeton University, Stanford University, top institutions in Germany and France—have produced impeccable experimentation. Nevertheless, their experiments have attacked a number of tenets held to be sacred. They did not fit the prevailing scientific view of the world, so it must be wrong. Acknowledging these new ideas would require scrapping much of what modern science believes in and, in a sense, starting over from scratch. The old guard was having none of it."

Changing medical and scientific paradigms is a process. Some people will shift, others won't. Accepting new ideas that challenge accepted beliefs is not a new issue. Accepting the Earth as round and the sun as the center of the solar system took time even though new facts rebuked accepted truths.

Even today, it is a common reaction to try and undermine the evidence rather than adjust our beliefs. Yet, our universe is continually expanding. This expansion lends itself to our ability to explore beyond previous boundaries and develop new theories regarding the quantum world, and allows the veils between the quantum world's dimensions to become thin enough for science to validate new findings.

Let's release the need to defend accepted theories and dismiss any information that contradicts them; instead, try approaching challenging new ideas with a healthy balance of skepticism and open-mindedness. We can choose not to ignore, as many doctors and scientists still do, the ground-breaking implications of the advances in quantum physics research.

I have great respect and gratitude for Dr. Isaacs' skill in repairing my spine. As Director of Spine Surgery at Duke Medical Center, he is certainly tops in his field. Dr. Isaacs wrote a validation letter regarding my injury and recovery; it is available at the end of this chapter. Even though the letter describes the seriousness of my injury, I wanted more clarity.

Five years after my injury, while I was preparing this book, Dr. Isaacs did a telephone interview with me and my friend Jodi, who was present with me in the hospital and who had talked with him often.

During our interview, he said he remembered showing Jodi my MRI on the computer right outside of my ICU room. She remembered that, too. This was shortly after surgery when I had very little function. He showed her the gray areas and tried to prepare her to not expect me to regain much more mobility. In the interview Dr. Isaacs re-explained that the grayness, called "signal" in medical terminology, is direct injury to the spinal cord, which the MRI clearly showed. He said, "The signals show up as different colors on the MRI. In my mind it doesn't make a difference whether the signal is blood or swelling. If you have a spinal cord injury that you can see on the MRI, it's pretty graphic. Historically, it would be devastating—one you would not survive." (My MRI is available at http://www.CallingBackYourPower.com.)

I arrived at the emergency room as a quadriplegic. I had slight movement in one foot, none in my upper body. When he visited me in the ICU, Dr. Isaacs made clear the seriousness of my injury and verbally shared, "Most people with your injury are dead at the scene because they stop breathing. The remaining few are quadriplegics." Later he said, "You had the same injury as Christopher Reeve." And, "People like you don't exist."

My recovery defies the Western medical view. Yet, those unwilling to be open-minded to an expanding universe or adjust their traditional beliefs will dispute the scope of my injury. I have observed other holistic results that perplex conventional doctors. They rarely ask what one did to achieve the results, but show support by saying, "Continue what you are doing."

In the interview, Dr. Isaacs' was comfortable giving credit to my faith for my results and since he, in his words, doesn't have my faith, he can't understand the scope of my recovery. He said, "I'm presented with a woman who got a lot better, a lot quicker than would have been comprehended, so I am trying to make sense of it in my mind."

Concerning unexplainable healings, conventional doctors continue to reach for possible Western medical explanations. I understand that. It is their training. Regarding regaining my breath, though, no possible medical scenario explains why, the very moment I did my affirmation, a bolt of energy instantly went through me. The second bolt of energy also came instantly after my second my affirmation. That is not a coincidence. Yes, it is a result of my faith—faith not only in my oneness with a Higher Power, but faith in our mind power and the laws of the quantum world.

Lynn McTaggart, in *The Field*, shares more: "At the very frontier of science, new ideas are emerging that challenge everything we believe about how our world works and how we define ourselves. Discoveries are being made that prove what religion has always espoused: human beings are far more extraordinary than an assemblage of flesh and bones. At its most fundamental, this new science answers questions that have perplexed scientists for hundreds of years. At its most profound, this is a science of the miraculous."

Quantum physics shows us that the mind and Spirit work outside of time and space, expanding our understanding of what we call miracles. My belief in the interconnectedness of my mind, body and spirit allowed me to stay calm and receive the power of that which is beyond the physical me, yet one with me. I used mental attention and personal will to create quantum events within my body, events that may appear as miracles to others. I'm alive and fully functioning today because I tapped into the *anything is possible* scientific model of quantum physics.

God, Spirit, Source—Organizing, Intelligent Energy Fields

Most scientists agree that all living species and objects have their own distinct, measurable energy field. Even an inanimate object, like your chair, has an inner "aliveness." This energetic quality is the powerful, organizing intelligence—I call it God, Spirit, I AM, Source—found within all things, seen and unseen, animate and inanimate.

Every object, person and thought has its own corresponding energetic vibration. The vibrations we expose ourselves to have an effect on us and on our environment. The vibrations of love and happiness are higher and healthier than the vibrations of anger and resentment. Pure spring water has a higher vibration than polluted water, fresh squeezed orange juice has a higher vibration than soda and the vibration of fresh organic vegetables is higher than that of vegetables grown using pesticides.

Einstein showed us that the vibration we perceive as hard matter is mostly empty space with patterns of energy running through it. When quantum physicists look more closely at these patterns of energy, the research reveals that the act of observation itself affects the results. When they observe light patterns looking for waves, they see waves; when they observe light patterns looking for particles, they see particles. In other words, this energy—light patterns—is malleable to human intention and expectation. Expectation alone causes your energy to interact with and affect other energy systems.

Consciousness obeys the laws of quantum physics. I think of the quantum world as the power source for the world of possibility.

The Power of Intentions

Dr. Masaru Emoto, a Japanese researcher, in his book *Messages from Water*, provides factual evidence that human consciousness—through words, intentions and sound—affects the molecular structure of water. Dr. Emoto's work clearly demonstrates the effect of the environment on water. This is profound information. Your body, like the Earth, is about 70% water.

Words Are Powerful Energy; Choose Them Wisely

Lots of people notice that they feel drained when they spend time with negative people or, conversely, how their mood improves when they are around positive people. This happens because everything in our universe has a vibration, a consciousness, and interconnects with other vibratory fields. This includes every cell in your body. Your cells can absorb and record the vibrations of your own thoughts and beliefs and the words of love or hatred directed at you from others. Your body is even absorbing the negative vibrations of the words or thoughts that, in anger, you direct toward others.

Those who improve their words and intentions not only feel better but, because their energy field is interconnected with those of other people, they contribute to improving the collective consciousness—humanity's combined thinking. Positive words and thoughts improve the energetic environment of your home, work place and beyond.

Besides being good words to live by, the Bible verse "Do unto others as you would want done unto you" has increased significance when you consider its energetic impact.

Your Inner Essence

In his book *Universe of Worlds*, Robert Grant shares, "Think of God as the butterfly and ourselves as the caterpillar. The winged beauty of the butterfly is already patterned within the caterpillar as it grows and changes from the caterpillar to the chrysalis."

All living species have a spark of divinity, an essence. Quantum physics refers to this essence as an infinite, invisible stream of consciousness that you are one with, not separate from.

You Are So Cool!

There are healings happening all over the world through the use of energy medicine that works with a person's energy field to stimulate the powerful, combined healing capacity of the mind, body and spirit. Later I share testimonials of clients who have healed their cancer, pain and arthritis; canceled scheduled surgery; and much more—all through seeing their body, thoughts, emotions and beliefs as energy and allowing us to re-pattern that energy field.

You don't need to understand fully this energetic work in order for it to benefit you. You may not understand the intricacies of computers and cell phones but you use them because they work, they add value to your life. I invite you to adopt a similar approach to the practice of the teachings within this book. You will be guided to and will resonate with the information that is best for you at the time you are open to receive it.

I wouldn't have had the same results if my injury had happened two years earlier—my belief in mind, body and spirit was not as solid. At the time of my injury, I had grown deeper into my awareness and practiced these teachings daily. I believed I was pure energy connected to an intelligent energy field, moldable by my thoughts and intentions. I believed in the power of my mind and my body's healing potential.

Thoughts and intentions are creative power. Awareness, belief and discipline can pro-actively convert challenges into more positive experiences for a healthier and happier life.

Get excited; you live in a world of infinite possibilities!

Dr. Isaacs' validation letter:

Duke University Medical Center
Robert E Isaacs, MD
April 4, 2007

Re: FOSTER,

SUZETTE FAITH ET561

Dr. Braden,

I am seeing Ms. Foster back today. She is now about a year and a third status post a mountain biking accident. She was doing a jump, landed wrong on her neck, and became quadriplegic, including losing her ability to breath. As you are aware, many patients in this condition will expire at the scene, never surviving to become hospitalized for treatment. Those that do, as in her case, are often found to have profound neurologic findings on physical exam. Given her combined fractures of C1 and C2 vertebrae and 50% translation at the C1-2 level not surprisingly the patient was found to have profound spinal cord injury at the time of presentation. Remarkably the patient has recovered dramatically.

Her recovery was truly dramatic, even early on, essentially gaining near normal neurological function within a relatively short period of time. This has only continued over the recent past. She actually presents to discuss today, after a severe fall while in-line skating.

The patient feels strongly that her improvement has been a direct result of her combining eastern medical philosophy and treatment to our western approach to her neck fractures. Regardless of the reason, we are quite thrilled and profoundly impressed with her recovery.

Even after her last spill, she looks great. Maybe one of these days we can get her to slow down before she "hurts herself" – I've tried!

Please feel free to contact me to discuss further with any questions.

Sincerely,
Robert E. Isaacs, M.D.
Robert E. Isaacs, MS
Director of Spine Surgery
Division of Neurosurgery
Duke University Medical Center
Box 3807
Durham, North Carolina 27710
919-668-5241 (office)
919-668-5095 (fax)

*Letter reproduced for *Calling Back Your Power*, original copy:
www.CallingBackYourPower.com

Chapter 4
It's Time to Put the Fun Back in Dysfunctional

Look not mournfully into the past. It comes not back again.
Wisely improve the present. It is thine. Go forth to meet the
shadowy future, without fear.
– Henry Wadsworth Longfellow

Happiness feels good and emotional freedom helps you get there. My clients and I have experienced emotional and physical healing when our buried emotional pain is identified and repressed emotions are felt and released.

Accepting that emotional pain's purpose is for the soul's growth helps allow feelings to surface. Clients transform this pain by surrendering the hold and perceived power it has over them. When they release the pain's emotional charge, they create a more positive energy pattern for themselves.

Clients dig up the courage to process emotions and possibly face the unknown. Processing and feeling the hurt dissolves the energy—emotion—causing the pain. Once the angst of the processing passes, people feel better. Ignored or partially felt emotional pain continues to attract more situations to people as energetic reminders that there are more layers to clear.

Every challenge or adversity carries with it opportunities for personal growth—for positive and powerful change. Look back over your life and re-examine the tough times. Notice how you grew from those experiences. Tough times aren't fun; yet you probably can admit that you learned a lot about yourself whether you chose to step up to the plate and deal with your issues or to spiral downward into despair.

Many people endured tough times as children. Consider that, from a soul perspective, these sad and dysfunctional childhoods have value. They provided the emotions and beliefs our souls came here to work through and, ultimately, to heal.

I have found peace in the spiritual awareness that we each divinely line up the people and experiences in childhood and life that perfectly show us our wounds—ones of unworthyiness, anger, resentment, guilt or perhaps some other emotional state. The Earth plane is like a huge classroom where you learn not just what your human self wants, but what your soul needs as well.

Cellular Memory

The human energy field holds memories of a person's past actions, personalities, relationships, successes, insecurities and challenging issues—in fact, all of their experiences from this or other lifetimes. The entire energy field, in and around the body, is like a computer, recording experiences as information. I refer to this record of information as cellular memory.

Negative experiences manifest as emotional blocks in your cellular memory, affecting your life even if you are not conscious of the experiences. I believe that from a higher spiritual perspective, you chose the setbacks of this lifetime in hopes of clearing the corresponding emotional blocks and cellular memory. In essence, you are here to address and clear the blocks of your soul's choosing.

Clearing blocks is similar to replacing a dirty air filter. More air can pass through when there is less dirt on the air filter. Similarly, more divine Light can enter when you clear emotional blocks from your energy field.

Doing the dirty work of facing your emotional pain has benefits: the ability to attract more easily what you want and, most important, to accomplish your soul work of raising your consciousness.

Facing my emotional pain prepared me energetically for my phenomenal recovery. I have had my share of hurts to address and lessons to learn. I didn't like experiencing the pain but, as I was willing to look at the pain, feel it, and, layer by layer, cleanse it out of my energy field, I moved to a higher vibration. My clearer energy field allowed me to receive more fully that lightening bolt of God-force energy.

My friends and clients find they judge their painful situations less as they understand that every perceived setback has a higher soul purpose. You are the accumulative product of your lifetimes. Your soul chose aspects of your cellular memory to bring forward this lifetime for healing. I invite you to allow this awareness to lighten the burden of your life lessons and move forward with greater confidence, perhaps even eagerly.

Preparing for This Lifetime

Many people agree that the greater aspect of who we are is still a mystery. But the veils between our human selves and spiritual selves are lifting and we'll understand more of the mystery as humanity expands its consciousness.

We incarnate with a game plan, a blueprint so to speak, of the potential experiences needed to heal our wounds and expand our consciousness. Consider the perspective of your soul preparing for the adventure of this incarnation. Your soul is so excited about this lifetime because, unlike in the spiritual realms, life on Earth offers contrasts and adversity; interspersed between the fun and successes are challenges.

For example, your soul knows you are ready for a relationship with a controlling person because she will teach you to stand up for yourself and set strong boundaries.

Your soul wants the experience of your family of four crowded into a three-room apartment for a couple of years to give you an opportunity to learn patience, appreciation for the little things and team work, and to see if you really got the knack of setting boundaries in that earlier relationship.

Your soul chose the contrast of being laid off for a year. It will be a struggle at first but your divine essence knows you are ready to release the false pride you have carried in your energy field for lifetimes and has given you an opportunity to accept help.

With soul choices such as these you are definitely going to be primed to feel more of the good things in life; specifically, self-respect, patience and humility.

Your soul knows that compared to eternity, this lifetime is like the blinking of an eye. It is your soul's intention that you learn to live in the moment and remain centered and open to what life offers. And your soul can hardly wait for that moment when it plans to whisper in your ear as you meditate, "Don't sweat the small stuff. And (after a dramatic pause)...don't sweat the big stuff!"

Your soul sees this lifetime as a play upon a stage. The leading roles will be played by "actors" you will call family, friends and co-workers. They will hurt you and push your buttons. At first you will want to blame them. But when you accuse another, pointing at them in anger, have you ever noticed three fingers are pointing back at you? Experiences offer you opportunities to look within and heal the discordant feelings.

It works like this. Do you ever find yourself getting frustrated or impatient with the actions of others? Consider when you do that it is a projection of that trait inside of you wanting to be healed. When you find yourself thinking, "I wish she could make a firm decision," look inside yourself. Discern if that is an indication of your own frustration with your inability to make a decision. In order to recognize something in others, you must first have it within yourself.

At times, you may insist that what you are observing in others is not a trait of yours. It may not be obvious but it can be in your energy field, though possibly from previous lifetimes, and being brought to your attention to be cleared. What you do not like in others is always an energetic projection of yourself. Even if you could change the behavior of others, it would not resolve your energetic blocks. You are the only one who can change your perspective and re-pattern the energy field of these vibrations. Blaming others and ignoring this feedback keeps the vibration of those feelings present.

The really good news is that this "mirror" has a positive side to it. The inspiring, uplifting things you see in other people are in you as well. When you see in others such things as compassion, genius, beauty, caring and affection, you're seeing a projection of yourself. You see these things because they are a part of you, even though you may not think that you are as beautiful or smart as the person you are observing. Trust that it is in your energy field now (remember, you are multi-dimensional) even if you are not expressing that aspect of you.

Let's get back to your lifetime. As you honor this bigger picture, you see that the roles of the leading actors were crucial. You understand why your soul has placed them in front of you—to force you to look at the issues your human mind wants to ignore. Like big dressing room mirrors, they each reflect back to you a clearer image of yourself. You are here not to change others or judge them but to change and appreciate yourself. And look at all the help you have— family, friends, co-workers and even strangers. These actors are your greatest teachers. Aha! That's the biggie your soul wants you to learn this lifetime.

Your soul knows that when you return to spirit realm you will thank your fellow actors for playing their roles so well. And you will honor the courage you had to take on the perfect experiences your soul planned for your life.

The Power of Forgiveness

Forgiving doesn't mean what another did was okay.

You are on Earth to experience love and peace, and forgiveness leads you in that direction. Many people attract opportunities in which others love them only conditionally, cheat on them or abuse them emotionally or physically. These trying times offer the contrasts for what their souls wanted them to discover: that they are worthy of respect, that they can set healthy boundaries and, ultimately, that they can forgive.

Forgiveness offers you a chance to release a painful weight and choose not to allow an experience to rob you of peace. Said in a similar way, forgiveness is refusing to participate in the harm of another's action. Forgiveness initiates the release of your bottled-up anger, resentment, and sense of victimhood.

Most of us are here to grant ourselves more self-love and forgiveness is an act of self-love: you gain more inner peace and allow in more love.

No one deserves to be beaten or betrayed. Yet it happens. Once my clients understand that their souls can grow from their pain and that their thoughts determine if they suffer or feel good, it is easier for them to address the hurt and move forward from a position of empowerment. They realize the power of not allowing their past to continue depleting their energy.

Forgiveness raises your vibration on many levels. Energetically, what you do for yourself, you also do for others and what you do for others, you do for yourself.

Forgiving others opens the pathway for others more easily to forgive you. When you forgive someone for taking advantage of you, you energetically forgive yourself for the lifetimes during which you took advantage of others. Forgiving those who have hurt you, ignored you or abandoned you not only lifts a burden off your shoulders this lifetime; it dissolves the blocked vibration of an inability to forgive that you carry from other lifetimes.

My Background—Growing Up

I will share my dysfunctional background not for comparison—many people have endured so much more—but to share that adversity or one's baggage can be transformed.

It's time to put the "fun" back into dysfunctional.

I was the youngest of four children born within five years. My mother left an abusive marriage when I was five. She had sheltered us from the abuse by stuffing her feelings and making excuses for her occasional bruises.

I was in my 40s and purposefully processing emotions when I realized my buried anger toward my father. Up until then, I honestly didn't feel I harbored any anger toward my childhood experiences.

The anger that came up was magnified by a memory of watching my father, consumed by unprovoked jealousy and excessive drinking chase my mother outside and around our house with a gun. No shots were fired but I recorded that into my cellular memory. I coped by blaming his erratic behavior on his drinking and unconsciously buried my anger. He worked intermittently; he wasn't able to care for himself, let alone a family. After the divorce he didn't have much time with us or help out financially. I watched my mother carry the responsibilities of raising us. And, I buried more anger and resentment about that. My father died of heart failure when I was 10. I buried that grief.

As I awakened spiritually, I felt guided to programs that, in part, had me facing these emotions. As I did, I got angry. I wailed. I felt excruciating pain in my heart. I hated the pain of doing this work but I stayed with the feelings. The "bad" emotional pain created a breakthrough, clearing lifetimes of stuffed anger and grief.

Growing up, the good, the love, out-weighed the bad. Mom worked hard to provide life's necessities. Considered one of the working poor, my Mom did her best to feed, shelter and clothe us. One winter, while drying my only winter coat on our big heating stove I burned a hole the size of a dessert plate through its lining. There were no Goodwill Centers nearby, nor extra money for a new coat, so I had to wear it. At school I was careful how I took it off or put it on. I did not want to explain to anyone that we couldn't afford to buy me a new coat.

Poverty can stimulate feelings of low self worth, anger and embarrassment. When these emotions are stuffed—often as a coping mechanism—they later manifest in different ways for different people. Some children get the power and attention they need by bullying or being disruptive. Others become withdrawn or numb their feelings with drugs or alcohol. Others use their experience as a catalyst to create a better life.

Even as an adolescent, I knew Mom was doing her best. Somehow that must have inspired my siblings and me to do our best. We all worked at a young age. When I was 11, I had a summer-long, 40-hour-per-week baby-sitting job. From then on, I bought or made all my own clothing. My Mom and sister Ramona taught me to sew and in high school I bought fabric and sewed many outfits. My wardrobe was extended when I realized I could fit into my brother Doug's pants. I loved his burgundy ones. He shared them with me until his friend caught on and teased him for wearing *my* pants. That memory still brings a smile to my face.

Mom modeled core values for us—integrity, an appreciation for an honest day's work and the desire to be of service. I am proud of my siblings and myself; we strove hard in both school and extracurricular activities.

I was drawn to sports. The physical activity gave me a fun way to get fit and I felt satisfaction from being part of a team.

Looking back at how much I really liked sports, I realize they must have also filled an emotional void. I couldn't control our standard of living. So I found activities that my hard work could impact, something I could control. I channeled my energy into field hockey, gymnastics and softball, and student government.

I loved contributing to my school community and was elected student council president my senior year in high school. In hindsight, I can see how my sense of unworthiness was playing out here; I'm sure this drive to excel was also serving my need to be validated. I was not emotionally secure from within, so I found validation outside of myself through activities.

I was inducted into the National Honor Society—a great honor and, simultaneously, a reminder of my family's financial straits. My mother couldn't attend the induction ceremony; her boss needed her at work and she couldn't afford the loss in wages. This is typical of the subtle yet difficult choices people must make every day. As an energetic being, I recorded this experience in my cellular memory: "There just isn't enough money." My mother probably recorded a mix of pride, guilt and resentment.

My spiritual journey taught me that, as a soul, I had chosen my childhood experiences including an alcoholic father and poverty. I also learned that my life had given me the very experiences my soul needed in order to dissolve the false beliefs I had accumulated. I became aware that my experiences would lead me to recognize and release the energetic blocks of fear, anger, unworthiness, lack mentality and the need to control outcomes. What a relief it was to learn that emotions and beliefs, imprinted in my cellular memory from this and other lifetimes, were just showing up again to give me another chance to heal them.

Time and experience have helped me develop self-worth and release unnecessary baggage. I have learned to let go of the need to control the outcomes of situations. I realized this baggage was rooted in childhood, in feeling I had no control over my situation.

I grew up wanting to control outcomes or people as my way of coping and trying to feel safe in the world. As I learned that I create my reality and that I am more than my baggage, I could let go of the need to control situations and people. I continued my journey and practiced the teachings I share in this book. I learned forgiveness and released judgment and anger. And then there is the umbrella over them all—faith. I give thanks that my life has offered me many chances to deepen my faith.

Our souls choose many lessons to address each lifetime. Of those, a few are considered major life themes. We attract situations in hopes of totally clearing, in this lifetime, the false beliefs associated with our life themes. We will know we have learned the lessons of our life themes when we stop attracting similar situations or have no fear around those scenarios.

My life themes were lack mentality and unworthiness. The lessons I have learned and finally have owned to the core of my being are: I am enough, I am worthy because I am one with God, and the universe is abundant.

My Background—Marriage and Family

There was fun and love amongst life's lessons. Happily in love, my high school sweetheart and I married after college. We shared interests in physical fitness, the outdoors, a strong work ethic and a desire to save money and live within our means. Considering my childhood of poverty, that felt good. It felt safe. We made cautious financial decisions, even though we were financially secure. As I look back, I see that I was living my life from lack mentality — those childhood feelings of "there just isn't enough money" were etched in my cellular memory.

When we married, we moved from Maine to Burlington, Vermont. My husband was in a retail management program and I worked as a dental hygienist. We enjoyed cross-country skiing and hiking in Vermont's Green Mountains. No matter the season, the fresh air and views of the quaint white churches and farms tucked in the valleys and the laughter of friends spending a day together all deepened our appreciation for this special time in our lives.

A few years later we moved back to Maine. Six years into our marriage, in 1987, our first daughter, Brianna, was born; our second daughter, Brittany, followed fifteen months later.

My husband and I were a great team. He climbed the corporate ladder while I took care of the responsibilities of our family and home. I loved being an at-home mom, totally immersed in my children's developmental years. I valued the routine of bath time, and at bedtime, crawling into the bed with my girls and reading aloud. We expressed our child-like wonder through finger painting, molding clay animals and making scratch biscuits and cookies together. We did lots of swimming in the summer at nearby lakes or in the 68 degrees Maine ocean waters and throughout the winter we went sledding.

In 1994, my husband's job transfer brought us to Cary, North Carolina.

Time and life commitments change relationships. My husband and I grew apart and after 18 years of marriage we separated on a trial basis. I remember writing in a notebook two years before our separation that our marriage, as I knew it, was over. Part of me didn't want to accept it but I was silently dealing with emotions of failure and grief. I often cried myself to sleep. But those two years gave me time to process my emotions. I focused on the positive, knowing that our trial separation would either make our marriage stronger or move us forward to healthier separate lives. The separation gave us clarity and we divorced.

My daughters were playful and respectful. They were bright, beautiful and creative, and even though they had very different personalities they got along exceptionally. Then, the hormones hit. Our home had hormonal teenagers and a pre-menopausal mom. We had our share of emotionally charged days...I mean, opportunities to grow. We became each other's teachers. Ugh!

Brittany's unresolved pain from the divorce was intensified by those hormonal changes and she expressed herself through rages of uncontrollable anger, crying and depression. She refused to participate in counseling, even when coerced to go.

I appreciate Brittany allowing me to share her struggles; not something she is proud of, but she understands that our experiences may help others.

As with each person who pushes your buttons or doesn't act the way you would like, Brittany has been my perfect "teacher." I was forced to look head on at my stuff—issues of control, self-respect and boundaries. Brittany's behavior was erratic and irresponsible. She was dealing with a lack of coping skills, depression and escalating anger. She struggled. I struggled. I continued to look for a program that could support her. I prayed for guidance. I heard about and researched therapeutic boarding schools and felt hopeful. They appealed to me because they provided daily counseling and peer support while the participants continued their schooling.

A minor needed both parents' agreement for enrollment in the program and her father refused to send her away for help. He blamed her behavior on mother and daughter dynamics. I disagreed. Brittany's refusal to get any professional help forced me to do one of the hardest things I've ever done.

It took me two months, with a friend's daily calls of support and coaxing, to get up the courage. Holding to my boundaries of what was acceptable behavior in my home, I insisted she leave during her sophomore year in high school. This devastated me. As a mother, I wanted her with me; I wanted to be the one to help her. She didn't want my help. She didn't want a counselor's help.

She went five minutes away to live with her dad. Her sister joined them. What I was hoping would be six months turned into two-and-a-half years, the rest of high school.

Her dad realized this was more than a challenging mother and daughter relationship; he struggled with parenting her too. A year later, in December of her junior year in high school, we learned that she had been using cocaine for three months. I lobbied again for her to go to a therapeutic boarding school. Her father still refused.

We got her into a local drug program for teens that met three times a week. She stopped using drugs. That was a big step but I was still concerned. It seemed she was looking at her anger issues, but only on the surface. And she wasn't developing enough coping skills to handle her emotions consistently.

Her senior year, Brittany wanted to go on a spring break trip with her friends. Her friends did not use drugs but it was still a thought-provoking decision because, on one hand, I didn't want her exposed to any spring break partying; on the other, we knew she would be on her way to college soon and would need to be able to handle that environment. Brittany had stayed clean, been drug tested weekly and was actively participating in her group counseling sessions. Her counselors, her dad and I agreed to let her go with her friends.

During spring break, I got a dreaded phone call at two o'clock in the morning. Her friends had called EMS and she was now in the hospital. She drank too much alcohol while combining it with cocaine and Klonopin, an anxiety drug. The hospital staff monitored her and released her the next day.

We were so thankful that she was okay. But, this was a very painful time for me. Brittany would turn 18 years old soon; as a legal adult I couldn't force treatment on her. I also knew that unless she got serious help, her dad and I would not allow her to live with either of us. This broke my heart. Employing "tough love" means having to accept the pain of its potential failure—of her continuing down this destructive path.

I chose to do an intervention. Those present included me, her sister, close friends who had been with her during spring break and another adult, our neighbor Karen, who Brittany loves and respects.

I had done my research and had a few program options for her. She agreed to get help, feeling she had to go because she would have no place to live.

I must have been holding in lifetimes of fear and anguish; when she agreed to go, a deep, guttural, fear-based sound escaped from me. That sound felt ancient. Regardless, my heart felt relieved. She went to an out-of-state, three-month drug rehabilitation program. I was deeply grateful. I had renewed hope.

She did well for two months. Then she broke the rules, the consequence of which was to leave the program. Before she returned home, she did drugs again. This culminated in an experience that literally scared her clean. She called her dad crying and agreed to cooperate and get drug tested regularly. As she walked into my house, after a long embrace, she asked me to do energy healing on her. Energy healing is something she had not previously wanted and still rarely chooses. She was ready to feel better.

She started her freshman year of college soon after. Her drug use became an issue of the past. Thank you, God! Throughout college, though, she has gone through ups and downs while still dealing with anxiety, depression, lack of coping skills, and inconsistency with counseling and medication. While she had some really good months, there were also times that she spiraled down. She sank to her lowest point twice, attempting suicide each time.

Through sadness and tears, I had to reach deep into my heart and call forth all the faith I could muster. I trusted her soul came here to work on all of these issues. I knew spiritually that I had agreed to walk this path with her. I trusted that all was in Divine order and that if she really needed to exit the Earth plane then she would do that no matter what I wanted. On the other hand, I was a mother, having a human experience that was very painful.

Since early 2010, she has increasingly made responsible choices with her life.

The principles I speak of within this book kept me on track most of the time. During the times that I was worried sick, the same teachings got me back on track. I would work with my fear and affirm through my tears, "She is in God's hands, what better place to be." That was very comforting to me. It still is. I trusted that Spirit was supporting us and, at the same time, not taking away the valuable soul lessons we all needed.

I relentlessly repeated this mantra: "Who am I, not to allow her to experience what her soul needs to experience in the way she needs to experience it?" It centered me in the moment. It gave me strength. The mantra also reminded me that we are all part of a bigger spiritual journey and it helped me step out of my own way and trust we'd get through these roller-coaster times. And, of course, she was and is always in my positive thoughts and prayers.

Brittany participated in a Dialectical Behavior Therapy program, available for teens and adults, for 18 months. DBT Skills Training includes, on a weekly basis, a private session with a counselor and a group session. It teaches skills to help manage thoughts and feelings, relate more effectively and handle distress without acting impulsively. It is valuable to those who have trouble letting go of self-defeating behaviors.

What a difference time makes! Brittany, a senior in college, smiles a lot and is taking more responsibility for herself; she handles disappointments better, has released some anger, appreciates her family more, maintains honor roll status in college, enjoyed her internship last semester and found a part-time job this year in her field of studies. Growth is a process and her dad, sister and I are so proud of her progress.

Over last Christmas break, she volunteered at a dog rescue program and adopted one of the pups. She took one that, because of previous neglect, would run from everyone. "Nugget" trusted Brittany and, after two months, the puppy was exposing her fun personality. My heart sings as I observe the unconditional love Brittany and Nugget have for each other.

My holistic healing practice helps many people with anger, depression and drug problems. Brittany has mostly avoided holistic treatment with me or other practitioners, saying she doesn't believe in it. That has been my lesson to learn—a hard one for sure, to see my daughter suffer and not want my help. I know that I, on a soul level, "signed up" for her to be my teacher. That awareness has lessened the sting. I still remind myself that my girls know my holistic avenues are an option if and when they choose to explore them.

They have also helped me to let go (okay, mostly let go) of needing to change their unhealthy eating habits. I eat a totally raw, vegan diet. And that works for me, and their dietary choices, well, they work for them. Though, it does feel good to see Brianna making healthier dietary choices. I remind myself that change will happen if and when it is in their divine timing, not mine. Yes, they help me practice minding "my business," not theirs. I'm getting there.

Both girls continue to have fun and experience life — including learning lessons and dealing with life's consequences. My daughters continue to help me become a better person. Over the years they have helped me see my blocks of stubbornness, control and fear. As I embrace what each of our souls came here to learn and experience, I am more and more able to honor myself and my daughters' choices.

As parents we feel we know best, wanting to protect our kids from harm and unnecessary hurts. Maintaining a spiritual perspective has given me the awareness to keep stepping back, sharing my opinion yet allowing my girls to figure things out in a way that is best for them and learning from their decisions. I am learning that my way doesn't have to be their way, and I understand that their choices, even the "wrong" turns, are actually helping them unfold along their soul paths.

Along my life's path, I felt more freedom and checked off some major life lessons as I recognized that the people who have disappointed me and hurt me are my divine teachers guiding me to higher consciousness.

Are you ready to find the fun in dysfunctional?

Emotional freedom, the way life should be.

Chapter 5
The Power to Choose

I know this world is ruled by infinite intelligence.
Everything that surrounds us – everything that exists – proves that
there are infinite laws behind it. There can be no denying this fact.
It is mathematical in its precision. – Thomas A. Edison

You expand your avenues to create a better life as you look at challenging situations and difficult people from a spiritual and energetic perspective. Most of us were taught to see our problems and how to fix them from the physical perspective only.

Viewing them from an energetic perspective allows you to influence the vibration around your problems, which energetically aligns you with more positive outcomes. You have the power to choose your perspective. You can choose to think differently about your challenges and to *decide* what to focus on.

When you access your power to choose, at each moment you are building momentum to create anew. This is possible because you live in an energetic universe that abides by energetic laws and your choices influence everything around you. As you experience your world from this dynamic, you will realize you do not need to change your problems, you just need to change the way you choose to *see* your problems. Decide what you want to create from this moment forward.

Keep in mind these truths: Spirit does not limit you. This multi-dimensional universe is abundant. Life does not need to be a struggle.

Universal Laws

Most of us don't leap right into enlightenment—that higher consciousness of knowing, of trusting and accepting "what is," and of being at peace with all of our experiences.

Understanding the energetic power of universal laws is important if you desire an easier, healthier and happier life. These laws are at work in your life whether you have heard of them or not, and whether you believe in them or not.

Opening to the power of these laws is like walking along the stepping stones that mark a path to deeper awareness of the energetic world in which you live. When you stay in conscious alignment with them, you have more power to influence and change your experiences.

Universal laws are the foundation of this book and are interwoven throughout its pages. The law of attraction simply states that like attracts like, energy flows where attention goes, and whatever you focus on expands. It is also a non-discriminatory law; whether you are focus on what you want or on what you don't want, you will attract whatever you fervently focus on and give emotional energy to.

Until you experience the benefits of the law of attraction first hand, the idea of it may cause some confusion or doubt. This happens because all of your life you have been taught that you are *only* a physical body, and the first thing you need to improve your situation is more "physical" things—more money, a better car, or prescription drugs and surgery. Similarly, you have been taught that if you want more out of life you must physically work harder and for longer hours to get it. You've been taught to see your world only from a physical perspective—one that includes limitations and fears.

Your soul chose to be here on planet Earth in this time-space reality, knowing you were equipped with all you need to face limitations and fears, to create your life on your terms. The law of deliberate creation speaks to this ability to use your mind and choose your thoughts and intentions deliberately. Your thoughts and intentions create feelings and these feelings create the vibrations that you emit, which, in turn, determine what you attract into your experience. With deliberate thoughts and feelings, you attract more of what you want. The law of allowing reminds us of the importance of getting into alignment so source energy can flow through us, improving the vibrations we emit. The result? Improved experiences.

The law of sufficiency and abundance speaks to the spiritual truth that you are innately enough and the natural order of the universe is prosperity.

There is also the law of pure potentiality. You are infinite potential. When you realize that your true Self is one of pure potentiality, you align with the energetic field of consciousness that supports you in manifesting.

You are part of this spiritually expanding universe. You have an opportunity to take your present understanding to a deeper knowing—to the truth of your being. Be empowered. Choose to look beyond the learned conditioning of physical limitation and fear, and of seeing your life from only one dimension. Be willing to shift your belief system, even turn it upside down if need be, for a more fulfilling life.

The law of detachment affirms there are no mistakes in the universe. Trust that each experience has a purpose and is for your highest good. Learn from each experience. Try to understand why you attracted it and align with your creative power. At the same time, don't be attached to a certain outcome. When you can give up your need for the result to be what you expected or wanted, you open yourself to infinite possibilities.

The law of polarity includes the idea that you are both

a spiritual being and a physical being. Efficiency increases in life when you first take action steps on the inner realm, using your mind and perspective to get into energetic alignment with what you want. Then, take action steps on the physical level. Aligning yourself energetically saves time and allows in more peace and balance.

You attract more blessings with each positive thought of love, peace, kindness, joy and compassion. Think of yourself as a magnet, drawing to yourself that which you focus on and magnetizing all of your life experiences—your preferences, blessings and even the curses. Expecting your preferences strengthens the likelihood of manifesting them. You will align to that which is for your highest good when you also add the feeling of joyous expectancy for a particular outcome, even when you do not understand how this could possibly come about.

However, you will align to chaos or misfortune when you approach a situation expecting difficulty and chaos and focusing on all the ways things could go wrong or have gone wrong. Our world abides by these universal laws. It cannot be otherwise. Negative feelings of anger, resentment and judgment attract like vibrations—negative situations—to you. These feelings actually block or lessen the likelihood that you will receive that which you do want. Some negative people find success in one or more areas of their lives because that is how their destiny plan was spiritually set up. In general, though, consistent negative and fear-based thoughts block you from achieving an all-around wonderful life.

If you work or live around people you do not like, you can improve your situation by adjusting your attitude. Realize you are in the driver's seat and can choose to feel differently about those people. When you change your attitude you transform your energy field—the atmosphere—to one in which everyone benefits and feels better, especially you.

Each thought carries with it a corresponding creative

or destructive energy field. The good news is you alone are responsible for the thoughts you think; choosing a more positive thought is always an option. Set an intention to monitor your thoughts and become more aware of the vibrations that are rippling out from you.

To monitor your thoughts, stop several times a day, at the top of each hour or after each phone call or meeting, and ask yourself, "Was I thinking and speaking from a positive perspective?" This practice will help you be more cognizant of your thoughts. With practice you will change a thought to a more positive one the split second before you speak it.

Team up with a good friend and gently remind each other to speak more positively. Discuss this ahead of time and confirm you both want this kind of support. You may decide to use a gentle reminder to turn worrying around, such as, "Did I hear you say, 'I got invited back for a second interview,'" when you had just heard her fretting about an upcoming interview. Or, you can use a reminder word, such as "positive," as a hint to choose more positive words.

Besides your words, your imagination is powerful. Create in your mind a picture of the life you would *love* to live, and then give thanks in advance for what you want as if it has already arrived. Say, "Thank you, Spirit, that I now have the right and perfect job for my highest good and the highest good of all," *before* an interview. Act or speak as if you already have the ideal job because there is no concept of time in the realm of Spirit.

Use your feelings to magnify your creative power. Gratitude and love are the highest vibrations there are. Coming from love is always best, but it is difficult to feel loving when life is hurtful and chaotic. In those situations, find something to be grateful for. Be grateful for what you want, again, as if you already have it. Affirm, "I am so happy and so grateful that I now have a job that is for the highest good of all." The highest good of all includes you and your family and whoever else may be affected. Always affirming "for the highest good of all" allows for the best possible outcome, especially when you do not understand why certain things are or are not happening for you.

If you are laid off and your family's finances require your daughter to go to a community college instead of the college of her choice, trust that, at some level, it is for her highest good too. Affirming that you are guided for the highest good of all reinforces your trust that Spirit has your back, even when you don't understand it. Spirit is aware of your soul lessons and the future opportunities that you are not privy to from your Earthly perspective.

Consciously monitoring and shifting your thoughts and feelings is a life-long practice. You, your family and your world are worth the investment you make in yourself when you take the time and create the discipline to align yourself to goodness. Challenges are changed into triumphs.

Maybe you are wondering how you could have "vibrated" your way into some of your dilemmas. Accept your confusion. We often don't get it. The more you analyze a situation, the more you give it energy and the more you keep the problem active. See the challenge as temporary. Then, call back your power—the awareness that your thoughts can also lift you out of the potholes they created no matter the depth.

People find they raise their vibration and move upward in spiritual consciousness as they consistently monitor their thoughts and feelings. This higher consciousness will strengthen your "magnet" to attract your desires more easily, experiencing an easier and more fulfilling life unfolding before your eyes.

Cherokee Tale

There is a Cherokee tale about two wolves that speaks to the law of attraction. One evening an old Cherokee chief told his grandson about a battle that goes on inside people. He said, "My son, the battle is between two "wolves" that live inside each of us.

"One wolf is named Evil; it is a wolf of anger, envy, jealousy, sorrow, regret, greed, arrogance, self-pity, guilt, resentment, inferiority, lies, false pride, superiority and ego.

"The other wolf is named Good and it is a wolf of joy, peace, love, hope, serenity, humility, kindness, benevolence, empathy, generosity, truth, compassion and faith."

The grandson thought about what his grandfather had told him for a minute and then asked, "Which wolf wins?"

The old chief replied, "The answer is simple, my son. The one who wins is the one you feed."

Besides this Native American tale, references to the law of attraction are found in many cultures, probably all cultures, and in all the spiritual texts. Master teachers have taught this law for over 5,000 years: thoughts are powerful creators, physical healing or changes in experiences are of the mind first, and intentions are the root of change.

In the Jewish Book of Proverbs you will find: "As a man thinketh in his heart, so he is."

From the Qur'an, part 23, surah 36 (Ya-sin), verse 82 translates from Arabic to "Verily, His command, when He intends a thing, is only that He says to it, 'BE!' and it is!"

Christianity is based on the teachings of Jesus Christ and in one of his famous sermons Jesus directed his followers to ask for what they want with the faith and belief that they already had it. In fact, he taught that anything you ask for in a spirit of faith and belief, you will get. In the Bible, Matthew 21:22, you will find these words: "Whatsoever ye shall ask in prayer, believing, ye shall receive."

These are just a few examples of a timeless spiritual law that has been available to humanity for thousands of years; today, energetically, it is commonly called the law of attraction. With practice, it guides you to experience life deliberately, not haphazardly.

Change what shows up on the outside by first changing what is happening on the inside—the vibration created by your thoughts and feelings and what you are focusing on.

Habitually concentrating on negative and worrisome thoughts attracts more negativity to you. These negative thoughts keep building upon the previous negative thoughts until you are creating problems and situations you would not have chosen purposely. The good news is it is not your past or present situation that will determine your future.

Your future is created by the power and focus you give to your thoughts and feelings right now, focusing, with joyful intent, on the good you want in your life. Accept the power of your thoughts. Accept the powerful Being you truly are.

You can improve your outcome in a precarious situation by staying calm and hopeful. Yes, I know it can take deep breathing, self-talk and much practice. But staying calm energetically aligns you with the more positive experiences you prefer.

Focusing on a particular scenario from the position of an angry victim actually blocks you from the very blessings you need in order to move on. If you find yourself automatically reacting as you always have, screaming and blaming others, for example, your anger is vibrating to the universe, "No thanks, I really don't want any help. I like all this chaos." I recommend that you go to a private space where you can feel the anger fully and allow it to dissolve.

Make peace with whatever situation you have attracted and know you can greatly influence the outcome. Look for the good in your current conditions.

There is a wonderfully funny story about a set of young twin boys. One was a pessimist who never appreciated what he had. The other had an optimistic temperament and he was always finding the good in his life. Some scientists decided to study these twins to determine why they had such different personalities.

They put the pessimistic twin in a room full of toys any boy would love and they put the optimistic twin in a room full of horse manure. When they went back to observe how the boys were doing, they found that the pessimistic child had broken all his toys and was crying because he had nothing to play with. To the scientists' surprise, the other twin had taken a shovel and was digging, knee deep, in the horse manure. When asked what he was doing, he replied joyfully, "With all this shit, there has to be a pony somewhere!"

Daily, like the young optimist, find the best feeling attitude you can muster, determined not by what you are dealing with but by your acceptance of the power of your thoughts. Make the best of a challenge and allow yourself to feel hopeful and positive. Allow the best solution to be revealed.

Practicing this journey helps you trust that challenges come to teach you something your soul wanted you to learn. Especially review repetitive patterns—life themes—showing up to be addressed and healed. Face the emotions associated with them and you will experience significant breakthroughs along your spiritual journey and deepen your belief that all experiences are in divine order.

My belief that all is in divine order is what allowed me to stay in my power and regain my breath. I even call what happened to me an incident, knowing that there are no accidents in the universe. I knew I was connected to Source and I knew that even this incident was somehow in divine order. I had no clue to why I had attracted it. My faith in the bigger picture allowed me to trust it anyway. Trusting the bigger picture that all is in divine order opened the door wide for the healing energy to enter.

The "How" Is None of Your Business

You were probably taught to work harder and take control of situations when life gets tough. You learned that *you* need to figure out *how* to make things better. You were told this for "your own good," but accepting these beliefs is limiting.

Happiness and success in your personal and business worlds is far more the result of making better use of your mind than it is of how well you control your outer environment. It's not your job to figure out "how" to fix your problems.

Practice believing in your worthiness for success and focus on your desires. You will tap into the interconnected field of consciousness and the universe will divinely guide your desires to you and more! Promise yourself that you will allow God—Spirit—to handle the details, the "how" of turning around your situation. Put your desire out there and then get out of the way. Let go and let God.

Allow the beauty of life to be in the journey. Each day becomes a stepping stone to trusting, using the tools available and getting out of your own way.

Builders can build homes more efficiently with the right array of tools. If these tools are not available, the job can be frustrating, extremely time consuming or possibly done poorly. Even with the right tools, if the builder's crew chooses not to use them because of their limited experience with them, the overall productivity and quality of the crew's work can be diminished. Fortunately, there are crews who will choose to invest the time it takes to learn how to use the tools because they realize a little effort up front and consistent use of quality tools will reap great rewards.

This analogy speaks to the teachings in this book. You have untapped, freely available tools already within you. Raising your belief in the power of these tools and your consistency in using them will help you attract the right people, opportunities, resources and blessings for your highest good.

Expect the quality of your life to increase, with more joy, harmony, health, abundance and spiritual growth. This book, your manual so to speak, will help you make good use of your inner tools and see your situations from a different angle—a fresh perspective.

This fresh perspective reminds you that you block your creative power when you focus on prior unsuccessful results or on that doubting Thomas in your mind. Let these teachings inspire you to pick up some of these tools and commit to using them.

Results differ from one person to the next because of their differences in soul lessons, old programming and beliefs, in how they approach life and in how deeply they can believe in these principles and in themselves. Many people get results with the law of attraction. Others, because they haven't understood its relationship with their overall vibration and beliefs, don't get their desired results and give it a bad rap.

You can sincerely say affirmations and focus on wants, but unresolved anger and resentment just below the surface of a smile affects the overall vibration emitted to the Universe. The vibration blocks you from getting what you really want.

The more you use these tools in everyday life the more your results will improve. With daily practice, they become familiar and comfortable. The next chapter's stories are examples of using these tools.

Remember your power to choose. Be willing to deepen your awareness of a world beyond physicality. Be willing to commit to your spiritual growth and recognize your destiny is entwined with your intent and desire. Be willing to accept the wonderful results that are available for you.

Beyond the Law of Attraction

Humanity is experiencing a time like no other. High frequency light waves are entering our solar system, causing universal energies to shift us to higher vibrations. The lower emotional vibrations of anger, resentment, unworthiness and fear are such different and discordant vibrations from those coming in.

This phenomenon is drawing our fear-based vibrations to the surface for healing. We are being given an opportunity to embrace our soul journeys and upgrade our lives. There are no limitations to what we can accomplish. It is our birthright to create joy, abundance and harmony.

This transformational era offers you an opportunity to stretch yourself and integrate all of who you really are—mind, body and spirit. You are given a chance to release the limitations, beliefs and self-sabotaging reactions that have defined you and to embrace instead the essence of your divinity.

Spiritual evolution is a given, though the amount of pain, disease and problems you experience can be mitigated. You attract situations and people to bring your lower vibrations to your awareness. Of course, from a logical, human-mind perspective you imagine you wouldn't choose such challenges; but from a spiritual perspective, these challenges show you what is on your "soul plate" to be transformed.

Your soul chose to participate in the process of life— the inherent emotional and spiritual growth offered to you under the guise of your hurts and challenges. But expect to reduce suffering when you consistently view your life experiences from an energetic and spiritual perspective, trusting that there is a divine purpose in all events, even the setbacks. Let go of the need to understand the purpose or control the outcome of situations. Know instead that these circumstances are nudging you forward to gain experiences for your soul's highest good.

When you experience any amount of lack or discord, you are seeing events through the distorted, limited view of your human mind. Spirit mind cannot see anything but an abundance of what it is—wholeness, perfection, love, joy, peace and harmony.

Creating Experiences from Your Soul's Vibration

Your vibration attracts your experiences. Nevertheless, a car accident, a lost wallet or a serious injury, such as I experienced, doesn't always mean you had a negative vibration.

You attract situations for many reasons, possibly to have fun, to meet people, to learn lessons, to be a teacher to others, to align yourself with something you will need later, or to balance karma. You attract every experience for a higher purpose. The purpose will not always be obvious but when you can trust that your experience has a higher purpose, your calmer energy field will help you handle it better and align you with the best possible outcome.

I was happy, well along my spiritual path and daily integrating these principles into my life when I fell and broke my neck. Each time I went biking I visualized myself safely ending my ride and putting my bike back into my SUV. That day was no different. And before I attempted the teeter-totter, the infamous obstacle, I visualized myself successfully riding over it and I wrapped myself in the protective Christ White Light.

And, I fell and snapped my neck in two.

It was my faith that everything always happens for a reason that allowed me to harness my inner power and not spiral into fear, anger or "Why me?"

I experienced a divinely orchestrated injury, an injury that was part of my destiny. This is illustrated by the synchronistic events before and after I broke my neck:

- Charlie and I rode weekly, just the two of us, for one and a half years prior to my injury. Our friend Andy "just happened" to join us that day. Seems like Spirit provided more support to handle the emergency.
- I took my cell phone out of my backpack and showed Charlie my ICE—In Case of Emergency—numbers, something I had never done before.
- Andy needed us to change our biking time from morning to afternoon; the director of Spine Surgery at Duke University Medical Hospital "just happened" to be on call in the emergency room that afternoon.
- I had been a side sleeper all my life, yet I started sleeping on my back about a year before my injury. I thought it strange to have changed positions, but it became so comfortable. Obviously, my higher spiritual Self prepared me for my fate. I had to sleep in that position during the months of recovery; that position was now natural and comfortable to me. Then, about a year and a half after my injury, without consciously doing so, I slowly acclimated back to sleeping more on my side.
- Two days before I broke my neck, I "just happened" to watch a Tom Kenyon video on sound healing. During the video, I followed along as he demonstrated a meditation using breath, sound and movement. He shared the names of the spiritual doctors whom he invokes. I wrote the names down and was particularly interested in the two neurosurgeons. Spiritual doctors assist energy facilitators in their sessions; I planned to invoke them for a multiple sclerosis client. Instead, two days later, I was in the woods, on the ground paralyzed from head to toe. After I regained my breath, I invoked the names of those two doctors.

I believe my traumatic experience was in divine order. Thankfully, the intelligent universe arranged for blessings to help make it as easy as possible. I give thanks that we are all one with this higher power.

You are a student in this game of life. You magnify your chances for an easier recovery when you acknowledge there is a purpose for the setback. As you learn from it, you eliminate more quickly from your energy field the patterns that attracted the setback.

The improved energy field shifts you to a higher consciousness and lessens your need to attract similar scenarios. However, if you do attract another one, then know it is because there are more layers of the same emotional wound to be healed. You can choose your perspective—to be frustrated that it has come back around or to be grateful that you are fine-tuning your energy field.

Trust that Spirit sees your energy field and the big picture of your soul's destiny path. Spirit always has your back, no matter what it initially looks like. Know that every situation has an important purpose. Breathe in the comfort and the peace that awareness offers. Knowing this is easy. Owning it takes practice.

You might be wondering why these principles seem to work in some areas of your life but not others. You may be blessed in relationships and health but unable to attract consistent financial success.

Think about a repetitive financial problem. Now, entertain the idea that this "problem" is related to one of your soul's "life themes." This problem is, once again, showing up to offer you another opportunity to clear a life theme dealing with financial insecurity or lack mentality. You are spiritually evolving, and in spite of the money you deserve, your evolution requires that this challenge be visited again. This can happen even after months or years of financial success. You may not be making poor decisions or being irresponsible. It's simply time to attract an experience that will take you to your next evolutionary level. Remember, you are a spiritual being having a human experience to grow your soul.

Even if you are already practicing that "what is" has a higher purpose, staying in gratitude, and focusing on what you want with the feeling of already having it, you may still attract a financial setback. Even with a committed relationship with God, the I AM, trust you are attracting it to go to your next level of spiritual growth. You may be clearing this fear vibration from other lifetimes. Regardless of the reason, one lesson here is for you to deepen your faith and accept what you may not understand—to cease trying to make sense of it all.

Being angry and frustrated at something you can't understand serves the moment and the questioning human mind but it blocks your energy field and sabotages your potential results. Analyzing it keeps that discordant energy present. Trusting that it has a higher purpose and that a solution will be revealed deepens your faith.

To deepen your faith and advance in consciousness, you get to practice accepting what is for as many times as it takes. When you are knee-deep in your struggles, realize that what you really want hinges on your willingness to release the need to understand it. Allow the process, the expansion, to unfold for your destiny path's highest good.

When you are ready for your next breakthrough, your higher spiritual Self will guide you to the right experience, book, person or program to positively shift your awareness and ease the challenges of your journey.

I was guided in such a way to Rasha's book *Oneness*. It is one of my favorite books, helping me take all I know and embed it deeper into my core. Rasha beautifully shares, "For what has been required of this transformation is a confrontation, within the depths of your conscious awareness, of the negative patterns and the stagnant energies that you have carried within your energy field. Repressed emotions, negative inclinations, habitual behaviors, addictions, and victim consciousness have been raised to the surface, blatantly, so that you would be able to scrutinize the evidence of the misguided energy harbored within your physical form."

Another of my favorite passages from *Oneness* is, "One becomes a leaf on the wind, embodying a willingness to be carried with the momentum of the process, knowing unquestioningly that one's best interests and one's well-being are being seen to in every possible way. In a sense, one becomes the wind while retaining the self-perception of the leaf."

Now, go and confidently allow in more peace. Spirit has your back!

Chapter 6
Imagine It. Ordain It

Every moment of your life is infinitely creative and the
universe is endlessly bountiful. Just put forth a clear enough request,
and everything your heart truly desires must come to you.
– Shakti Gawain

I love opportunities to practice the law of attraction.

I decided to offer my energy healing services at a Body
Mind Spirit Expo where rows upon rows of practitioner-
sponsored booths reveal energy healing, whole health foods
and supplements, intuitive readings, book stores, and jewelry
and gems of all colors and sizes.

It was to be my first. I even talked with two people
who each sincerely discouraged me from participating; when
they had participated, they hadn't even earned back their
booth rental. I appreciated their comments, but I had been
working with the law of attraction and trusted this as an
opportunity to co-create with the Universe. I chose not to let
their experiences influence me.

It felt right for me to be there. I signed up to offer
introductory 20-minute healing sessions—helping people
release their emotional blocks and feel better physically.

I prepared energetically for a successful event by
intending that these experiences would be highly valuable to
all involved and focusing on the end result. I wrote names on

a mock sign-up sheet, anticipating a full schedule. I visualized a post-expo phone conversation in which I told a friend about all the people who appreciated their sessions and who were interested in further healing sessions and classes.

I leveraged my experience with the law of attraction and ignored what others told me about their negative experiences. My actual sign-up sheet had spaces for names every 20 minutes. Throughout the day, the list was filled out over an hour in advance. I enjoyed meeting new folks and helping them create energetic shifts.

The law of attraction came through again. Throughout the two days I worked a nearly full schedule.

I often reflect and learn from others' experiences; as in this case, even from their disappointing results. I try not to allow the past, mine or theirs, to undermine my efforts and expectations. The power of my creative energy is in my present focus and intentions. Over time I have noticed that the more I practice the law of attraction, the more I deepen my faith in it and attract more consistent results.

Creating with Short Notice

I thank Spirit and the law of attraction for the cool experience I created when I went to buy my car. My salesman encouraged me to place an order for the car I wanted because the few that did come in sold quickly. I decided to wait a month before ordering to make sure I didn't change my mind. I stayed busy with life and, with each passing day, purchasing the car just wasn't on the top of my priority list. Surprisingly, eight months went by.

Then one morning I woke up with an inner knowing that this day was the day to go to the dealership. I arrived at the showroom. It was filled with the smell of new leather and shiny silver, black and red cars strategically placed on a marble tiled floor which reflected the silver lights hanging overhead. I followed the salesman to his glass cubicle.

While he was writing up my order, he told me that a gentleman had just traded in a similar car the previous day. It was the same fire-mist red I was ordering and had only 1,800 miles on it. To me, the synchronicity indicated that I was definitely co-creating with Spirit. We test drove it.

This car was the next model up, loaded with options, and was priced at $10,000 more than the one I intended to order. I learned while doing my car-buying research that dealerships never reduce their prices for my preferred model. And, my law of attraction training prepared me to give more attention to the creative power of the Universe than to what dealers usually did. I had accepted the intuitive nudge from Spirit to get there and continued with that momentum. Sweet.

I like fair negotiating, so I decided to meet them halfway and offered $5,000 less than their asking price. I recognized this as my first big opportunity of utilizing the law of attraction but to be unattached to the outcome. If I didn't receive this car I would place my order. I trusted that with either outcome, Spirit had my back.

I had five minutes to add my creative energies to what Spirit was already orchestrating. I visualized my tall salesman in his starched white shirt weaving through the showroom as he returned to his desk telling me that the general manager had accepted my offer. I visualized signing the contract and driving off with my new red convertible. I was confident and peaceful because, whatever the outcome, I trusted I would have the right and perfect car for my highest good.

Spirit, we are so cool! I drove off in my fire-mist red convertible—for $5,000 less than the asking price. Spirit had my back and that car had my name on it.

I saw the general manager a few days later. Curious about the no-haggle pricing policy I had heard about, I asked, "When was the last time you reduced my model by $5,000?" He replied, "Never. I have never taken even $100 off." His comment affirmed what I had been told. His next comment made it clear that Spirit was all over it. He said, "I wondered later that night why I did that."

Thanks, Spirit. I trust it was my belief in my oneness with Spirit and my use of universal laws that allowed me to avoid waiting for six months and, instead, start having more fun right away.

Creating Just for Fun

Life should be fun and easy so, sometimes, I just play with these principles.

I had dated three men who each drove a Harley Davidson motorcycle. I enjoyed the rides and the camaraderie of meeting other Harley riders at area restaurants. Motor-cycles, 20, 50 or at times 100, would be parked outside these restaurants as their riders enjoyed a pre-ride breakfast or a Southern "home-cooked" dinner. They proudly revved their souped-up engines and showed off their bikes' custom paint jobs—creative designs such as drawings of eagles or of women with long flowing hair. Harley owners are from all walks of life. The ones I met opened their hearts to strangers and to good causes.

When we rode, I loved being the passenger and feeling the wind on my face while taking in the sights—my favorites were the weathered and dilapidated tobacco barns.

I imagined hard-working farmers who ended their days with tired backs and calloused hands. I felt inner peace as I passed by the horse farms, soaking in nature— acres of meadows dotted with oak trees and ponds, outlined with white wooden fencing. I blessed the owners for maintaining their property—a visual gift to those who passed by.

I had a continuous smile on my face riding the curvy highways along the Blue Ridge Mountains of western North Carolina. My eyes took me on a tour of green shrouded mountains, country churches in distant valleys and, right at the roadside for us to enjoy when passing by, steep granite walls and cascading waterfalls.

I realized how much I enjoyed riding and decided to get my own motorcycle license. I attended a weekend Basic Rider Course and received my license soon afterward. A few weeks later I broke my neck. Ugh! It doesn't feel right to get on a motorcycle anymore so, instead, I now get to appreciate all that divine beauty from my convertible but still with the feeling of the wind on my face. And, I ended up with the following great story.

Practicing the law of attraction was becoming natural to me, so I used it here. I committed to learning all I could during the motorcycle safety class. I asked myself, "What would successful learning look like?" So, I affirmed and visualized my desired end result, that I received the highest written and practical test scores in my class. Then, I got out of my own way and enjoyed the class.

I practiced many of the outdoor techniques with the motorcycle provided. The figure eight exercise was the most challenging. The goal was to stay within a rectangular area, about 20 by 50 feet, while driving in a figure eight path. I was doing fives, nines, and even a 12! But I could not do a figure eight.

I kept a light-hearted attitude and focused on what I did have power over, my thoughts and attitude. I ignored how poorly I was doing with the figure eight and stayed true to the law of attraction. I felt grateful in advance for receiving the best written and practical test scores.

You can imagine the surprise I felt and the shocked look on the instructors' faces when, during the riding exam, I performed the figure eight exercise perfectly. The only time I did it correctly was when it counted for my test. Oh, I love embracing my oneness with Spirit.

Some riders in the class owned their own motorcycles and had clocked as much as 4,000 miles. I wasn't the best rider in the group but I knew how to leverage the law of attraction. I did score the highest grade in both tests because I used the ever-available power of my mind, I didn't take myself too seriously, I gave no power to my mistakes and I visualized myself reaching my goals. All three steps are important elements of the creative process.

Improving Your Athleticism

Before I broke my neck I enjoyed slalom skiing on area lakes a handful of times each summer. On one such occasion, at nearby Jordan Lake with several friends, I decided to try wakeboarding—a surfboard-like platform for riding behind a motorboat.

I was with friends who could make a 360-degree rotation on their wakeboards, while catching air, look easy. In the heat of the sun, the women's bodies glistened, the men just sweated. An air temperature in the high 90s was all the encouragement we needed to jump into the 85-degree water.

They encouraged me to be patient; learning to get up on a wakeboard would take several tries. That was good advice; being reminded to stay hopeful is always helpful. However, I had access to another tool—visualization.

Before I jumped into the water I visualized riding a wakeboard. When it was my turn to get cooled off, I jumped in and squeezed my feet into the bindings. I let go of the chatter of my friends as they called out bits of advice. I crouched in the water with my legs close to my body and positioned the wakeboard perpendicular to the surface. As the driver was creating a slight tension in the rope and as the voices quieted, I went within—to my true potential. In my mind's eye I saw myself popping up out of the water with ease. I saw myself wakeboarding. I didn't focus on the individual things to remember. I just focused on popping up.

I felt ready and yelled, "Hit it!" I heard the loud engine and felt the rope tightening. I continued to visualize myself wakeboarding. Something interesting happened. I actually popped up easily.

You may want to celebrate with me, but hold off. In a few seconds I realized I was plowing horizontally through the water instead of having the nose of the wakeboard forward. I had no idea how to turn my board forward. My friends, not thinking I'd actually get up, hadn't given me further instructions. They were yelling to me now, but I couldn't hear. One friend had his arms positioned as if holding the rope bar and repeatedly twisted one hip backward. He knew what I should be doing. I knew what I should be doing. I just needed to figure out how to do it. Then I remembered the power of my mind.

I visualized my board positioned correctly with me still riding it. I needed to use my mind and my body. My body acquiesced; it naturally brought forth strength, tightening my core muscles and helping me grip the bar and stay relaxed at the same time. My mind and body came through for me and got me successfully turned around.

I used the same technique when doing my first surface 180-degree and then a 360-degree rotation on the wakeboard. I visualized and affirmed it done before I even attempted it. I was not graceful at first but I accomplished the turns.

Saving Time

How often have you wished for more hours in the day? Often, more time equates to less stress. People, myself included, find that valuable time and energy is saved by staying tuned in to the greater aspect of who we are.

I got to practice this one night on my way to a weekly East and West Coast Swing dance event. It was easy to go solo because the event attracted single men and women who, like me, went for the fun and to improve their dancing. Driving down the highway listening to my Meatloaf CD, I realized I had left the $20 bill I needed for the entrance fee and for the parking garage on my kitchen counter. I had a choice to turn around or to use the opportunity to co-create with Spirit. The venue was 30 minutes from my home and I was already running quite late. I decided to trust Spirit to reveal the blessings I needed.

So I affirmed there would be free, on-street parking available. I also affirmed that someone I knew would be easily available and willing to lend me $20.

I found on-street parking. Thank you, Spirit. I walked along the city sidewalk. As I approached the building and climbed its wide steps leading to the spacious stone floor piazza I smiled. Out of the approximately 200 dancers, the two men I would be most comfortable borrowing money from "just happened" to be two of the three people outside getting fresh air. I was grateful and as I approached them, I thought to myself, "Spirit, we are so cool! Thanks for showing me easy!"

Saving Money

I volunteered to do a printing project for a nonprofit organization and had emailed my work order to a print shop. I got the call that the job was completed and was shocked at the price—$420. Ouch! I was comfortable donating the cost of the printing, but I thought it would cost around $100. The printers usually give a quote when you drop off a job but, since I had sent it via email, they and I had both overlooked that step. I planned to ask the manager how he could help me out.

There is power in affirming and praying with others. The Bible says, "For where two or three are gathered in my name, there am I among them." I set an intention with a friend that afternoon. We thanked Spirit in advance for a 50 percent discount and new cash to cover this expense, whatever the amount. We affirmed the cost would be for the highest good of all.

The law of attraction works. When it doesn't seem to be working, I take the time to check my vibration, my attitude and my predominant thoughts. I ask myself the following questions and I encourage my clients and you to do so, too: Do you doubt it will happen? Are you sabotaging yourself with a limited belief? Do you believe it is possible to reach your goal? Do you still have old, debilitating programming of unworthiness? Did you believe others, even from childhood, who told you that you couldn't do anything well? Do you walk around often in anger, frustration or other negative emotions?

This self-monitoring becomes part of the journey. Give yourself some time for introspection and really consider these questions. I recommend using a self-healing technique called the Emotional Freedom Technique (EFT). It helps dissipate the emotional stress created from your fears and limiting beliefs. A link for EFT is at CallingBackYourPower.com/links.

Remember, what you consistently think and believe creates your prominent vibration. It is your energetic vibration that draws your experiences to you. If I earnestly said affirmations for what I wanted, and then went about my day doubting it would happen or vibrating with an underlying anger, I would be lowering my vibration and blocking my desired results.

When you say affirmations, feel the excitement as if you already have what you want. Trust that how it will happen is Spirit's job. Then get out of your own way and allow Spirit to orchestrate your results.

I walked into the print shop the next day with an inner peace, knowing Spirit had my back. I trusted that whatever the outcome, it would be for the highest good of all and that I would be fine. I trusted that new money would easily flow to me to cover the bill. In my mind, I thanked the manager for adjusting the cost of this project however he could. I had focused on what I wanted, the 50 percent discount, and then got out of my own way and trusted Spirit to reveal the best solution for all of us.

I met with the manager. I told him about the nonprofit project and then I asked how he could help me. It seemed like he surprised himself even. He gave me a 50 percent discount. He said, "We don't normally do this. I won't do it again, but I will today." I love co-creating with the universe.

The law of attraction is a powerful tool. Use it and have fun.

If you can imagine it, you can ordain it.

Chapter 7
Tapping into Spiritual Guidance

*The world is changing so rapidly, and many people are
paralyzed with fear and anxiety about the future. The angels can
guide us through these changes, and give us solid guidance that we
can trust.* – Doreen Virtue

Do you want an easier life? Great because you are one
with a powerful, divine, organizing intelligence which is ready
and willing to guide you in creating that easier life. Yes, an
easier life! Can you feel that? Can you feel the possibilities?

Think of this intelligence as your personal support
team working relentlessly behind the scenes for your benefit
and available 24/7. Support increases as you stay conscious of
your connection with your "team" and then are willing to ask
for and accept its help.

Staying connected—believing in and creating a daily
relationship with the Divine--ensures the support from this
invisible intelligent force field which, in our Western
experience, is often referred to as God, Spirit, Source or the
Universe. There are many levels of consciousness that are part
of this divine presence. They include what many know as
angels or spiritual guides.

Each angel or guide have their own specialty and come
and go as your needs change. They may be general helpers
that guide you or loved ones that have died—transitioned to

higher consciousness—or spiritual specialists like doctors, scientists, musicians, athletes and the like. Whatever your need, they are here to help. Your spiritual team can orchestrate the most fantastic sequence of events, create your most treasured desires or set you up for your spiritual journey's highest good.

Are you asking yourself why you haven't taken more advantage of this free and loving team that is just waiting to help you? Be gentle on yourself. You have been taught since birth that you live in a world made of physical objects. Thus, you look for solutions from only a material aspect; you work harder to make more money and you change jobs, partners, and homes in hopes of being happier. Very often these are short term solutions leaving you once again feeling unfulfilled.

As you deepen your belief in and embrace the wholeness of who you are—mind, body, and spirit—and understand that you are one with, not separate from, this infinite, intelligent force field, you are paving the way to an easier life. It is then your choice as to how much you partake of this ever available stream of support.

Your beliefs, intentions and expectations are what fuel the momentum of this divinely benevolent team. It supports you, yet does not do your emotional work for you or interfere with your free will.

Your relationship with your team is similar to a healthy relationship between a child and his parents working together on a science fair project or math homework. The parents make themselves available for brain-storming with their child to develop some ideas or shopping for supplies. Yet the parents know their child will not grow in confidence or learn self-discipline if they help too much—even though they could easily do the project or solve the math problems in half the time. Well, okay, maybe some of you could do those math problems. My point being, the purpose of the project or homework is to help the child advance in school and to increase his or her self-worth, not just to get it done.

Similarly, you chose this earth school—this time-space reality—to grow your soul, to develop confidence, self-love, self-worth and healthy boundaries and to release limiting beliefs. It is not in your divine plan for your team to do your dirty work. And, like a parent, they see your trials from a higher perspective and know the ultimate benefit they offer. Your team is here to support your growth and they see your challenges not as problems, but rather as lessons and opportunities for growth.

Your experiences of success, happiness, and health already exist in the here and now. Like apples on a tree, these experiences are within your reach, waiting to be plucked from the tree of life and enjoyed. Don't let me lose you here, just be opened to or trust that we are multi-dimensional spiritual beings and there is much we do not yet understand about the mystery of our spirituality.

You are more than a physical body. A daily connection to Source—your team for spiritual guidance—will improve your ability to blend your third-dimensional life with your higher spiritual self, allowing in more joy, health, and prosperity. During your journey you attract the guidance, people, and impulses you need to act at the right and perfect time which, in turn, increases the flow of creating with ease. As you see the results of your beliefs and intentions, you deepen your faith in these disciplines.

Later on I share more specifically how to be in the ready state, allowing in this wonderful guidance for your highest good.

You obviously benefit from the electricity running through your home *when* you plug into it. And similarly, you have the opportunity to benefit more when you plug into divine guidance. Your support team is here to give you free spiritual guidance on minor and major issues and they will always find the easiest way to bring it to you. With an open mind you will recognize the signs you are given even though they may be different from what you expected or wanted.

There is a lot of truth in those words. You have access to divine answers and guidance daily; be open to *seeing* what you need to see for your highest good. Affirm: "Thank you, Spirit that I hear, see, and know what is for my highest good and thanks for bringing it to me in a way I can recognize."

Some ways to feel a daily connection to Source are prayer, gratitude, affirmations and developing a daily discipline of looking within, and to, layer by layer, face and heal your emotional wounds.

Even those who may not purposely do a particular spiritual practice but live with a pure intent of love and kindness in their hearts and share their gifts of service with others are embracing their connection to divine guidance.

There obviously are many ways for you to feel your connection; you will find what resonates with you. In reality, you are always connected, though limited beliefs and experiences may prevent your awareness of this connection.

If you are looking for more deliberate ways to awaken your connection, you can memorize some of my affirmations and requests that invoke this divine help. I've included them at the end of this chapter. Soon you'll be coming up with your own, customizing them to address your specific needs. Keep in mind, when I use the word Spirit, it is for ease of understanding; Spirit is not outside of you, you are not separate from Spirit, but one with you.

If you were to get regular spot-on guidance for all areas of your life, wouldn't life be easier? I regularly ask for clear signs when making decisions. It is so cool to see the unique ways in which my guidance shows up.

To increase your success rate in recognizing the signs Spirit gives you, remember that you are worthy of receiving blessings and that *expecting* clear signs attracts them to you. In observing my clients and peers, the more open they are to being helped by Spirit—invisible intelligent consciousness—and the more they trust their intuition and listen to their heart, the more they recognize the signs given them.

The times I don't get the guidance I ask for, I trust all is well anyway: that there is a purpose for me to "feel" the answer within or that the answer will show up at a future time for my highest good.

Spiritual Guidance—Even When You Didn't Ask For It.

Sometimes Source just wants you to know you are loved. In 2000, when I was newly aware of my connection to Source, I had bunion surgery and pins were placed in my foot for temporary support. I prayed for precise surgical technique and ease in recovery.

After the surgery, I continued to intend total ease and comfort with my recovery and I directed healing energy to my foot. I stayed off my foot as the doctor had recommended and with my belief, intentions and conscious connection to the Divine, I took no pain medicine and experienced no pain.

What I found most interesting was the sign Spirit gave me when I went in for the pin removal. Several minutes after the doctor anesthetized my toe, a very obvious white line crept up my leg beginning with an outline of a heart appearing on my foot.

My doctor and I were intrigued; he even took a picture of it for me. He explained that this white line, traveling along the route of the lymphatic system, always goes in a straight line. It never makes a curved line, let alone a heart shape! This was my first, in-my-face experience of being shown that a greater intelligence was with me and sharing its love. We are so cool!

Spirit Can Affect Technology

And sometimes you may get clear guidance even when you haven't specifically asked for it. One evening during a half-hour drive home, I listened to some Abraham-Hicks tapes of messages that come through Esther Hicks from Abraham, the name given to her team of spiritual guides. The first tape I grabbed wouldn't play. It seemed to be stuck both times I tried it. So I grabbed a different one and listened to it.

On this tape, Abraham was guiding a husband on how to energetically and emotionally move through his wife's affair.

I got home and within a half hour, a friend called. Extremely distraught, she asked if she could come over for some support—she had just discovered that her husband was involved in a long term affair. When she arrived I shared with her the same guidance I had just heard on the Abraham-Hicks tape. Even though she was emotionally exhausted, this particular guidance helped her feel her pain with a higher understanding.

Neither she nor her husband is open to my spiritual approach and energy healing, yet I "just happened" to be the first friend she called, something I wouldn't have expected. Even though it was extremely difficult for her, her husband commented that he was totally surprised at how well she was handling the situation and he actually made an appointment for energy healing for himself. This was certainly a difficult time; yet with this extra spiritual guidance, they handled the demise of their twenty-year marriage in the best way they could.

Knowing Source always has my back and with an understanding of synchronistic events, the next day I tried to play the first tape that had appeared stuck; it worked fine. Isn't it cool how Source, knowing the bigger picture, orchestrated this sequence of events so that I was guided to listen to the tape that would best support my friend? Staying plugged into Source certainly has its benefits.

Spiritual Guidance—Out-of-the-Blue Thoughts

Remember how I listened to the out-of-the-blue thought to go order my car. Thoughts that just pop into our minds are very often impulses from the Divine. You'll read in chapter 16, Creating Your Financial Comeback, how paying attention to an out-of-the-blue thought got me to check on a stock I hadn't planned on selling. In fact, I hadn't checked on its price in over a year. I felt guided to sell it and it sold at the highest it had been in several years. Spirit, you are so cool!

Spiritual Guidance—Following your Intuition

A strong intuitive sense can show up as a deep feeling to do something, a thought you keep thinking or an inner knowing that can't be ignored. All are ways through which you may be getting divine guidance. And, keep in mind, the more you listen to your intuition, the stronger it will get. "Mother's intuition" and "sixth sense" are other names that refer to this infinite, informational energy field.

Spiritual guidance finds interesting ways to support us. Several years ago I felt a strong urge to participate in a weekend program at Edgar Cayce's Association of Research and Enlightenment (A.R.E.) in Virginia Beach, Virginia. I could have easily talked myself out of going because Virginia Beach is a four-hour drive from my home near Raleigh, North Carolina, and even though the conference subject was interesting, I went because I intuitively felt drawn to be there.

There were 200 people in attendance at the opening night dinner. A gentleman and his wife came in late which prevented them from sitting together. He, David, joined my table and by the end of dinner we were comfortably conversing with each other.

David had been living with intense pain in his right hand and that evening he told me the pain level was at a nine or ten. The pain prevented him from turning the ignition key with his right hand. Playing the piano at church was his passion; he hadn't played for a year.

I shared with him my life's work and mentioned some client results. I offered to do energy healing while we listened to the after-dinner speaker. David was a very skeptical scientist yet was intrigued with the results my clients experienced. And the depressing prognosis he had received from his doctors—two hand surgeries with no guarantee that he would ever play his beloved piano again—made him more open to what he didn't understand. So, during the after-dinner program, I held his hand between mine and set the intention for him to receive for his highest good. Then we each enjoyed the speaker while the energy in his hand was being repatterned.

The excruciating pain went away. The pain, though much less intense, did come back 24 hours later. David asked one of the speakers during the A.R.E. program why, after there had been such great results, the pain returned. Even though the answer was the same one I would have given him, I'm sure the skeptical scientist was more comforted hearing it from a credentialed speaker.

He was told that symptoms often go away at first because of the healer's consciousness and if they return it is because the client hasn't released all of the associated emotional energy blocks. He got what he needed—great results and a reason to explore this more.

The synchronicity here was that we actually live two miles from each other in Cary, North Carolina, yet we had to meet in Virginia Beach, Virginia, 220 miles away.

Also, note that Source used the path of least resistance to guide us. David, being the skeptical scientist, would have strongly resisted coming to me for healing in Cary. Our first meeting seemed best to be in an environment where David felt comfortable enough—where researchers and scientists were the speakers—to entertain ideas that were new to him.

Always pay attention to that inner feeling, even when you do not yet understand it. Source works behind the scenes, even as our shopping angel! It was a Sunday and on my way to church, I decided to skip an antique show I had earlier planned to attend that afternoon. As I walked out of the sanctuary, I bumped shoulders with others also making their way down the aisle. We congregated in the social area, reconnecting with each other while eating sliced fruit and donut holes. Before I left, I had a strong feeling that I was supposed to go to the antique show after all. I had no idea why but I went ahead and followed this feeling.

Two weeks prior I had mentioned to a friend that I wanted to buy an amethyst geode. A geode is a rock formation that is sold broken open and polished on the edges to reveal a cavity lined with purple crystals. They come in many sizes; I was looking for one about ten inches high and was willing to spend $200. The powerful organizing intelligence of the Universe knew my desire, and I soon discovered why I was given clear intuitive guidance to attend the antique show.

I took my time walking down each aisle. My eyes scanned back and forth over the booths. I stopped at the ones with one-hundred-year-old chests with marble tops or rockers or side tables.

I felt drawn to a booth with stone carvings and gems. To my delight, there on display was a two-foot tall, $950 amethyst geode. It wasn't what I'd expected to see at an antique show, though, I must admit, being one million years old, it was the oldest item there.

The Universe sees itself and each of us as abundant; I was guided to a much nicer geode than I had planned on buying. I approached the man who, surrounded by religious and spiritual figurines, was squeezed into the remaining small space behind a table covered with an array of colorful geodes. I simply asked him what his best price was. His answer, $550! He said it would sell for $1500 in Miami.

The original price of $950 was a typical price for a geode of that size so perhaps you understand my surprise with the huge discount. I really liked this large geode and had wanted one for some time to enhance the energy in my healing room. I trusted I was guided there for this find and took advantage of this blessing. Thanks, Spirit!

Suggested Affirmations

Call your Higher Power the name of your choice. For ease here I will use Spirit.

"Thank you, Spirit, that I hear, see and know what I need to hear, see, and know in a way I can receive it.

"Thank you, Spirit, that I am making the most difference in the least amount of time for the highest good of all."

"Thank you, Spirit, for showing me the best solution for the highest good of all."

Requesting Signs for Guidance

"Thank you, Spirit, for showing me clear signs and guiding me for my highest good with this decision."

"Spirit, if spending money and time now on this program (or accepting this job, or going to this destination for vacation, etc.) is for my highest good then please show me three obvious signs within 24 hours." (Or 1 week or whatever length of time is believable for you.)

Upon going to bed, say "Spirit, thank you for giving me clear guidance in my dream state concerning hiring this employee." (Or, dating this person, using this contractor or traveling to this country, etc.)

You are one with a non-physical Spiritual team. Enjoy deepening this relationship. Enjoy being blessed.

Chapter 8
Divine Synchronicities

We are here to awaken from the illusion of our separateness.
– Thich Nhat Hanh

Synchronicities are events divinely orchestrated for your highest good. Pay attention to them. They seemingly appear out of nowhere, yet often, in hindsight, their meaning, blessings or guidance is clear.

The perfectly aligned and timely ways in which events come together can perplex you, a mystery to your mind. I invite you to analyze them less and instead embrace your partnership with a multi-dimensional, intelligent Universe. And accept that Spirit always has your back and guides you for your highest good.

Synchronistic events connected me with the Hawaiian Spinner dolphins. In 2006, a client gave me Doreen Virtue's *Healing with the Fairies* as a Christmas gift.

Summer came and I finally pulled it off my bookshelf. I found myself eagerly crawling into bed each night to read more. One night I was particularly intrigued as I read about Doreen's wild dolphin swim experience with Captain Nancy Sweatt in Hawaii. I put the book on my lap, closed my eyes, and visualized myself swimming side by side with dolphins. Adventurous enthusiasm and curiosity arose within me; I abruptly stopped reading, left my cozy bed and went upstairs to my office to peruse Nancy's web site. For your convenience, at www.CallingBackYourPower.com/URL there is a link to this website and URLs for other people and products I mention.

Even though I had never entertained the idea of a dolphin excursion, I sat quietly at my desk, seriously considering the timing for one. The previous two years had been dedicated to recovering from my broken neck and other personal concerns. The thought of swimming with the dolphins was so intriguing, but I decided to shelve the idea and focus on expanding my holistic life coaching and energy healing practice.

Spirit had different plans. The next morning I felt compelled to listen to a spiritual CD, something I seldom do in the morning. I chose the one by Felicia Rose. Since I hadn't listened to this CD in over a year I had no recollection of its songs. I only remembered that she had a beautiful voice.

The *first phrase* on the *first track* was captivating: "To swim in the exotic sea." Wow! Hearing this, my inner Being immediately *knew* I was to experience the dolphin adventure. I said out loud, "I've got it, Spirit. I'll go sooner!" Knowing this synchronistic event had been orchestrated by Spirit, my whole Being was smiling. Then, to clarify the message, the *third phrase* echoed "with the dolphins and whales." Double Wow! I love those absolutely clear hits of guidance.

We are one with such a cool Universe! We don't have to know how it all happens. We can just be thankful it does!

I played telephone tag with Nancy Sweatt, the owner of Dolphin Journeys and captain of its excursion boat. In the meantime, Spirit nudged me to "Think Big." I asked myself, "For this trip, how would 'thinking big' look?" Mind you, I knew no one in Hawaii. But for me, thinking big meant experiencing the Hawaiian dolphins and doing some speaking and teaching. It also meant an all-expense-paid trip or, at the minimum, a business write-off.

I have learned that the job description for my partnership with the Universe includes being clear in my desire, expecting it, seeing it as already done, and then getting out of the way and allowing the Universe to do what it does—handle the how. The guidance I received through the song that morning gave me confidence that Spirit had my back. I felt as if a friend had planned a spectacular trip and invited me along.

Because it is so important I'll say it again. *Your work is not to figure out the how.* You and Spirit are one. You are a team. Your job description is your business and Spirit's is its business. Let Spirit figure out the how and you can stand back in awe of Spirit's creativeness.

Spirit sees the big picture and aligns you with the easiest, most direct way to accomplish what is for your highest good. Guidance becomes obvious and consistent as you embrace that you are connected to this divine source—a loving teammate that is always there, and (in all ways) willing to help you.

Nancy and I dealt with a six-hour time difference. We finally talked by telephone two weeks later. Our conversation confirmed my belief that everything was being divinely set up and that my thinking big was paying off. Nancy and I talked, not for the twenty minutes I presumed we would, but for 1½ hours. We felt an immediate connection; we comfortably talked and excitedly discovered how our spiritual journeys were interwoven.

I shared my "Thinking Big" ideas. Being creative and accommodating, Nancy suggested that I plan my trip for late October because four women had scheduled dolphin excursions for three days in a row and she could use my help on the boat and in the water swimming with the dolphins.

I paid for two dolphin excursions, giving me five encounters with the dolphins. Nancy told me she occasionally opens her home to workshop facilitators and invited me to stay with her. I asked how long I should stay and she responded, "Stay as long as you can. It's beautiful here!" I said, "Okay, then let's plan on two weeks!" To allow us more privacy, I ended up subleasing her on-site rental apartment and was blessed with her energy and support daily.

While we were still working out the details for my trip, Nancy introduced me to the contact person at the West Hawaii Center for Positive Living. I was invited to give the Sunday morning message and present a workshop. I enjoyed meeting and sharing with people ready to go to their next spiritual level. Even Nancy joined us that day. My thinking big paid off!

Captain Nancy has great love and respect for the dolphins in their natural habitat. During the dolphin excursions I felt a surge of unconditional love from the dolphins and trusted they felt it returned. Happiness was tickling every cell in my body.

I was mesmerized by the dolphins' intelligence and playfulness and I found them to be otherworldly. An overwhelming feeling of Oneness, safety, and love enveloped our group. Words cannot describe the deep peace and heart-expanding emotions we felt.

I continued to be awestruck as I connected eye to eye with those enlightened creatures. We watched as pods of dolphins performed what appeared to be synchronized dancing, moving in spiraling formations of sacred geometry. My connection with the Hawaiian Spinner dolphins is etched into my core!

The scientific order Cetacea includes the marine mammals commonly known as whales and dolphins. Spirit clearly guided me to strengthen my connection with cetaceans. Six months after my trip to Hawaii, I was on a humpback whale excursion at The Silver Bank, 70 miles off the coast of the Dominican Republic. Joan Ocean, who is spiritually connected to cetaceans and has written books about her experiences with them, led this trip.

I had specific guidance to go on this trip, too. I had never heard of Joan Ocean and "just happened" to receive an email about her and felt guided to peruse her web site. I immediately contacted her office. This was two months prior to the trip I was interested in and I was surprised to find it already full. I intuitively knew I would be on that trip and asked Joan's assistant to put me on the cancellation list. Ten days later she called with an opening.

If an experience is for our highest good and we are not energetically blocking it, then, of course, the "how" is divinely worked out.

At the end of this chapter in appendix 8-1, you can read more about my experiences with the dolphins and humpback whales and the messages they bring to us here on Earth.

Spiritual Guidance—More Synchronicities

Spirit will guide us in any area of our lives. For example, Spirit got my attention and guided me to a natural way to increase my daily mineral intake.

I hadn't eaten table salt for years. And I wouldn't have given Krystal Salt a second thought if it hadn't been for the clear guidance.

I found myself cleaning out my nightstand. I decided to move two volumes of Dr. Christine Northrup's newsletters to my filing cabinet. Each volume had a year's worth of monthly newsletters in it.

If you have ever experienced cleaning out drawers filled with articles and magazines, you may understand how easy it is to spend more time reading than organizing. That's what I usually did. But this time, while fanning through the pages of 24 months of newsletters, the only article that caught my eye and which I read thoroughly was one on a pure, highly mineralized salt that is mined from ancient Himalayan salt beds. I set this newsletter aside, feeling guided to order some of this salt.

I hadn't realized I was receiving guidance until a few days later when it became "Krystal" clear at a spiritual program I was attending. Guess what they were selling? Yes, pure, Himalayan Krystal Salt. I read the literature on its health benefits and talked with the sales person. Because of the guidance I had been given, I trusted that the salt would be for my highest good and I purchased this natural dietary supplement.

You can find more information regarding the value of Himalayan Krystal Salt in appendix 8-2.

Being Guided for Lasik Surgery

The Universe orchestrates situations for your highest good. A great example of this was put into motion during the weekend of my motorcycle safety course. I was pleased to learn while chatting with other women during a break that Lasik surgery could now be performed on an eye which had astigmatism.

I had astigmatism in my right eye and only needed vision correction for that eye.
Even though I seldom read the paper, a few days later I "just happened" to pick one up and also "just happened" to see in it two ads for Lasik surgery. Hmm. Coupled with my new information from the previous weekend, the synchronicity of the ads got my attention.

One ad mentioned an upcoming informational meeting to explain Lasik surgery. This eye center "just happened" to be five minutes from my home and the meeting was scheduled for a convenient evening. I went. I listened and asked questions and intuitively felt aligned with the doctor who was speaking and would perform the surgery.

I decided to have the Lasik procedure. It was the end of October and with the holidays ahead, I decided to go ahead and schedule my surgery for the last week of December.

I was told that one of the prerequisites for contact lens wearers is to stop wearing their contacts for the six weeks prior to the surgery and instead, wear eyeglasses. I wore one contact and kept a spare one handy but I didn't own a pair of glasses. My driver's license does not require me to wear corrective lenses; I needed to decide whether to buy eyeglasses I would need for only six weeks.

I love being one with this very cool Universe with very cool infinite intelligence and a very cool ability to orchestrate events way beyond our understanding—we don't get to decide "how" it's done but it sure is nice that we get to participate.

This guidance showed up in October 2005, a few weeks before I broke my neck. In the emergency room, they took out my contact lens. I didn't have the finger function to put it back in and since I was home recovering, my uncorrected vision was sufficient. And in December I had my scheduled Lasik surgery. Hmm, I figured Spirit set it up; conveniently arranging this surgery to follow a time when I did not wear my contact lens for seven weeks—the doctor recommended six weeks without my contact. I also avoided the need to buy a pair of eyeglasses.

Watching for Guidance in Everyday Life

Spirit uses whatever avenues are available to get our attention. Here's a story about another time I "just happened" to be reading the paper.

I had asked for guidance to confirm an inclination I had to attend a sponsorship business program in San Francisco.

Sponsorships were set up to be a win-win-win for a non-profit, a business that wants to support that non-profit, and businesses, like my holistic healing practice, that offer a valuable product for the non-profit.

I asked for clear guidance to confirm if traveling, learning, and using my time and financial resources for this purpose would be for my highest good and the highest good of those I serve.

Again, Spirit guided me to the newspaper and even though, really, I don't read the paper very often, I was drawn to read a particular article. Soon, the reason became clear. The woman in the article was from (guess where?) San Francisco.

I thanked Spirit for that clear guidance and felt amused at how Spirit so easily gets me to notice what it wants me to notice. That same paper had another obvious piece of guidance for me, a half page ad with the word SPONSORSHIPS written in huge letters. Being more amused, I said aloud, "Okay, I got it." and I made plans to attend the program.

Spirit has your back and, combined with your inner knowing, is the best business consultant you can have. Once, while I was considering how best to promote my business, I was guided to attend a four-day program in New York City for which I needed to be accepted.

I felt good about applying and then gave the outcome over to Spirit, trusting all would be in divine order. I affirmed, "Spirit, if it's in my best interest to go, thanks for having them accept me. If not, have them deny me."

Spirit knows the big picture of where we are going, what is needed for our journey, and how to get there as easily as possible. Trusting Spirit helps us move out of our own way and go with the flow of the spiritual momentum at hand.

I was quite surprised when the administrators of the program got back to me, gave me the pros and cons of my participation and then said it was up to me to decide whether to attend or not. My request for an easy decision— to be accepted or denied—hadn't worked. The program gave me 24 hours to decide. I felt it was valuable yet I questioned the timing of it.

I decided to ask for more guidance. I asked for three specific signs regarding New York City. When I joined several friends for dinner that evening, the car parked next to the door of a restaurant in Durham, North Carolina, had a New York license plate. Okay, that was my first sign. Out of the five friends at dinner, three of them mentioned New York City in three different contexts. I received four signs before the night was over and confidently made my decision to attend the program in New York City.

Spiritual guidance, through synchronistic events, supports our journey—blessing us, helping us make decisions, or simplifying our lives. Even more important, to me, it is a loving reminder that we are never alone during this Earth journey.

APPENDIX:
8-1 Hawaiian Spinner Dolphins

When I swam with the dolphins, I intuitively felt their messages for us. The obvious one is to play more; less obvious is that they hold love and wisdom for us and Mother Earth and that they are here to help us raise our spiritual awareness.

Sound healing—toning, singing mantras and playing the crystal bowl—clears old programming and balances people at the cellular level. Swimming with the dolphins directly immersed us in their tonal and vibratory gifts. Our playing with the dolphins spoke to one of my affirmations: "Thank you, God that I am clearing blocks with ease, gentleness and grace and through joy and laughter as often as possible."

As with other forms of energy healing, the dolphins' energetic gifts assist us in transcending false beliefs and negative chatter as we ascend to higher consciousness. They help us spiritually awaken to higher levels, making it easier to bring forth our creativity, passion, and abundance. Our mental, physical, and emotional health also improves, allowing us to react to challenges from a position of love and acceptance, not fear. We become open to a new mindset and deepen our appreciation of the natural beauty that surrounds us.

Humpback Whales

The Silver Bank, a temporary home to about 3000 whales, is the first sanctuary in the world designated especially for humpback whales. During mating and birthing seasons, only three vessels carrying a total of 60 visitors a week may visit there. Based on their research, the Whale Commission believes that small numbers of people do not disturb the whales. Actually, the whales often initiate encounters with humans.

For one week, I lived with 16 other adventurous souls on a 120-foot boat. We spent 6-8 hours a day on small boats called tenders from which we observed and then would swim with humpback whales that were from 50 to 70 feet long.

The curious calves would swim within a few feet of us. From the safety of our boats we watched powerful males chase each other, breach and leap out of the water, and court females.

At night, gathered in the dining area, we continued to be immersed in the energy of the whales as we listened to Joan Ocean share from her twenty years of experience with the whales and dolphins. At bedtime the songs of the whales echoing in my mind lulled me to sleep.

Joan taught us that dolphins and whales are energetic helpers between Spirit and Earth. The cetaceans' continuous vibration of Love helps humanity handle the changes inherent in raising our consciousness. They serve as catalysts to heal and nourish our planet, too. The properties and frequencies of the ocean water are more conducive to the assimilation of these vibrations than any other area of the planet.

In her book, *Dolphin Connection,* Joan tells about a channeling experience during which she asked the dolphins, "In what ways can working with you and whales serve Creation and mankind?" They answered, "…our wisdom is that of the past and of the future. We have been joyously awaiting this time of evolution for the planet, sending our healing rays to the earth, assisting those who are aware of us, and, soon, to release the wisdom of the ancients to the sensitives of the Golden Age. The time is quickly approaching when humans will have ears to hear this knowledge, and will begin to benefit from it. This information comes as Truth and Beauty. It is the information of Love. It is a combination of technical-scientific data with the vibrations of Universal Love. In your world these aspects have been separated."

The dolphins and whales will continue to teach us, deepening our awareness and appreciation of them. I invite you to tune into their divine frequencies and wisdom, either intuitively tuning into them or physically connecting with them in their natural habitat. Allow them to expand your heart as they have mine.

I am so appreciative of the clear guidance I received which led me to experience these beautiful creatures.

Appendix 8-2 Krystal Salt vs Table Salt

Of the 84 mineral elements found in the human body, 72 are believed to be essential ingredients of a healthy diet. The 250-million-year-old Krystal Salt contains these 72 mineral elements in a perfect crystal matrix, resulting in a much higher life force field (crystallization is nature's way of storing life force).

Homer called salt a "divine substance." Plato described it as "especially dear to the gods." The Celtic word for salt means holy or sacred. From the beginning of recorded history, salt was exalted and believed to be synonymous with virtue. Jesus referred to his followers as the salt of the earth. Salt was so precious that spilling it was considered a bad omen.

The difference between Krystal Salt and table salt is in the processing. Table salt is salt which has been chemically cleaned and purged at very high temperatures, thus yielding pure sodium chloride but removing the important minerals. It is white and looks sparkly clean and, with the addition of aluminum hydroxide to prevent caking, it pours easily-- people love it.

The downside is that it no longer has the mineralizing and balancing effects of natural salt.

Krystal Salt rocks can also be purchased for use in making brine—sol—to use as a daily supplement or to put in bath water. Because it contains an ideal proportion of all 72 mineral elements, the same found in the human body, Krystal Salt's brine is an antioxidant.

Once it is introduced in the body, a profound regeneration of the cell membranes becomes possible. Many studies have been done in Europe on Krystal salt. Renowned biophysicist Peter Ferreira and Dr. Barbara Hendel, naturopath, co-authored the book *Water and Salt: The Essence of Life.* This book details the powerful healing qualities of Himalayan crystal salt and water. It explores the myths surrounding salt and water, two of the most important substances on the earth, and how Himalayan salt and water "can act as a catalyst for a new, healthier and independent life." Peter's two-year study of 400 people using crystal salt is impressive.

Many feel the rediscovery of natural, pure, Himalayan salt may become one of the most important health discoveries of the twenty-first century. I invite you to consider adding Krystal Salt to your diet. Check it out, ask to be guided and make a decision that feels right to you.

Chapter 9
The Creative Genius of Spirit

Faith is not something to grasp, it is a state to grow into.
– Mohandas Gandhi

Life experiences give you the opportunities to grow your faith and embrace your connection to your non-physical team—Spirit. This connection allows you to receive spiritual guidance in a myriad of ways, creating more ease, peace and prosperity in your life.

Spiritual Guidance—Through Dreams

I get specific information and guidance through my dreams which gives me assurance, comfort and clarity whether the decisions I need to make are big or small.

One morning several years ago, I awoke with a strong memory of a dream. I felt guided to immediately write down everything I remembered and to call a dream interpreter I had heard speak a few months prior. The dream was unclear and events appeared to jump around. Nevertheless, I sensed I needed to understand it. The dream interpreter helped me grasp its meaning—the man I was dating and I were going in two different directions. This wasn't going to change and it was time to move on. The dream clarified feelings I had, though had not yet acted on. It helped me trust that this break-up was for our highest good.

Spirit had given me the inner knowing to write my dream out in detail and make the call. Thus began my experience of getting great guidance via my dreams.

If you are interested in getting dream guidance too, keep a notebook and pen at your bedside. At bedtime thank Spirit for clarity regarding a concern and intend that guidance, for the highest good of all, will come in an easy-to-understand dream and that you will remember it when you awake. Be open to receive any dream, requested or not, that will support your journey.

Write out your dream immediately upon waking and include every detail you recall. Be as clear as you can with the beginning, middle, and end events. Then have fun using your intuition, meditation or a dream dictionary to understand the depth of the dream. Or, call a respected dream interpreter for support. I only used the interpreter's help one more time. My guidance dreams soon became straightforward enough for my understanding.

I had a straightforward dream right before I found out about my daughter Brittany's drug use. She and I were sitting in separate inner tubes but holding hands and experiencing a wild, out-of-control ride on huge ocean waves. As scary as it felt, we never did let go of each other and we eventually ended up in flat, serene water and then up onto dry land.

Brittany had experienced emotional ups and downs. This dream assured me that whatever we had to face, as scary as it may feel, we would go through it together and end up fine. Even though I wished we didn't have to go through more challenges, this dream gave me comfort.

Guidance, comfort and blessings came through those two dreams even though I hadn't requested either dream. If I ask for guidance and don't get it, I trust I will know what I need to know at the right and perfect time. I have learned that any dream that comes right before I awake, requested or not, is valuable or comforting.

I was very comforted by Spirit's message to me regarding my grandmother. Her health was declining and we knew she would be passing soon. With her in Maine and me in North Carolina, I prayed for her. On November 24, 2004, right before waking, I was given a special message. Just as the words of a special bulletin roll across your TV screen, my special bulletin appeared across the screen of an unrelated dream:

> *As a person must fade at midnight to find*
> *the depths of their soul, they will again rise to the*
> *Everlasting Light of Eternity.*

I called my family to share the message. Even though it appeared through an unconventional avenue, they all found comfort in it.

I thought the word midnight was just poetic. Instead, the message ended up being literal and timely. My beloved Gram Bea died close to midnight, November 24, 2004, the same day I received my message.

I was so touched by the Divine's loving message in the form of our special bulletin that right after receiving it, I sat down and wrote Gram this poem. My sister Ramona read it at Gram's bedside after her passing and I read it later at her funeral.

> *Lady of Love*
> *We may have caressed your hair and kissed*
> *your cheek one final time...*
> *But as we tenderly let go of your hand,*
> *There is comfort as we send you on into the Light*
> *With our blessings and a love that is as strong*
> *and eternal as you are.*

Lady of Love, we bless you. We honor you.
And may we allow the love that you have
shared in this lifetime
And the love that is present here today to
Heal our core and abide in our hearts forever.
We Love You!

That dream guidance emotionally supported me and my family. However, dreams can support us in any area of our lives.

One area for which I get dream support is my business—I trust Spirit as my business consultant. For example, one night while preparing for bed, I asked for dream guidance about investing in a year-long mentoring program. The next morning I had a dream right before waking. I saw myself intensely working alongside the program's teacher. With this very clear guidance and the knowledge that Spirit sees the big picture, I confidently invested the time and money.

Another dream I had right before awaking, without specifically asking for dream guidance, gave me valuable insight about hiring a specific assistant.

In the dream, this prospective assistant and I were about to get on one of two available buses to go to a meeting. The next part of the dream had me arriving at my destination without her. I assumed she had gotten on the second bus so I waited. But, she hadn't.

Because I trust the value of my dreams right before I awake, I looked at its possible meaning more closely. I realized, as qualified as she was, that, for some unknown reason, she "wouldn't get on board with me." I didn't over analyze it, or try to convince myself otherwise. I trusted my guidance and hired someone else.

When you receive information in a dream, please make sure the guidance feels good to you. If you feel any resistance—resistance and uneasy feelings block the reserved blessings awaiting you—I recommend holding off on taking action based on the dream until you get clarity regarding the resistance.

It may be that you have a fear-based belief in financial lack, making it difficult for you to spend money, or you are hesitant to step outside of your comfort zone to change jobs or sell your house.

Whatever action you take should feel good to you. If, later, you realize you missed a great opportunity because you were too fearful to take action, look at that and learn from it, but don't be too concerned. Just like your automobile's GPS guidance, your guidance will reroute you to the next best option to move you forward—maybe without even having to "make a legal U-turn."

Dreams are an aspect of my spiritual GPS system. They give me clarity in many areas of my life, from choosing financial advisors, assistants, programs to attend, and vacations to meeting and interacting with clients and even the men I have dated.

Spiritual Guidance—Through Songs and Objects

Spirit uses obvious paths to get messages to you. Guidance can show up in the words of a song playing right at an opportune moment for you to get the wisdom you are ready to hear. Remember the message that convinced me to swim with the dolphins—it was in the first song on a CD I hadn't played in a year.

You may be guided to play a CD or to switch radio stations just at the right time to hear a song whose words may be the trigger you need to allow yourself to let go of grief, anger, or resentment—releasing painful emotions is part of the healing process, part of your soul's journey.

Another way Spirit may guide you along your journey and get your attention is to allow a book to fall from a bookshelf. Pay attention and read the book that fell. A loved one who has transitioned may move a family picture on a table to let you know they are with you—and that they still have a sense of humor. Often this is done repeatedly; each time you move the picture back, you soon find it out of place again.

The Universe is also very savvy at getting your attention through computers. Spirit uses Google search to guide clients to me. One time it was very obvious that Spirit guided a stranger to me.

Cheryl called me one day and shared that she was moving from California to Raleigh. She said that she had searched "energy healers, North Carolina" and my name and website came up first on the list.

I knew immediately that she was being guided because I was building my healing practice and knew my website hadn't had enough hits to warrant the first position. I interpreted our connection as Divine.

Our conversation was easy, like old friends meeting up again. We're staying in touch until she actually moves here. Understanding synchronicities, I Googled "energy healers, North Carolina" and I perused the first ten pages and didn't find my listing. There were 225,000 healers listed and when Cheryl Googled me, thanks to this invisible intelligence, I "just happened" to be listed first. Spirit, we are so cool! Again, you don't have to understand how the Universe pulls this off. Just be open to spiritual guidance and grateful for its gifts.

Spiritual Guidance—To Bless or Be Blessed

You can be guided to bless others or others can be guided to bless you. You may have experienced this, for example, when you felt guided to do something out of the ordinary like buy groceries for a stranger standing behind you in the checkout lane.

There is more to an incident like this than just feeling good about helping someone. This blessing could be an answer to their prayer or a message reminding them that with all the pain in the world, there are still kind people. The Universe may have orchestrated a karmic payback between the two of you; you may have stolen from or taken advantage of that person in a previous life and this good deed balances out that energy between your souls.

If the intuitive nudge you receive seems intrusive to the other person, I recommend you ask Spirit for a clarifying feeling on whether following your intuition is truly for the other person's highest good. This is something only you can discern at the time. You don't need to see the big picture, though trusting that Spirit does, makes following spiritual guidance easier.

Spirit, seeing the big picture, makes shopping easier. One year my ex-husband took my daughters shopping for Mother's Day to buy me the white, wooden birdhouse with a smooth copper roof they knew I wanted.

They pulled into a gas station just a mile from his home to fill up the gas tank. Imagine their delight when they spotted the birdhouse "shop" on the edge of the gas station parking lot. A gentleman, who travels around our county setting up shop at parking lots, "just happened" to be there for the day with his handmade, wooden, copper-roofed birdhouses. Pretty cool, isn't it. Overthinking about how this was orchestrated is a waste of energy. Just be thankful it can!

And everyone was blessed. That gentleman sold another birdhouse, my daughters were happy with their gift for Mom, my ex-husband, in saving his precious time, was willing to spend considerably more money on the only size available—a 2-story, copper-roofed birdhouse, and, as for me, the birdhouse was larger than I had envisioned yet it ended up being the perfect size for its place in my garden. Thanks,

Spirit, for orchestrating all of this and for knowing what would look great in my garden!

Another example of a divinely-set-up situation that benefited the needs for all involved was when I visited Nashville, Tennessee.

I went with a group of West Coast Swing dancers and was hoping I would get a chance to see the city. The schedule was too tight to set up an organized tour ahead of time. But I trusted Spirit would help me. I affirmed, "Thanks, Spirit, for guiding me to a nice, local person who is attending the event and would enjoy showing me around, and also would appreciate an energy healing session with me as a thank you gift." I mentioned my desire to the woman who had organized the event. She said she would give it some thought. Several hours later she introduced me to a gentleman who was pleased to take me on a tour of Nashville. And he "just happened" to have back pain so he definitely benefited from our energy healing session.

Spiritual Guidance — On Short Notice

Our beliefs allow or block the wisdom that is available to us. The following true stories support the belief that a non-physical team is here to help us and even on short notice, we can get clear guidance.

I had been dating Michael for a month when he and a friend decided to take a weekend trip to the Outer Banks, a 3½ hour drive from Raleigh. Michael called me on Friday at 2:00 p.m., apologizing for such short notice but also excited to invite me to the Outer Banks. He had just found out his friend could no longer go and now he was hoping that it would work out for me to join him. It would give us our first extended amount of time together.

It felt right to go have some fun and get to know Michael better, but I had a full weekend planned and there was one event that I didn't feel comfortable changing without guidance. I was leading a five-week class in my home on Sundays where I shared spiritual teachings and emotionally supported the participants. I was conflicted. I wanted to honor my commitment to be there AND I wanted to go have fun with Michael. My human mind decided the best choice was for us to drive in separate cars so that I could drive home early on Sunday. But that idea didn't feel good because it took away all the fun of sharing the drive there and back.

I wanted my decision to be easy so I depended on my ever-present spiritual support team that sees the needs of the group and would guide me to the highest good for all.

You can request clear and obvious guidance in a general way or ask for guidance to come in a very specific way. It depends on your comfort level. I use both approaches. Again, belief is the key.

If you can't believe you can get clear guidance, you won't. When you ask for guidance it is important to trust the outcome even if it isn't your preference. When you ask for the highest good for all, you are getting out of the mindset that it has to be your way. You trust that the outcome is right for all involved, which includes *your* highest good.

Trusting the process brings peace to my heart. Keep in mind that I had only a few hours to decide. I called Amy, a friend and participant in the group, and told her about my opportunity. My request to Spirit was, "If going with Michael is for the highest good of all, then have Amy suggest, without any hinting from me, that I postpone Sunday's gathering."

I had to leave a message for Amy. Ooh, not what I wanted, though it did give me an opportunity to practice staying centered by trusting that "All is well." I gave it over to Spirit. Aligning with the law of attraction, I focused on what I wanted—I thanked Spirit that Amy would return my call within 45 minutes and if it was meant for me to travel both ways with Michael and enjoy the whole weekend with him, then she would suggest I postpone the class. I chose to be very specific in my request for clarity because other people's needs were being considered.

Wow. Amy called me back within a half hour and after hearing of my opportunity, emphatically said, "Just postpone the gathering. Don't worry, go and have fun." And I said, as I often do, "Spirit, we are so cool." Life is always in divine order. I also trusted that each member of the group would personally benefit from the date change as well.

Spiritual Guidance—Connecting with Others

Spirit is often guiding you if you hear or see the same person's name repeatedly in a short period of time, a strong suggestion for the two of you to connect. This information can help you feel more comfortable when choosing a doctor or a dentist, an accountant, a new company to work for or even a future business or personal connection. Spirit even has fun in this way by acting as my Divine dating service, getting me to meet certain men.

With any relationship, you are guided to people for life lessons, love, personal or business support, karmic balancing or whatever else you are ready to experience with them. Can you think of times you met people in uncanny ways?

Spiritual Guidance—Some Are Not Ready to Receive It

When I see others suffering or feeling helpless, I naturally want to intervene to lessen their emotional or physical pain. But, I also know that they attract situations to learn from and until that soul lesson is learned, it's for their highest good to experience what they have attracted.

When I feel an impulse to offer my help, I tell Spirit, "If it's for the highest good of all for me to work with this person, show me clear signs." A well-known, local woman had breast cancer and her doctors had told her it couldn't be healed and managing it would be the best she could expect. I knew Western medicine was doing the best it could for her and I also knew that she could magnify her options and increase her potential for full recovery if she would use the combined healing potential of the mind, body, and spirit. I felt if she could be open to what she probably didn't yet understand, then she could get results that Western medicine wasn't expecting.

The woman had been quoted in the newspaper as saying, "This is in God's hands." Two friends, Jodi and Amy, and I prayed together, "God, if connecting with me is for her highest good, then please open the door for this connection." Our part was now done. We trusted God would guide the rest.

And we were guided. Within a few weeks, Jodi went to a certain deli for the first time and she "just happened" to see the woman there. Jodi trusted this encounter was divinely set up and spoke with the woman for a few minutes, mentioning my work and my recovery, and then gave her a business card so she could follow up if she chose.

She didn't follow up. Yet, it appeared God was trying again to get this woman's attention. A few weeks later, Jodi stopped by that same deli. This time she waited at an outside table while her order was prepared. Who "just happened" to drive up and park right in front of Jodi? Yes, the woman with breast cancer. She stayed in her car, talking on her cell phone. Then she looked up at Jodi. Jodi smiled.

The two times Jodi visited that deli, she saw the woman. I believe God opened the door for the woman two times, her probable prayers being addressed. Though, her answer must have come in a different package than expected. She didn't recognize God in these random meetings or, if she did, she wasn't ready to walk through a non-traditional door.

This woman did what felt comfortable to her—stayed with traditional treatment, handled her cancer with grace and died a few years later. God often sets up opportunities for us to help others but we need to honor those people whether or not they are receptive.

When Julie, a friend from high school with whom I rarely connect, was diagnosed with stage 1 breast cancer, she perused my web site as she had occasionally over the past several years. She called me and was talking fast, her thoughts jumping around. She said she was scared and confused about how to proceed. To encourage her, I shared the results one of my cancer clients had after five energy healing sessions. The client's follow up tests, even a year later, came back negative—no sign of any cancer.

I told her most people aren't familiar with the combined healing power of mind, body, and spirit. Many people return to wholeness using only alternative avenues while others prefer to incorporate both avenues—holistic healing with traditional medicine. We discussed her non-invasive energy healing options. Julie was definitely feeling overwhelmed and I suggested she pray for guidance.

She got her guidance. During another phone call, Julie told me that "the weirdest thing happened." While she was researching traditional cancer treatments, an unrelated page "just happened" to pop up on her computer screen—a page with *my* bio information on it.

It was my bio from the Sound Healers Association's practitioner page. She had never visited that web site and if she had it would have taken four more mouse clicks to get to that page. It just showed up.

I trust it was Spirit trying to get her attention and confirm it would be safe to use holistic healing. Her spiritual guidance surprised her with this blessing, yet her fear and beliefs blocked her from seeing it as one. If she had been able to trust the guidance she received, her fear would have been naturally diminished.

Julie recognized her intense fear and made the decision most comfortable for her—a lumpectomy with six weeks of radiation. I respect people for checking out all their options and choosing what works best for them. She also supplemented with Superfood, vitamins, my twice monthly tele-classes and distance healings and focused on all she had to be grateful for.

We keep in touch and I am very proud of her. She continues to improve her health by addressing emotions she had buried and by eating a whole food diet. Most important, she moved on from a marriage that, for years, had been emotionally dead. She is now extremely happy and enjoying a fulfilling relationship.

Pay attention to unordinary happenings. People unexpectedly say or do things. Web pages show up or disappear. Lights flicker or bells or phones ring. Objects move or hide. Lost objects reappear. You take a different road instead of your familiar route. Voice mail messages are deleted.

Spirit can do these things and anything else it deems best to orchestrate a message that you need, or to help you for your highest good. The creativity of spiritual guidance is infinite. Ram Dass reminds us, "Everything in your life is there as a vehicle for your transformation. Use it!" So, have fun tapping into the genius of Spirit.

Chapter 10
How Spirit Comforts and Guides You

Participate joyfully in the sorrows of the world. We cannot cure the world of sorrows, but we can choose to live in joy.
– Joseph Campbell

Divine guidance can bring you much comfort, especially when you are grieving the death of a loved one. Energetically, "transition" is a truer word for death.

Upon death you transition from the denser earth plane vibration to a much higher vibration and consciousness in the spirit realm.

I embrace the perspective that even though the physical body dies, your eternal soul returns to its full spiritual expression and lives on in a higher dimension—once again whole, and feeling more joy and peace than you could ever have imagined from your earthly, human perspective.

Whether the loved one is a human being or an animal companion, those of you still living on the earth plane are naturally saddened by your loss. Grieving is a normal process. Yet, while you grieve *your* loss, their consciousness is still present. At death, their soul, a pure Light body, vibrates so quickly that most can't see them on the earth plane—yet, you often can sense their presence.

Many of you have felt your loved one's presence or had a very real dream of them after their death. This is not your imagination. Your loved one is there to comfort you and connect with you. Enjoy the experience and allow yourself to feel the peace it is meant to bring.

They bring you peace from the other side by letting you know they are fine and are still with you. Once in spirit, a loved one's sense of humor may come through as the phone or door bell ringing at the same time they used to call or get home. They may have your favorite flower or collectable appear seemingly out of thin air and in the oddest places.

When a loved one is dying, I always recommend that he and family members decide on a sign that can be used from the other side to let the family know he is safe and spiritually present. The following stories share about the comfort this brings.

Using Red Cardinals as a Sign

My client Chuck was dying and setting up a sign for him to use after his transition brought the family more peace. They chose a bird, the red cardinal.

Chuck died at the end of November and when family members walked into the floral shop to order flowers for the funeral their eyes were drawn to a Christmas tree. It was decorated only in red cardinals. Did Chuck guide them to choose this florist because the tree would be there or did Spirit guide the florist to decorate a tree with cardinals? It doesn't matter. What matters is the presence or "presents" of love.

The love continued. Chuck's family saw cardinals in many places. A few weeks later, one daughter instantly felt a connection to her Dad when she spotted a woman with a red cardinal on her sweatshirt, and Chuck's wife, Betty, received a cardinal night-light for a Christmas gift from a friend who had no knowledge of the cardinal sign.

The sweetest of all the sightings, a display of the comforting love that continues from the other side, was a pair of cardinals that appeared around 8:30 every morning—for

126

three months straight—strutting back and forth on the railing of Betty's deck. They had not been there prior to Chuck's transition.

It's been a few years since his passing. Even so, every day Betty hears the cardinals calling to each other. They tend to save their appearances for special occasions. One winter, the cardinal's red feathers were a welcome sight against the white of a rare North Carolina snowfall. And often when Betty has had an especially tiring or challenging day, they have stayed longer to help ease the stress. Betty and Chuck's children and grandchildren still feel Chuck's presence regularly and love how cardinals are always part of those special times.

I talked with Betty recently and asked her how much the cardinal sign has helped her. She was at a loss for words. After pausing for a few moments, she said it's allowed her to get past not having him with her physically because she knows he really is here. And even though she knows she can talk to Chuck at any time, the cardinals give her a physical presence to which she can direct her words. Chuck was a Marine and was called Sir by many of his coworkers. When the cardinals appear, she now talks to Chuck, her beloved husband of fifty years, calling him Sir—an endearing name that keeps him close to her heart.

Using a Martini as a Sign

My friend Valerie was dealing with the painful reality of her father's inevitable transition. When his death was imminent, her out-of-state siblings came to be with their father.

I suggested to Valerie that her family come up with a sign for their father to share with the family after his passing. Valerie's personal spiritual work had given her much peace and comfort, though it wasn't the path her father, Tom, and her siblings had chosen; she wasn't sure if they would be open to the idea. Together, we prayed, "God, if this idea is for the highest good of all, reveal the ideal timing and have Valerie easily share this."

Right before her siblings boarded a plane to fly home, the timing felt right to share her idea and the words flowed out of her mouth. Her brother agreed and shared the story of a friend who had done the same thing with his grandmother. Valerie's two sisters were now more accepting. Their Dad loved a good martini, so they decided that would be their sign.

The next day, Valerie took her Dad's hand and told him about the martini sign. Mind you, her Dad wasn't open to her beliefs. Yet, that day, he totally understood what she was telling him and agreed to let them know he was fine. He thought a martini was the perfect sign. Two days later he transitioned.

When Valerie told me they had chosen a martini, I was a little surprised. At first I thought they chose a difficult sign. I caught myself limiting Spirit, and said, "That's an uncommon one...but Spirit can arrange anything!"

Within 24 hours of her father's passing, the most skeptical sister found her eyes drawn to a glittery greeting card. She picked it up and realized she was looking at a drawing of a martini glass.

That evening Valerie's husband had a dream in which his father-in-law drove by in a red convertible holding up a martini. The next day Valerie "just happened" to see a martini wind sock high up in a tree at a restaurant. That same day, she talked to a friend who saw a Christmas tree decorated with martini glasses and thought of Tom. That evening, another friend saw a martini skit on "Saturday Night Live." He thought of Tom because he knew Tom loved martinis and had recently passed, but the friend had not been told about the martini sign. The next day another sister opened up a recipe book—to the very page that "just happened" to be a photo of a martini.

A month after Tom's passing, Valerie's friends were at an art show and came upon a booth full of paintings of martini glasses; one painting, in full view, was a martini glass that held three Yorkshire terriers. Knowing about the martini sign, they couldn't wait to call Valerie. Valerie has three Yorkies.

Even though it has been two years since Tom's passing, his wife and children continue to have uncanny sightings of martini glasses.

Valerie, who just had a birthday, shared with me how her Dad made it clear that he was celebrating with her, too. A friend took her to lunch at one of her favorite restaurants. Valerie ordered the specialty salad she had ordered many times before. It was always served in an Asian bowl, but on this day, her birthday, it arrived in a big martini glass. No one had asked for that. Can you imagine the guy in the kitchen struggling with this whim to serve the salad in a martini glass? Blessings to him for following his guidance.

You get the picture. Tom, who hadn't believed in an afterlife, was now having fun helping his family process his passing in as light a way as possible. Valerie reports that they have found the martini signs to be anchoring points for them to connect physically with their Dad, giving everyone great comfort and joy.

Your Pets Will Comfort You

Pets are such an integral part of our lives. The death of an animal companion is a major loss and often difficult to deal with. People find comfort in knowing that their pets can communicate back to them with wisdom and guidance and with signs that all is well. For example, a pet may communicate by allowing its mannerisms to come through another pet; a dog may now carry its leash in its mouth or now wait by its food dish for a hug before eating, mimicking the familiar mannerisms of the dog that had passed.

A friend of mine had an aunt who found it very comforting when she physically felt her cat return every night after his death to curl up at her feet as she drifted off to sleep.

A few days before our ladies' weekend at Wrightsville Beach, North Carolina, my friend Jodi's elderly dog had to be put to sleep. It is an act of love to help an animal companion's soul leave its physical body and move into the higher vibration of the spirit realm—back to pure positive Light and love.

On our way to the beach, Jodi asked her dog to show us balloons as the sign that he was fine. Jodi believed he was running across fields of green grass in the spirit realm, though her grieving heart welcomed the consoling.

As we drove into the hotel's parking garage, we saw loose balloons floating around. Then we saw an SUV full of balloons with "Just Married" written on its windows.

The next morning we awoke to more balloons. A man had several kites for sale on the beach in front of our hotel window. He also had about twenty flat nylon lawn ornaments, balloons, attached to thin posts propped up in the sand.

The fun with the balloons continued as we made our way home. An unusual choice for us, we '"just happened" to stop at a barbeque restaurant for dinner. Even though I was a vegetarian I knew I could eat the baked beans and coleslaw. We all laughed as we approached the counter to order. We now understood the nudge to choose that restaurant because several bouquets of balloons greeted us, one near each cash register. The balloons comforted Jodi and gave us all happier hearts.

These examples are a sweet reminder that our loved ones who transition are never really gone from us. They may be expressing their full essence in another dimension, but they can still tune into us and lighten our day.

Spiritual Guidance May Seem to Change Its Mind

Spirit sees your soul's destiny path—where you've been, where you're going and everything with which you are energetically aligned. Guidance is given to you with the big picture in mind, moving you forward with the best opportunities for growth, or setting you up for more blessings. Guidance can make sure you are at the right place at the right time, provide for karmic balancing, or help you to be of service to others. Keep in mind that you are an energetic being— vibrations in motion. You attract the experiences your soul needs for its growth.

Energetically, there may be a strong propensity for certain events to lead you in a particular direction so Spirit guides you accordingly. Then, Spirit may need to shift gears and move you in a different direction for your highest good. At first glance, you may feel you were led down the "wrong" path.

Even though you may not understand why things happened as they do, trust that Spirit always has your back and is guiding you for your highest good. Trust that you got the lessons and experiences that you needed and now what is for your highest good requires that you head in a different direction.

This different direction, especially a disappointing one, may challenge your acceptance that all is in perfect and divine order. This was my experience. For months, many doors opened. Then a few crucial doors closed.

For several years my vision was to secure a triplex apartment building for a non-profit which helps homeless families get into a temporary apartment, find jobs and learn life skills.

Of course, Spirit knows the big picture and knew of my idea. So one day I got an out-of-the-blue phone call telling me about an ideal property, a triplex in our downtown area. The next step was getting the grant money I needed from the town and county to make my vision a reality. I affirmed the highest good for all. I visualized 3 families using these apartments, and I thanked Spirit in advance for all the blessings that made this happen.

My friend Lyle offered to donate his time and expertise to my vision. He's a builder and developer who's familiar with the town and county grant processes and regularly receives grant monies for his low-income elderly housing projects. Lyle had the history and business success that the town and county needed to see as party to my grant request. I said, "Thanks, Spirit!"

The doors continued to open. I had a meeting with the appropriate town committee head and was told that because the triplex fit their vision to improve housing for the homeless, they would support my project with or without the county. This was a blessing since they generally wanted the county involved as well. I said, "Thanks, Spirit!"

Because of my desire to help the homeless, I committed to give the necessary time to accomplish my vision, but I needed funding so I approached a local bank for support. Repairs had to be made to get the building ready for occupancy, so I requested more than 100% financing. The bank supported my vision and agreed to the financing. They even told me they never finance 100% and, yet, here they were agreeing to finance *over* 100%. I said, "Thanks, Spirit!"

My desire was to secure a property for the non-profit to help more families get off the street, but not to handle the day-to-day responsibilities of owning a property. The non-profit, as they did with their other rental properties, agreed to handle the maintenance on this triplex. I said, "Thanks, Spirit!"

This was my heart-centered project to help the homeless. I would use the grant money to pay my monthly mortgage. I would not see any profit until the property was sold which couldn't happen for at least 11 years. At that time I would pay back my grant money. My hope was that by then I'd be in a financial position where I could gift the building to the non-profit.

I stretched myself mentally and time wise for five months learning about grants and town politics, creating spread sheets for budgets and repairs, attending meetings, getting estimates and following up with contacts. So many blessings supported this project. And I said, Thanks, Spirit!

Then five months into it, my phone calls were not being returned by the town committee head. Eventually, it became obvious the project was no longer the town's priority—the committee head even made comments during a meeting that contradicted what he had told me earlier. I was totally confused. Yet, I believe everything is *always* in divine order, no matter what. I stayed in my power and faith and prayed to God, "If this is for the highest good for all, please reveal a viable solution."

During the last week, even the non-profit wasn't returning my calls or available to attend the town council meeting supporting *their* cause. I was perplexed for sure *and* I was recognizing the signs—the project was folding right before my eyes.

When it became exceptionally clear that it was not going to happen, I called Lyle and shared the news. I was surprised and disappointed, but accepted that the project was not meant to be. Again, because of my deep faith that everything happens for the best, I accepted what is and grieved for only a minute.

My old self would have spent days feeling totally frustrated for wasting months of my precious time and blaming other people for leading me down the wrong path. I would have been baffled by and angry at the politics that allowed something that would benefit so many go so wrong.

Part of my soul's journey has been to find a way to feel good and not suffer emotionally when things don't go as expected. I am thankful that I accepted that nothing was "wasted" and that everything that had happened was exactly what each of us players in this game of life needed. I was able to thank God for all that I had learned, for the wonderful people that had been on board with me, and for the goodness that makes my town so special. And I said, "Thanks, Spirit!"

Spiritual guidance helps us move through life with a lighter step whether we are grieving loved ones or animals that pass, or business deals that fall apart.

And remember, no matter what, it's all good. Acceptance creates a non-resistant energy within you—a field of energy allowing in the next experiences and blessings for your highest good.

Enjoy the mystery.

Chapter 11
Diamonds in the Rough

I have come to the frightening conclusion that I am the decisive element. It is my personal approach that creates the climate. It is my daily mood that makes the weather. I possess tremendous power to make life miserable or joyous. I can be a tool of torture or an instrument of inspiration; I can humiliate or humor, hurt or heal. In all situations, it is my response that decides whether a crisis is escalated or de-escalated, and a person is humanized or de-humanized. If we treat people as they are, we make them worse. If we treat people as they ought to be, we help them become what they are capable of becoming.
– Haim Ginott

This quote is one of my favorites. Ginott says it so powerfully. You are the writer of your life's script—each day you make a choice to give your power to productive thoughts, beliefs, and attitudes or to destructive ones.

Let the phrase "diamonds in the rough" remind you of your power just waiting to be recognized. Great pressure turns coal into diamonds. Yet the rough diamond looks dull and lifeless when first removed from the black carbon. A skillful lapidary transforms the shapeless stone into a beautiful gem— the brilliance inherently present within the rough diamond.

As with the great pressure that turns coal into diamonds, life's "pressures" allow you the opportunity to transform yourself and shine with the full brilliance that you innately are.

The following story about a client, I'll call him Rob, is a great example of how challenges offer us growth opportunities. When I met Rob, he had just moved here from another state to get a fresh start after a recent bankruptcy and impending divorce.

He had accepted a full-time position but it didn't work out. He hoped to find more full-time work. He hadn't. His wife, also without a job, moved back in with her parents. Throughout their 30-year marriage, finances were always a concern and over the last ten years, intimacy and healthy communication were lacking.

Rob was scheduled that week to fly back to his home state to meet with his wife to further discuss their impending divorce.

Rob had four back surgeries in eleven years and, most of the time over the last three years he dealt with chronic lower back pain. His pain and the subsequent scenarios around it interfered with his ability to work and contributed to feelings of unworthiness, anger, resentment and fear over his future. Through recent phone conversations his wife tearfully pleaded with him to reconsider his plans. He felt guilt over moving forward with the divorce.

Months before our sessions, he had considered suicide.

He admitted he has a habit of wanting instant results. He became frustrated with anything less than his expectations of perfection and complete success. He was open to the lessons of the Universe but, trained as a scientist, he shared his skepticism toward the mystical.

In spite of being an overachiever, Rob acknowledged that he had a negative self-concept, rooted in never feeling his father's approval. Also, as a child he was teased about being the fat kid in the neighborhood. Throughout his adult years, his false belief of "I'm not good enough" was fed by years of unfulfilling relationships, lack of intimacy in his marriage, fear of rejection and a constant drive to improve and do better.

After a few sessions, Rob caught himself reinforcing his negative programming, his "stories" that kept past challenges and false beliefs energetically alive. He has experienced how these limiting beliefs affect his ability to receive the full benefit of our energy sessions. After a healing session his pain completely diminishes but then, when he thinks according to his old negative beliefs, the pain returns.

He came to me for healing when his chronic back pain became severe. During our sessions he learned about the mind, body and spirit connection and how undealt-with emotions cause energy blocks which lead to pain and disease. He now understood that his body was giving him feedback via the pain that, despite narcotic analgesics and lying on an ice pack, had him screaming and fighting back tears with his slightest move.

The lower back is located in the second chakra, one of seven non-physical energy centers within the body. Other areas in the second chakra that can be affected by negative beliefs are the sexual organs, large intestine, pelvis, appendix, bladder and hip area. The lower back is affected by long standing emotions dealing with a lack of finances or financial support, or by an obvious or underlying worry regarding money. Even those who enjoy financial success but regularly worry about their money in some fashion—wondering if their investments will last or who will take advantage of my wealth—will create health issues in the lower back, second chakra. Carolyn Myss shares in *Anatomy of the Spirit* the general mental and emotional issues associated with each chakra. The issues that deal with blame and guilt, money and sex, power and control, creativity, and ethics and honor in relationships create second chakra imbalances.

Rob's family had stressed over money for years. He felt powerless in a marriage which was devoid of an intimate sexual relationship. He blamed his wife for their problems and carried guilt for moving on from their marriage. Considering his bottled-up emotions, I wasn't surprised when he told me about the back surgeries. The root cause, the emotional blocks, had never been addressed.

Rob and I "just happened" to meet at a social event shortly before his back pain began screaming at him. He called me when it got worse. Our life coaching sessions helped him understand how the themes of past life beliefs are continued in this lifetime—his were unworthiness and "not enough money." He began to see his pain as an indication of the need to address those false beliefs. He chose to look at the root cause of the pain.

Rob's in-person and distance healings included rebalancing his energy field with energy healing and sound healing—sound frequencies created by my voice, crystal bowls and tuning forks. The healings provided immediate relief. And, he learned that neither I nor Spirit could do his emotional work for him. He was raising his awareness and finding relief through meditation, affirmations and Epsom salt baths. He was sincerely trying but still needed to own the teachings to shift his beliefs enough to remain energetically balanced. His feelings of low self-worth, the anger he kept just below the surface and expressed at the least bit of frustration, and the guilt he felt in moving on from the marriage threw his energy field out of balance again and again. Thus, the relief from the healings was short term.

Rob wrote the following about his experience. "It sounds so easy to just release the negative energy of unworthiness, fear, resentment and anger and allow the positive energy of love, abundance and peace to flow in. I am certainly not choosing pain over peace. For me, I do feel like a diamond in the rough, though it has not been easy to shift my old programming.

"On my way to letting my Light shine, Suzette is helping me to recognize that it's the accumulation of negative thoughts that build into an avalanche of despair. I am making a conscious choice to redirect those thoughts toward acceptance and surrender to my Higher Power. When I am alone and become present in the moment, meditative and receptive to the love and abundance of the Universe, I allow in and accept the higher vibrations. The pain and feelings of unworthiness magically disappear. Even though it fills me with awe and gratitude in the moment, I am not yet effective at sustaining the higher vibration. I slip back on the roller coaster that redelivers me to my feedback—emotional and physical pain.

"Over the last several days, I couldn't move without feeling waves of burning electricity down my left leg in spite of the narcotic analgesic. I was allowing myself a big pity party and couldn't focus on the empowering suggestions Suzette shares. I hadn't talked with her for several weeks and I was expected to make a five-hour airplane trip the next morning. I considered a 911 call that night.

"Then Suzette phoned to check in with me; what a coincidence. She says, "Not." She reminded me to take my power back and to tap into the teachings from previous sessions. She helped me release the anxiety surrounding my "need" to make that flight the next day and the challenges of the ensuing several days of the trip. She helped me surrender and trust that Spirit would guide this trip, if I was to go at all, and for the highest good of all. She reminded me to get out of my own way and to receive the abundant healing energy that is always available, as long as I don't block it with my persistent fear-based emotions. I became more centered. I gave my pain and my trip over to Spirit. I had to. I could no longer manage it on my own.

"Suzette agreed to do a half-hour distance healing later that evening. I set an intention that if it was for my highest good to make the trip in the morning, my pain would be relieved when I woke up.

"The next morning, I was not only able to make the flight, but I no longer required narcotic analgesics. My back improved each day in spite of my drive of over 800 miles in a rental car before my return flight to Raleigh.

"Suzette helps me lighten my need to totally heal these emotional blocks *yesterday*. I am seeing financial issues, anger and unworthiness as themes my soul wanted me to heal this lifetime. I am working with the power of the mind and am relaxing the need to be so perfect or to carry the burden of my wife's emotional pain. I am focusing on the possibilities instead of what is.

"What is? I am out of a job. I don't like it but I can see how my life needed this to get my attention in a dramatic way, I had ignored looking within all these years. I did not see four back surgeries as a hint. I did not see a life time of financial stress and feelings of 'I'm not enough' as a hint. And now, my body, once again, got my attention and I'm ready to see it for the message it brings. I'm ready to recognize and release the root blocks. The saying, 'When the student is ready, the teacher appears' is valid here. I'm ready for my bliss. I'm learning that I deserve it."

Rob learned the hard way. But you don't have to wait for the Universe to create pain and drama to get your attention. Perhaps it's time to feel and let go of the fear-based thoughts and false beliefs that have held you hostage in your mind. Perhaps it's time to grab an imaginary Kleenex and "wipe clean" the lenses through which you, like many others, have interpreted your life—lenses blurred by negative experiences, erroneous beliefs, hurts and even events from other lifetimes.

If so, then intend to dissolve the grip that your fears and beliefs have on you. By creating lighter and happier feelings, your ability to more easily handle and deflect stress and chaos will strengthen. Also, your body will respond with more energy and improved health because you have opened to a greater flow of life force energy. Often symptoms of disease and illness will go away because you are clearing their root cause—those undealt-with emotions.

Learning and Growing Through Relationships

Time and a new perspective offer a sense of appreciation for relationship challenges. People often look back at these challenges and realize they grew from them. And they begin to appreciate these relationships for exposing the issues they chose to work on this lifetime.

The feelings relationships stimulate in you are the result of past hurts and dramas, yours and theirs. Relationships, especially with immediate family members, are generally part of a predestined plan for each of you, together, to experience joy *and* growth. You each decided to reunite this lifetime to heal karmic situations or to mirror to each other the emotional wounds in your energy fields that need healing.

Let's consider two adult women who grew up in the same family and were exposed to the same environment of parental behaviors and beliefs. They have different outlooks, unique life experiences, and different emotional wounds even though they spent their childhoods with the same dysfunctional parent, perhaps an alcoholic, a workaholic, or one unable to demonstrate love.

If you could look at each woman's astrological birth chart which explains their soul blue prints, you would see that each chose to incarnate this lifetime to have different personalities and to heal different emotional wounds. The same environment shaped and scarred each woman in a different way; each received opportunities to learn their respective lessons in that same household.

In response to a controlling and abusive father, one daughter may have become very promiscuous, wanting to find love and attention in any way she could. The other daughter may have become withdrawn, afraid to do anything that might upset the people around her. They lived in the same environment but, depending on what each of their souls needed for spiritual growth, they experienced it differently; each looked through lenses—honed by their specific lifetimes—and saw what they needed to see.

An empowered perspective can free you from an emotional jail cell. If your partner, a family member, or your best friend gravely disappoints you, consider that the amount of suffering you continue to incur is directly related to your thoughts and perspective on the situation. Coaching or counseling support can help you see your pain from a healthier perspective—a view from outside the emotional jail cell.

Your thoughts, your body, and your environment are informational patterns of energy. Changing an energy pattern is simply a matter of changing your thoughts and perspective. You can't change the problem, but you can change the way you *see* the problem. And changing the way you see the problem breaks down the wall of resistance you built with your emotional "blocks" of anger and frustration. The end result is your ability to feel good no matter how others are treating you. This good feeling creates an energy pattern that attracts more blessings to you.

To create more good feelings, look at every hurt as an opportunity to grow. This is the inner work your soul came here to do. Consider, for example, the feeling that arises when a friend pushes one of your buttons. Anger or resentment pops up. See the feeling as a red flag signaling that an emotional wound has been re-opened. Recognize that your friend is just showing you a hurt that was never sufficiently healed. Practice not reacting to your friend's behavior. Consider it, instead, as an opportunity to discover where the root charge of this hurt lies within *you*. Look back at your childhood or other past relationships to find the first time you felt that way. As you recognize that this hurt is connected to an old wound, an old pattern, you can choose to see your friend's behavior from a fresh perspective—as a gift, showing you what still needs to be processed. I admit it often takes time to see your uncomfortable situations as gifts. Yet, the sooner you do, you call back your power.

To process the hurts from these situations, when you are alone, allow yourself to feel the emotions. You may feel like crying. You may even experience deep sobbing, moaning or deep emotional or heart-centered pain. You may get angry. You may wonder, "Why me?"

Giving yourself permission and the space to feel this pain allows the pain to be dissolved. Then, as the feelings are expressing, call on your Higher Power and ask for its help as you set an intention to clear the emotions from your entire energy field, including other lifetimes. And with the deepest gratitude you can feel, affirm: "Thank you, Spirit that I am clearing the root cause of this hurt from this or any other lifetime with ease and gentleness."

Consider receiving energy healing sessions to move these blocks quicker than you can do alone. Once the root issue—the false belief or old programming—is addressed and healed, that button will rarely be pushed again. If it is, you can recognize that there are more layers of the same emotion to be addressed and you have the tools to handle it.

Like attracts like, so the beauty of clearing old patterns is that your new energy field will attract nicer experiences and kinder people into your life. The purpose of this work is not to change people; it is to adjust *your* attitude and focus. Yet, generally, when you change, they will change, too. And even if they don't, you will have found a way to feel good in spite of their behavior. It is possible that you may feel less comfortable around them and, eventually, the relationship may end. The good news is you will attract new relationships that feel good.

Changing Your Perspective

Positive changes in perspective help develop healthier relationships. **REAP** is an acronym, a tool, that can be used to improve any relationship. The following is an example of how a person who feels disrespected in a relationship might use this acronym.

R—**Release** the feeling.

E—Shift the **Energy.**

A—**Affirm** what you are worthy of.

P—Focus on the person's **Positive** qualities.

First, tell your body, "I **R**elease this feeling of disrespect." Take a deep relaxing breath and repeat the affirmation.

Next, affirm, "My thoughts and intentions are Energy that I can choose to shift." Loving intentions shift energy, so send love to the other person. You receive that which you give so you both benefit from this love.

Affirm what you are worthy of. "I am worthy of respect and healthy communication." Take a relaxing breath and repeat the affirmation as often as needed throughout the day.

You get what you focus on. So, focus on one or two of the **P**ositive qualities of the other person. "He is generous." "He is a jack of all trades." "He is trying." You can't be focusing on their positive traits and be angry at the same time.

REAP improves both your reaction to another person's action, and, ultimately, your vibration. Energetically, you are not condoning their behavior or being a doormat when you accept others as they are. Quite the opposite. Acceptance of what is allows you to align energetically with your real power, mind power which helps you handle your relationships vibrationally. When you focus on the imperfections of another, you keep that energy present and magnify your own anger, frustration or depression. When you choose to focus on their positive attributes you leverage the power of your intentions with the law of attraction.

In my clients' life coaching sessions, I help them understand the energetic benefits of shifting their perspective and choosing pro-active thoughts. Positive thoughts create more emotional harmony.

If the comments are not for them to carry, I help my clients not take the comments of family, friends or co-workers personally. Instead, I help them observe the hurtful action or words from a healthier perspective—they start to realize that when others are hurtful it is because they are hurting.

They see that it is the friend's feelings of fear, insecurity or need to control that are behind the hurtful actions or words. The friend may also twist my client's well-intended words around and end up blaming my client. Blaming others is the action taken by one who is unwilling to look within and heal unresolved issues. Otherwise, they would handle the disappointing interaction with a respectful conversation. I encourage my clients not to accept the blame if it is not their responsibility; as long as they and Spirit know the truth of who they are, *that* is enough.

Words that have helped me and my clients deflect the negative emotions of others are, "What others think of me is none of my business, as long as I'm being the best that God intends me to be."

Trust that even though it may not always seem so, others are doing the best they can with where they are on their journey. They are looking at their world and reacting to it through their own lenses of unresolved emotional pain—pain they may not be ready to heal. Their pain and reactions are not your baggage to carry.

If you attempt to "shoulder" the burden of another's action or opinion, you may find your own shoulders becoming tight and sore—your body wisdom physically reminding you of the impossibility of what you are trying to do. Or, if you aren't able to speak up for yourself, you may attract a sore throat. As you let go of that which is not yours to carry and learn to speak your truth in a loving and firm way, the pain in your body should dissipate.

You are a Masterpiece in the Making

Life is a journey. Rejoice in the good times and allow yourself to grow through the trying times.

Compare yourself to others only if it inspires you to your own greatness. Review how you handled a situation and learn from it without self-judgment. Judgment and emotionally beating yourself up lower your vibration.

If you are not pleased with the way you handled a situation, affirm that next time you will handle it better. It may not have been your all-time best, but it was probably your best at *that* time considering your own emotional blocks. The reaction is now part of your past and your power is in the present moment and in what you choose to focus on. Your reactions affect your energy field, and a healthier energy field helps magnetize you to preferred situations.

Honoring Other People's Journeys

Your path provides you with all the scenarios you need for your spiritual growth—the fun, the contrasts and the wake-up calls. Integral to your spiritual growth, though, is to accept that other's unique paths may not be the path you wish they were on.

Their paths offer the perfect way for them to gain clarity, have fun, and grow. Their experiences give them opportunities to let go of fears, unworthiness, resentment, anger and whatever else their souls chose to heal this lifetime.

Spiritually, one path choice is no better or worse, no more right or wrong, than another. Each challenging interaction offers a lesson. People who don't learn the lesson offered will unknowingly stay in unhealthy relationships or lifestyles or they will repeat those interactions with different people—all part of their journey to "get the lesson."

You may feel frustrated as you observe a loved one making poor decisions or suffering, from your viewpoint, unnecessarily—doing drugs, staying in an abusive relationship, or not living up to their potential. Nevertheless, observing their path offers you a chance to decide how best to react—another chance to let go of the need to control or the need to have them do what's "right" in your opinion.

There seems to be a consensus that those closest to us do not welcome our suggestions on how to improve their lives. In fact, if they are not ready to change or hear your suggestions, your help will appear as nagging.

Yes, I'm speaking from experience. I'm learning to trust that my daughters are on their perfect paths and to honor that their journeys are unfolding exactly as they need them to. They give me much to be proud of. In areas of disagreement, I still get to practice stepping back after sharing my concern. I find comfort in supporting them through prayers and intentions for their highest good: "Thank you, Spirit, for guiding them to hear what they need to hear in a way they can hear it. Thank you for wrapping them in safety and blessings." Then, each time any feelings of worry show up, I say, "I release this fear. They are safe and protected." There is power in loving them unconditionally as they work through their life lessons in their best way and in surrounding them with the pink energy of love while visualizing them happy, confident, or gainfully employed.

I learned the hard way that feeling bad for others doesn't protect or assist them; it just lowered my vibration. Peace came over me as I adjusted my perspective and trusted our soul journeys

Repeating the Lesson

Have you ever had a friend who divorced a controlling or alcoholic spouse and then turned right around and married another person with the same problem? We think, "It was obvious to me, why isn't she seeing it?" Yet, spiritually, like attracts like and the friend still had lessons to learn around those conditions.

A friend may have made considerable headway, or not grown at all with her first partner, but the bottom line is there is still something for her to learn. You can support her more easily by recognizing her soul lessons, thinking good thoughts about her and visualizing her happy with her self-worth, self-respect and boundaries improving.

The more my clients have trusted that they attract situations for a higher purpose, the easier it is for them to get out of their own way and honor the journey, the process. They realize when they have mastered the lessons from their challenges, they seldom attract similar situations. And if they do, by then they have trained themselves to remain calm and learn from them.

The Emotion of Judgment

Your buttons are being pushed. And it doesn't feel good. This red flag, not feeling good, is offering you an opportunity to honestly question what's going on beneath the surface. You realize that you are really upset about what someone else is doing or saying. You may even admit that you are judging their way as bad or wrong. Oh, great, it's another opportunity to grow.

Remember, you aren't here to mind other people's business; you can't change anyone except yourself. Take a deep breath. Consider that you have attracted this to bring the energy of judgment to your awareness and then to clear it. So let's take a closer look at the emotion of judgment.

First, feelings of judgment create a lower vibration that blocks you energetically from your own peace of mind.

Second, feelings of judgment are feedback. Resist the temptation to label them good or bad. They are just reminding you that you are letting others determine how good you feel. Perhaps you judge a friend as controlling, insecure, or unorganized, and you begin to get upset until you remember that you alone determine your thoughts and feelings.

Third, feelings of judgment, from a soul journey aspect, are good. Your soul is using the person you're judging to mirror back to you what is energetically present in you to be healed. As you think this over it may be obvious, or maybe not.

If you don't find within yourself the particular trait that you are judging, trust that you are being nudged by Spirit to see that this trait is in your energy field from another lifetime. And, that everyone benefits from you dissolving all judgment around this trait. I have found it interesting to see how another's melodrama shows me what I was not recognizing and acknowledging within myself.

Expect to feel better as you recognize feelings of judgment and then clear them. Use the following affirmations or others you like to reprogram your cellular memory and release judgment with ease.

Affirm: "Thanks, Source, for transmuting the root cause of this judgmental energy to love." Continue more specifically with "I forgive those who have hurt me and I forgive myself for any time I have judged others. Thanks, Source, for revealing the highest outcome for all."

The beauty of challenging situations is that they offer you opportunities to improve your inner strength, clear emotions residing in your energy field and to heal at the soul level. You would not purposely choose arguments or hurtful situations. Though, in hindsight, you usually can see how you gained wisdom and strength from them. As you finally learn the "lesson," you no longer need the "teacher," the friend pushing your buttons.

Remember, everyone is connected by invisible informational fields of energy--you are not separate from those you swear at or judge or hurt. Every action of one person has an effect on all others and the entire universal energy field. As you work on yourself, you are helping not only your own spiritual expansion but the expansion of the collective consciousness. As you grow, you are energetically being of service and positively influencing many others.

Sparkle like a diamond. Expansion lets you shine more and more of your natural brilliance. You are inherently the essence of the divine—pure Light, joy, love and wholeness. Awaken to the *All* that you *already* are and accept an easier, happier, healthier and more prosperous life.

Chapter 12
Good, Good Vibrations

Life is not about waiting for the storms to pass...
It's about learning how to dance in the rain.
— Vivian Greene

Are you ready to find a way to dance in the rain (or avoid the rain clouds altogether) and even enjoy the pot of gold at the end of the rainbow? Join others who are doing just that by consistently choosing good feelings, good vibrations, throughout their day.

Many times you increase the good feelings by recognizing and releasing resistance; feelings such as doubt, control, frustration, judgment or anger. Resistance is like a kink in a garden hose that prevents the flow of the water — your blessings. You also release resistance when you hand over your problems to Spirit and thank Spirit for transmuting them to love.

Letting Go of Controlling the Outcome

Read on and see how an everyday situation offered me the chance to deepen my faith and stay centered.

I remodeled my master bathroom. During the week prior to this project, I used my manifesting tools. Every day I visualized a positive white light around the master bathroom and I visualized myself appreciating it. In advance, I stayed in gratitude for the quality workmanship I received.

After the shower and floor tile were installed, my plan was to have the handymen complete the painting, lighting and wiring by Friday, allowing for some scheduling leeway; the plumber's fixture installations were set for Tuesday. But on Tuesday morning three handymen were still there. They told me they thought they could easily work around the plumber.

At 8:30 a.m., I talked with the crew chief and reminded him that the plumber was due in an hour. I asked the crew chief to please rewire near the mirror first so he would be out of the plumber's way. When I asked how long this would take, he replied, "Just a few minutes."

His words were very accommodating, his actions weren't. At half past nine he was only halfway through the rewiring. Actually, all *three* handymen were in my bathroom. Imagine the plumber in there too. It would probably be comical. Even though I like comedy, I didn't want it here. And I didn't want to have to reschedule the plumber. At that point, my old controlling self would have been having a certain l-o-u-d-e-r conversation with the crew chief, leaving me pacing back and forth.

What should a girl do? As I felt my frustration, a clue that I was not staying in my power, I remembered that I don't have to do this alone. I remembered the *creator* I am. I decided not to waste my creative energy on frustration and worry; I went within.

Some days, in order to stay centered and stress free, you give the circumstances over to Spirit. Some days that is needed often; as it was for me that day. I made a concerted effort to keep my old control issues and anger at bay. I allowed Spirit to handle the project from that point on. I thanked Spirit in advance for the project's perfect quality and timing.

I also said a powerful affirmation that has helped me many times to reclaim my power: "The most important thing right now is for me to feel good." I knew it was my responsibility to feel good no matter how messed up my plans were. I said to myself, "I'm chalking this up to being just another opportunity to not let others affect how good I choose to feel. Thanks, Spirit!"

As I stayed centered, I felt much calmer and truly did know that my connection to Spirit was all I needed. I continued thanking the Universe and affirming, "All is well." I sent love to all the workmen and affirmed a quality job would be completed efficiently.

As Spirit had shown me before, and according to universal energetic laws, my job was to get out of my own way, focus on the end result, and expect it all to work out. I put forth my best effort and *chose* to be calm no matter what happened.

Writing this a few years later, it all seems so petty. Yet, sometimes it is the petty issues that can pile up and derail our days. It turned out to be a great learning experience, an opportunity to call back my power and allow myself to manifest the right and perfect outcome.

The handymen, whom I had expected to be finished at least 24 hours sooner, left at noon. The plumber, who never called to tell me he would be late, conveniently drove into the driveway nearly three hours late, just as the handymen were backing out.

And I was thanking Spirit for once again validating the power of these teachings and for showing me the importance of relaxing *with* the flow of life. My friend Karen has a similar saying, "Flow with the go."

Control is definitely one of the traits many souls handpick for healing during their time on the Earth plane. So try not to judge it. Recognizing and shifting these traits transforms them into gifts to help you move along your path and accomplish your divine purpose. Do you agree? Are you beginning to be okay with control issues, depression, anger, jealousy or other traits you chose to work on this lifetime? If you haven't already done so, try accepting them when they show up; then do your part and feel them dissolve.

Learning to let go of the need to control creates more peace. Ironically, surrendering does allow you control, but it is control empowered by trust, not fear.

Many people, especially Westerners, find letting go to be quite difficult at first. Our culture is one that values striving, doing and accomplishing at all costs. Spiritual principle requires the opposite—relaxing, surrendering and letting Spirit determine *how* to orchestrate the best outcome. Your journey is finding a balance that feels right to you.

Befriend Your Feelings

Happiness feels good. Appreciation and love feel good, too. And the good thing about "good feeling vibrations" is that they energetically align us to the things or experiences we desire. Thoughts that don't feel good can be replaced with thoughts that do feel good. It's that simple and it gets easier with practice.

Your negative feelings are like the rumble strips alongside the highway. They provide feedback that you have veered off course. You feel the roughness of the rumble strip, and you know to quickly re-align yourself back into your lane. If you didn't heed this warning, you would be struggling with an unnecessarily rough ride, perhaps even a serious mishap. Just as responding to the rumble strips makes for a more enjoyable ride, responding to your negative feelings makes for a more enjoyable life.

Negative feelings are natural expressions and there are healthy ways to honor them without burying or ignoring them, or unleashing them on others. However, feeling sadness, frustration, anger, resentment, or any other troublesome feelings and staying there for days is like hitting the rumble strip and staying there for miles. Think about it, you just wouldn't do that. You would make a few adjustments to get back in your lane.

Why not do more "joy-riding" down the roads of your life by traveling in alignment with your good feelings. The effort you expend in shifting to more positive thoughts, to good feeling vibrations, is directly proportional to how peaceful your life will be.

Today's To-Do List to Feel Good
1. Make a decision to feel good.
2. Find ways to feel good.

Law of attraction teachings remind you to pay attention to the way you feel, and deliberately choose thoughts—about your concerns or totally different subjects—that feel good to you when you think them. When you are focused on feeling good, what others are doing or saying affects you less. If you are affected by their deeds or words, it is immediate feedback telling you that you have given them the power to determine how you feel.

People suffer because of the thoughts they choose to believe about what they are experiencing, not because of the experience itself. And conversely, all of your happiness and prosperity, all of your power, also rests in your thoughts. Wow! That makes you one powerful being! Are you ready to call back your power?

3. Get into energetic alignment.

Before you attempt to make any actual changes, I recommend you get into energetic alignment first; it makes the action part of the journey much easier. Positive affirmations and intentions allow energy to flow in a forward direction, making it easier to make and maintain desired changes.

Affirm daily that you are living a productive, happy and harmonious life—even before it is a reality. You do it beforehand because the universe and your body—being pure energy—don't know if your thoughts—also pure energy—are real or imagined. Affirmations are thoughts and thoughts are energy and they influence the energy fields in and around you. They help you dissolve negative cellular memory and limited beliefs while helping you attract an easier and healthier life.

For example, if you want a pay raise, energetically align yourself to that raise before approaching your boss. Leverage the law of attraction and your spiritual team for your highest good. Affirm a few times a day, with X being the new salary: "Thanks, Spirit, that I am appreciated and valued at work. I am making X dollars per week or more for the highest good of all." "Thank you for revealing the perfect timing for me to approach my boss. Thank you that I confidently said what I needed to say to get my point across."

Then, visualize your meeting flowing easily and your boss paying you an amount higher than you expected! Feel the excitement now that you will feel when that happens; it raises your vibrational field. Let the good, good, good vibrations course through your cells now, doing the happy dance!

Spirit "has your back" and is setting up the best parameters for your needs. Since Spirit sees the big picture which includes your boss's attitudes and daily stressors, trust your intuition and be flexible as to when to approach your boss. Make sure the timing *feels* right. If you need to set up an appointment to discuss this, affirm: "Thanks, Spirit, for choosing the divine time for my pay raise request."

Also, check your feelings to see if you really believe this can happen for you. All the right affirmations won't cut through a dense vibration of doubt and unworthiness. Yet, done with confidence, your affirmations will magnify the likelihood of you getting that raise.

If it doesn't happen, evaluate the reasons your boss gave you. You will sense how much you are appreciated or if it is solely about finances. Continually affirm that you are at the right and perfect job for your highest good. Even with a refusal you will at least know you put your best self forward and worked with the law of attraction.

4. Set some goals.

Belief adds momentum to these principles and your goals. Unless you are seasoned at manifesting, I suggest you set goals that are a stretch for you and that are also realistic in your belief system. Continually reevaluate and update your goals while you enjoy watching your new life unfold. Thank Spirit for the discipline necessary to achieve your goals. Will you have challenges and setbacks? Yes. But there is good in all things and the good thing about challenges and setbacks is the clarity they give you regarding changes you want to make.

The positive vibrations you felt in your affirmations are never wasted. They add to your overall vibration, creating an alignment with what you are to receive next.

Perhaps you want to improve your health, have more energy or lose weight. Again I suggest that before taking any action—even with the best of intentions—you get in energetic alignment first. Change can happen with ease and you'll more likely maintain your healthier habits when you co-create *with* the energetic universe. Yes, mash that Easy Button.

For 5-10 minutes, twice a day, say affirmations; consider the following or create some of your own. "Thanks, God, that I love myself unconditionally on my way to my perfect size and health." "I wake up each morning physically, mentally, and emotionally healthy and rejuvenated." "Thank you, body, for helping me make healthy food choices and for absorbing, assimilating and excreting for my optimal health." Visualize yourself exercising, preparing salads and meals and fitting into clothes that you have not worn in over a year.

Many people notice that they have more energy and desire to exercise. They'll find their taste buds changing and they'll "just happen" to choose healthier, nutritionally dense foods and treats. Improved discipline improves their blood test results and they just feel better because of the changes—

the ones easier to make than expected. And more importantly, these changes help facilitate the idea of making lifelong healthy choices instead of gravitating to a quick-fix solution.

Energetically, you can't attract what you want by continuing to focus on pain and suffering or by thinking of yourself as a victim. Remember, your negative emotions, thoughts and attitudes block the flow of receiving the very things you desire. Positive thoughts and feelings align you to attract what you want. Let me be clear. You don't have total control over what happens to you, but you do have total control over how much you *choose* to suffer regarding your experiences. As you embrace the power of your thoughts and know you are worthy of feeling better, you will more often catch yourself and choose more positive thoughts.

My client, John, hated his underpaid job. I helped him realize that his negative attitude was blocking the very thing he wanted—a better paying and more fulfilling job. He then understood from an energy perspective, it was his attitude, created by his thoughts, which attracted or blocked his desires. He felt more empowered to work on changing his attitude.

John chose to change his thoughts to ones that felt better until he secured a more appropriate job. John began to think of his job as temporary. He looked for ways to appreciate the people he worked with, and he valued his job as a means of income. Energetically, the changes he made in his thinking allowed him to shift his attitude and he felt so much better, even without a job change. He trusted his ideal job would show up in divine timing.

Another client accepted a part-time job that he didn't like. He took it as a bridge to going back to college. Once he understood the power of his attitude, he made some changes in how he perceived the job. As a result, he increased the amount of hours he worked, enjoyed his co-workers more, was asked to do more fulfilling tasks and got more compliments for work well done. He started enjoying his job, all because he shifted his attitude.

5. Incorporate affirmations and positive intentions into your daily routine.

Make this easy. When you rinse off the dishes, shower or with each weed you pull from your garden, affirm: "I AM releasing negative thoughts and fears." Also, make good use of your bathroom time. As you brush your teeth or release your physical wastes, intend that you are also releasing your limiting beliefs and emotional hurts.

A good practice is to look for areas in your life where a simple shift in perspective can have a significant impact. Notice the thoughts you think when you are doing activities and chores that you'd rather avoid, yet need to do.

Decide to clean the house with an attitude of gratitude instead of being frustrated that you have to spend your time cleaning. Think about those who are homeless, who have gone through foreclosure or whose home may have recently burned down. Your housecleaning chores will no longer seem like a burden.

Also, with a task such as grocery shopping, since you're going to do it anyway, a good attitude strengthens your vibration.

If you find yourself complaining, taking others' actions personally, or being angry, ask yourself, "Does this thought help me feel good or not?" "This thought makes me miserable; do I want to continue down this path of suffering?" Then, as John did, without changing the problem or the person, find better thoughts around the situation. Choose to find some soothing attitude about the activities you previously approached with frustration. Remember, today your job is to choose better thoughts to help you feel good.

6. Share your positive energy.

For even more "feel good vibrations," do simple tasks for others, even if they are not aware of them. Keep this easy;

fit the tasks into your daily routine just as you did with the affirmations. Send blessings of safety, patience and love to those sharing the roads with you. Compliment a peer or family member, thank a cashier for being there, or hold a door open for a stranger. Pay the toll for the person behind you. Be creative and have fun.

As you decide to make harmony more of a priority, you will create a healthier, happier, and easier life for yourself. And because you're happier, the changes you make will positively impact your loved ones and others in your life. You will not only reap the benefits but you will become a role model, showing others how to get through challenges and take charge of their lives.

Energetically it is a much smoother ride to get to where you want to go by first accepting where you are. Accepting where you are releases the resistance—the blocked energy. Thus, accepting "what is" emotionally frees you.

Your acceptance doesn't mean you want to stay there, yet, without the resistant thoughts and actions you are energetically allowing the flow of what you really want to come forth. Like attracts like. When you feel good, good things will flow to you more easily. Go for it and feel those *good, good vibrations.*

Chapter 13
LAFTER as Medicine

People say, "Laughter is the best medicine." Well here is "laughter" again, spelled differently, but still able to help with life's problems. I created the acronym LAFTER to help you memorize the following statements which are powerful keys to releasing resistance, staying centered, and attracting the life you deserve. LAFTER is available for download at www.CallingBackYourPower.com.

L   Let go of fear and limitations.

A   Accept the situation as temporary.

F   Focus on the desired end result.

T   Trust all is in divine order.

E   Expect your desired outcome.

R   Remain in gratitude.

Letting go of fear and limitations. Fear, worry and frustrations block you from receiving guidance and the blessings you desire. Affirmations help you let go of fear and limitations and allow you to stay in your power.

Affirmations shift your cellular memory and dissolve fear and limitations. They also help you stay centered times of chaos. By using a favorite affirmation with all of your smaller frustrations, you allow the affirmation to become etched in your memory. Thus, it becomes an automatic reaction to unexpected challenges. The use of an affirmation made the difference between life and death for me.

When I broke my neck and stopped breathing, I commanded in my mind, "I refuse to accept this limitation. God is my Source!" I used the same mantra I always used for any frustration. It had always empowered me to focus on what I wanted, instead of on my problem or worry. Here, it literally saved my life.

The law of attraction encourages us to use the most positive words and phrases possible in the affirmations we speak and think. For instance, if you don't want to fall on the ice while walking to your car, it is best to focus on what you do want—to get to the car safely. Unfortunately, most of us habitually focus on what we don't want. "I hope I don't fall" is a common thought, and the Universe aligns with the energy of your main focus. In this case it's the word "fall." The Universe does not energetically recognize words like "not" and "don't." Thus, you are inadvertently emphasizing what you do not want—to fall.

Despite the word "limitation" in my affirmation, "I refuse to accept this limitation. God is my Source," it worked miraculously. The pure intent behind my words was strong enough to override the word "limitation." Learn to write affirmations with the strongest positive energy and use the purest intent behind your words—both are significant in creating a great outcome. To maximize the law of attraction and my intent, I now prefer, "I am one with the infinite power of God." Or, "I am love." All the words are positive.

Accept "what is" as temporary. This statement reminds you to make the best of whatever you are experiencing. Think about it. Hating or being angry at what is causes you discomfort. Finding a better feeling thought regarding what is frees you from emotional bondage. Accept your not-so-good situation as a temporary experience, a stepping stone to where you want to be.

Focus on the desired end result. The law of attraction states that whatever you focus on expands. Your manifesting abilities increase when you focus on what you want, instead of on the challenge at hand.

In the hospital's emergency room, while fully paralyzed, I said to my friends and family, "This is temporary, see me dancing." I accepted my condition as temporary and focused on the desired end result. Refusing to give the seriousness of my injury any power, I trusted the healing capacity of my mind, body, and spirit, and focused on dancing again.

The doctors were perplexed with my remarkable results. Just as I had intended, one month after my injury, I danced at an annual Christmas dance. There was still much room for healing yet I celebrated my progress that evening.

Trust all is in divine order. Trusting that everything has a divine purpose allows you to *grow* through your challenge, not just *go* through it.

You are a part of a very profound universe, too profound for any of us to really understand. As you gain wisdom and adjust your beliefs, you expand your awareness and intuitively align with new thought patterns that assist you on your soul's evolution.

As I had on all previous bike rides, on the day of my incident I surrounded myself and my biking buddies with the "Christ white light," an intention of extra protection, and I visualized myself on the other side of that teeter-totter.

I still fell and snapped my neck in two. Some would question where the spiritual support was that day. I don't. My faith and daily devotion to my spiritual journey assure me Spirit always has my back. I trust everything is in divine order and that day was no exception. It was a necessary part of my destiny path. Because of my beliefs, I was able to stay calm. Without fear and resistance, I allowed in Universal energy—the bolt of energy—and regained my breath.

Expect your desired outcome. A state of expectation adds momentum to your intentions. Keep expecting the result you want, especially when you have no idea how or if it can happen. Eighteen months after my injury, it dawned on me that I never once considered the question, "What if I'm permanently paralyzed?" I always expected a complete recovery. I knew I am an energetic being and energy is neither created nor destroyed; it just changes form. It is what I expect it to be.

Remain in gratitude. Love, peace, and gratitude are the highest vibrations you can choose to feel. You can choose from one moment to the next to feel your power or to give it away. When you are exhausted from challenges coming at you, coming up with loving feelings is also challenging. Yet, to feel your power, no matter what you are going through, find something to be thankful for. Grab any idea and repeat it. "I am grateful for my refrigerator. I am grateful for my refrigerator." It may seem silly, yet it keeps you from spiraling downward. Your feelings of exhaustion will be replaced with increasing good vibrations. You can't feel gratitude and stress at the same time.

I had plenty to be thankful for. People with my scope of injury don't survive or, if they do, they seldom walk again. Each day I appreciated my increasing mobility. Being true to the law of attraction, I appreciated each step of my recovery as if I had already recovered. The Universe does not know what is real or what is imagined. It responds to the vibrations created by our thoughts and feelings. As I gratefully visualized myself biking and dancing, those visions became my reality.

LAFTER is the best medicine for what ails you. I am alive and healthy today because of these teachings. Questioning or not believing in any one of the LAFTER statements would have diminished my dramatic results.

Thankfully, I had honed my trust and belief in these principles before I needed to create my extraordinary healing.

Go forth, have more fun, and create with LAFTER every day.

Chapter 14
The Alchemy of Change

The stuff of our lives doesn't change. It is we who change in relation to it.
– Molly Vass

You are always unfolding to your greatness, forever a student practicing your skills in this experience called life. Moment by moment you have the choice to live life on purpose, to look within and consciously evolve. I invite you to remind yourself as often as needed that you are worth the investment of time, discipline, and courage it takes to live life on purpose. You are the key to your "yet-to-be!"

Life's ups and downs offer you opportunities to choose your perspective and raise your spiritual awareness. A heightened state of awareness has many benefits: attracting positive people and experiences, feeling happier for no specific reason, easily shifting from negativity, allowing in the energies for exceptional healing, trusting every event has a higher purpose, living in harmony and appreciating the simplicities of life.

Expect to simplify your life and evolve your spirit as you purposely release limitations, focus on what you want and think more positive thoughts. Also meditation and prayer heightens your evolution. The practice of going within, connecting to a Higher Power and staying in gratitude leads you to the easy, happy and healthy life you deserve.

Call back your power to create the life you deserve. Play your earthly role to the best of your abilities—having fun, taking time to enjoy the goodness that shows up, and, also, seeing the lessons in and growing from every setback. As you expand your consciousness and trust that everything happens for a higher purpose—divinely orchestrated just for you—you move more easily through the challenges.

Early on I accepted that everything happens for a reason but, as you will see in this next story, I needed my own, first-hand experience to really own it at my core, not just think I knew it in my mind.

Two years before I broke my neck I had my first "flying-over-the-handlebars" fall on my mountain bike. I was at Lake Crabtree County Park— where we did most of our single track mountain biking and the same place I later broke my neck. Approaching a T in the path, I had slowed to a crawl to make a right hand turn. My front tire got stuck behind a thick exposed root. My bike stopped. But I kept going—right over my handlebars.

It was a strange experience. I was flying but in slow motion. And, even a friend who had stopped to wait for us to catch up saw my fall and confirmed what I had felt. He said, "That was weird, you were falling in slow motion!" My next thought was, "Where were you, Spirit?" I had energetically set up protective energy around myself and my riding buddies and I must admit I was at a point in my spiritual journey where I expected this protection to prevent any accident. Oh, the learning curve of the spiritually naïve.

Before each ride, I surround myself and my buddies with the Christ white light, an intention of safety and protection. As I take my bike out of my SUV, I visualize myself, at the end of my ride, putting my bike and myself back into my vehicle, totally intact. I intentionally add the feeling of gratitude for another chance to have fun in nature. The more I practiced intentions, the easier it is to remember to use them. It had become natural and took only a few seconds to include Spirit in every part of my life.

I dusted myself off and before I got back on my bike I had an "aha" moment. I laughed at myself for questioning where Spirit was. Spirit *was* with me. It was Spirit that brought me, in slow motion, safely to the ground. I had flown over my handlebars and when I finally landed on the hard packed dirt of the trail, I not only had no cuts or bruises, there was not one scratch on my bare arms and legs.

Falling so gently deepened my faith that Spirit is always with me, even when, at first glance, it doesn't appear so. One truth I've recognized is that we are guided for our highest good, whether our limited human thinking agrees or not.

If that first fall had resulted in my spinal cord injury, I wouldn't have accepted "what is" so quickly and my untrusting mind would have blocked the initial energy surges I received two years later in 2005. Those two years allowed me the time to deepen my belief that all events are in divine order and deepen my oneness with Spirit. Belief opens the door for healing and other divine energies to enter.

Layer by Layer You Clear—Getting to Your Next Best Level

No one wants to experience frustration or emotional pain. Yet, as you accept that everything you attract has a higher purpose and understand the spiritual value of healing the pain, then you more easily move through the experience responsible for the emotional pain. You more easily go to your next best level of spiritual awareness.

It's important to know that you heal emotional pain layer by layer, clearing—healing—one or a few layers at a time. The good news is you address and heal only what you can emotionally handle at the time. Then, in time, your soul guides you to your next level of expansion where hurtful experiences, a relationship or even a movie or song trigger deeper layers of feelings around the same emotional wound. This causes the emotion to resurface again, giving you another opportunity to address the hurt and heal further.

Clients are often surprised when they find themselves still needing to clear emotional pain from childhood or a divorce, issues they thought were resolved. Actually, they resolved what they could at previous times. As people get stronger emotionally and ready to go to their next spiritual level, they are then guided to experiences to clear deeper layers of pain. It is a process.

There is a benefit to the process. Every time you clear a few more layers, your energy field becomes a higher vibration, a stronger "magnet" to attract blessings—the ones you want and those unexpected gifts that just happen to show up for your highest good. Sweet!

Dealing with Hurt

If someone hurts you, you may take their attacks personally—consciously or unconsciously taking on the misguided and hurtful words they spew on you. This creates false beliefs that your cellular memory records as true and you may wind up feeling "less than," allowing their words, actions or opinions to take your power. These false beliefs block the flow of energy.

Another common response—to avoid being yelled at, punished or mocked, or simply because you didn't know how to deal with your feelings—is to stuff your emotions. This response also blocks the flow of energy. And emotional blocks limit the amount of goodness you allow in.

Or you allow the feelings to simmer just below the surface and later emotionally erupt at the people with whom you feel the safest. Spouses may come home and lose their temper after they've kept their anger bottled up at work.

Children can be very mean, taking their frustration out on one or both parents. Children feel most safe to act their worst with those who love them unconditionally.

One thing to keep in mind is that when people ignore you, say mean things to you, or try to make you feel small or guilty, it is an indication of their own emotional hurts. Their pain keeps them from even considering that they need to deal with their feelings in a more constructive and healthier manner. This book is in your hands. So I trust you may be willing to look from a healthier perspective at the harsh approach of others.

When people hurt you, consider asking yourself, "What do I need to learn here? Why do I attract this kind of person or situation?"

To change who you attract, begin with awareness; let your awareness inspire you to take responsibility to feel your best. You can feel better by choosing to look with compassionate eyes, becoming more aware of the patterns and wounds on both sides. Give yourself permission to release your hurts and no longer feel responsible for theirs. By making these adjustments in your perspective, you can let go of the emotional charge other people's behavior triggers in you.

Shifting your focus from what others are doing *to* you to what *you* can do *for* you will depersonalize their actions— you begin to call back your power. You are choosing to make feeling good more important than the actions or words of others.

Remember, you are the only person you can change. By focusing on changing your perspective in any given situation—changing your thoughts, intentions and actions to more positive ones—you feel better and you may find yourself pleased with the results, as were my clients in the following stories.

The "Journey" Rewarded my Clients with Inner Peace

By taking responsibility for their own thoughts and expectations and focusing on what they wanted instead of what they were going through, my clients, Cathy and MaryAnne, experienced significant improvement in their relationships with those close to them.

Cathy, during her first appointment, shared that she was seriously concerned whether her marriage of 18 years would survive. Her patience with her husband was wearing thin. He was emotionally unavailable, disappointed and bored with his job, and drinking much too often. Even though she loved him, she was reaching her breaking point.

I shared with Cathy that marriage gives us huge opportunities for soul growth. And, if her marriage was meant to be according to both her and her husband's soul journey perspective, then she could trust it would shift to being healthy again. And, in the event her husband couldn't get on board to grow with her, through her efforts to feel better she would gain more clarity and soul growth, and freedom from an unhealthy marriage. She knew she was worthy of more and was hoping for a positive shift within the marriage.

MaryAnne felt disrespected by her co-workers. As hard as she tried, nothing seemed to make a difference; management usually took its wrath out on her anyway. As we were reviewing her past, she admitted that being disrespected was a pattern throughout her life.

Repeated patterns are soul lessons showing up to give you another opportunity to learn. If you ignore your role regarding the patterns, you will continue to create similar ones, over and over, until you finally decide to learn the lessons they offer.

As Cathy and MaryAnne came to see their patterns from a spiritual perspective, they agreed to consider that all was in divine order and for their personal growth. Personal growth is not always easy. Yet, the sooner you see its value, the sooner you can dig in and work through the challenging patterns and avoid attracting similar situations.

They wanted to attract better situations so they agreed to focus on what they wanted, not on what they were experiencing. And they both worked with forgiveness.

Cathy visualized herself and her husband doing household projects together, laughing, and enjoying family outings, and she saw him coming home from a new job he really liked.

When her husband was drinking, Cathy practiced thinking of his good qualities instead of spiraling into frustration and anger. She realized her frustration and anger carried energetic vibrations that coursed through her, depleting her energy and health, and negatively impacting her environment and even the universe at large. She focused on what she wanted, a healthy marriage. She affirmed that she and her family were worthy of respect and a loving relationship.

Cathy did a great job in getting out of her own way. She continued to release emotional resistance as she learned to trust that whatever happened would ultimately be for everyone's highest good.

Due to her anger, MaryAnne at first resisted the exercises I suggested, especially the suggestion that she send loving thoughts to her boss. But since she wanted results, she was willing to trust my guidance.

I helped her understand that others' actions are a result of their fears and undealt-with emotions and that she expands spiritually as she showers them with love. Diadra Price, in her book, *Grace Awakening Essence*, has a quote that speaks to this. (For your convenience, her website is listed at www.CallingBackYourPower/URL) This quote, in fact, her whole book, has helped me own these teachings to a deeper level. She says, "A consciousness of Grace seeks not revenge or punishment for a deed expressed from fear, but rather to express the love the mind of fear could not see."

MaryAnne visualized herself being happy at work and her boss praising her high quality of work. After learning that her intentions create fields of energy, she used her mind to bathe their offices in green healing energy and wrapped several co-workers and her boss in the pink energy of love.

She realized she had some false beliefs from her childhood—that she wasn't worthy of respect—and, because affirmations reprogram cellular memory, she affirmed several times a day that she was worthy of respect and feeling good.

Affirmation by affirmation, you chip away at false beliefs and replace them with the truth of your being—you *are* worthy, respectable, lovable, and joyful. The universe responds to your thoughts and feelings. Practicing these techniques and focusing on what you desire shifts the vibrations of relationships; true to the nature of this energetic universe, favorable results will appear.

So both women had to pay close attention to their thoughts and change ones like "That's how it's *always* been," or "They won't ever change." As you unwind your own thinking, you may find yourself engaging in a lot of self-talk, such as "That thought is focusing on what I don't want and it doesn't feel good. What thought will help me feel better?" Self-talk is good. Shifting your old tapes—the programming you accepted as true—is a process of catching yourself saying or thinking anything that contradicts the lifestyle you prefer.

During the first month of life coaching and healing sessions, dramatic changes happened in Cathy's home. Her husband stopped drinking heavily, got a better job, and they were enjoying being with each other again. Did she insist her husband change? No, she accepted the situation as temporary and in divine order. She trusted there was a higher purpose for the marital discord and accepted it as an opportunity for personal and soul growth. She embraced energetic laws and focused on shifting her own vibration. She not only got back a happier husband, but along the way she grew her soul by calling back her power, gaining self respect, setting healthy boundaries, and feeling better no matter what her husband was doing.

If she had done all this for herself and he had not changed, it would still have been in divine order. If one partner grows and the other does not or if they have learned all they can from the relationship, it generally dissolves.

You've been taught since birth that marriage is forever, though, the spiritual purpose of marriage is to love, honor and enjoy each other, and to be each other's "teacher." Thus, the length of marriage differs. A marriage can last a lifetime when there is love, freedom, respect for differences and growth.

Once MaryAnne committed whole-heartedly, she had great news to share at her two-week appointment; her boss was actually smiling and being very nice to her, a dramatic change from his usual behavior. As she continued to use the energetic techniques she learned, she consistently had positive results. Each success made it easier to reprogram "I am worthy of respect" into her energy field and cell tissues. She consistently called back her power. She cleared many layers of emotional pain regarding her lack of self respect.

More layers will reveal themselves as she is ready to clear more. Ugh—that means more relationships where others disrespect her. Yet, when that happens, she will have the right tools in her tool box to handle them with grace. Every day she gets to choose whether to let others talk down to her, snap at her or blame her or to embrace her power.

In the following testimonial, MaryAnne summarizes beautifully how you can influence the behavior of others when you understand your interconnectedness.

"'I don't know what's going on! Everything went so well.' said my manager after the first meeting.

'This has been a magical week,' my manger said after the second meeting. 'I was prepared for a fight both times, but everybody has been really cooperative and congenial.'

"What my manager didn't know was that Suzette was clearing the conference room's negative energy, and we both were sending Light to the participants while setting intentions for everyone to be a respectful team player. But my manager was right. It has been a magical week.

"I got to the second meeting 30 minutes early; my steps seemed guided in that direction. My previous manager also arrived 30 minutes early; he'd misread his calendar. Alone in a giant room, the two of us had the best conversation I think we've ever had. You wouldn't have known we'd never gotten along.

"For several months now, to clear any discordant energy, Suzette has included my company's campus in her twice monthly, group teleconference healing sessions. I can see attitudes improving. I can see individuals accepting more responsibility for their actions. I can see more cooperativeness and less competitiveness. It definitely isn't politics as usual.

"Coincidence? Synchronicity? Call it what you want. My manager called it magic. I call it a blessing. Suzette calls it Calling Back Your Power."

By shifting to a positive perspective, you energetically open yourself to the ever-present flow of the goodness you desire. Your desire may be for others to treat you nicer, for your problem to be worked out with ease, for an unexpected flow of cash or other blessings. Or maybe you want to be bathed in the good feelings that will result when you let go of a perceived problem, a situation depicted so well by my next client's story.

Jan called me needing emotional support. She was very distraught; feeling the pressure of her world crashing down around her. I knew she practiced these principles and still, some days, as she said, she just seemed to lose it and wind up feeling disconnected to Source.

Remember the importance of being gentle with yourself by allowing yourself the journey of evolving. As you learn to lighten up, you can shift from "losing it" to feeling better quicker. You may find yourself only giving an issue your attention for a day and then the next time a few hours, then minutes, until you are so tapped into your mind power that the issue no longer pushes your buttons.

On this particular day, Jan just needed my help to call back her personal power. She understood that fear was causing her reaction and she could see the negative power she was contributing. I reminded her of the power of her thoughts and to start focusing on and visualizing how she wanted the problems to be resolved. I suggested she affirm, "Thanks, Spirit, for revealing the best outcome for all involved." I had her tap into the power of gratitude. She spoke of things for which she was grateful. I had her cough—a powerful technique when used along with a sincere intention to energetically clear blocks. In her case, she coughed out anger and fear. I could sense calmness come over her.

After 20 minutes, she had released the fear and felt like her happy self again. She was ready to stay in her power and continue focusing on what she wanted. Bear in mind, her problems had not changed. Nothing had changed on the outside, but by calling back her mind power, she changed the way she viewed her problems and let go of the grip they had on her.

Without demanding others or the situation to change, my clients had to do their "inside" work before they could see any results on the outside. It is not what happens to you that matters. It is, rather, the attitude and perspective you adopt. What you choose from life's buffet of choices will determine how smooth, successful, and fun your life will be.

As you work at improving your life, think of yourself as an archaeologist who has to get through a lot of rubble, rock, and tedious work to find the treasure. The treasure is being happier and healthier, and reaching your goals while maintaining a harmonious life. Are you ready for your treasure?

Chapter 15
It's All Good

Learn to get in touch with the silence within yourself, and know that everything in life has purpose. There are no mistakes, no coincidences, all events are blessings given to us to learn from.
– Eilsabeth Kubler-Ross

Getting to the point where you can trust that all experiences have a higher purpose takes time and practice. Once you can trust that for some reason it's all good, you'll more easily accept the opportunity to grow—the lesson—in each challenge. Acceptance of "what is" releases resistance and allows in the blessings.

As I was learning to trust, I would tell myself to "put my big-girl panties on." This reminded me that I am not privy to all the details from my earthly perspective. Embracing this helped me release the need to control outcomes. You may be thinking. "Ouch, not care about the outcome, that doesn't sound right." Yet, the operative words here are *"the need to control"* outcomes.

You can learn to accept that it's all good even when the outcome appears so wrong in your eyes. You may not like the situation. You may not have chosen it. But this journey helps you learn to trust in the big picture. Remember, Spirit sees the big picture and is responding to your vibration and your desire "for the highest good for all."

Often you can look back and understand why things had to happen the way they did. Embracing that your situation has a higher purpose helps you trust it's all good even when you don't understand it, even in hindsight.

Trusting that you are part of a master plan and Spirit sees the big picture helps you move beyond worrisome thoughts such as, "How will I get through this?" Or, "What will happen now?" When you worry, you block energy flow and you suffer more often. Call back your power and practice shifting your worry and dissolving fear by affirming, "Thank you, Spirit for revealing the best outcome for the highest good of all." Then, let go of the need to control the situation and trust.

Consider this scenario. You are confused and sad when you don't get the offer for the dream job you *know* you deserved. Then weeks later, an even better opportunity shows up; you accept the offer, move to a new, great town and meet your life partner. Looking back, you realize that not getting that first job was a life-altering blessing, though, without seeing the big picture, it felt like defeat.

You raise your vibration when you trust from the onset that in every disappointment there is a blessing or lesson. Yes, this takes practice. And *you* are worth the effort. Just remind yourself that acceptance of what you may not understand releases fear and aligns you with your ultimate desire.

Let's ponder this for a moment. Abraham, a group of non-physical ascended masters that shares wisdom through Esther Hicks, says "Fear only exists when you do not understand that you have the power to project thought and that the Universe will respond." Or, said another way, fear is the result of believing your worrisome thoughts. Energetically, fear and suffering are of the mind, not of any given situation or perceived threat. Fear is not present when you examine your fearful thoughts and change them to ones of acceptance and empowerment.

Byron Katie, in her book, *A Thousand Names for Joy* comments when asked, "Isn't fear biological? Isn't it necessary for the fight-or-flight response?" She answers, "Does your body have a fight-or-flight response when you see a rope lying on the path ahead of you? Absolutely not—that would be crazy. Only if you imagine that the rope is a snake does your heart start pounding. It's your *thoughts* that scare you into fight-or-flight—not reality."

It is your thoughts around the problem that either escalate it or deflate it. It's really that simple. But believing and practicing that is part of our journey.

Experiences—Soul Journey Necessities

Experiences aren't always fun, but they are usually part of a soul contract and stepping stones to future blessings and spiritual evolution. My neck injury was a necessary step along my soul path; I actually needed to break the bones in my neck.

The neck, located in the throat chakra, is the chakra that affects our ability to speak our truth. In reviewing past lives, I had learned of many lifetimes where I was either killed or tortured for speaking my spiritual truth. Thus, my cellular memory recorded that it was not safe to do so. My destiny this lifetime is to help expand consciousness, so it was imperative to clear any cellular memory of, "It isn't safe to speak my spiritual truth." The breaking of my bones was a necessary physical occurrence to help me energetically clear the cellular memory quickly.

My recovery from my broken neck also allows me to be, as part of my soul contract, a bridge between Western medicine and energy medicine. Great, I get to check that off my soul's to-do list. Remember, Spirit sees the big picture and coordinates the necessary experiences. The following experience demonstrates how, injured again, I "stepped on those stones" and trusted that the experience was for my highest good.

A year and a half after breaking my neck, I fell while rollerblading. It was a serious fall on my butt in my cul-de-sac—a cul-de-sac that was at the end of my driveway—a driveway that goes down a very steep hill. Oops. Did I sign up for another fall?

Well, you know by now that my answer is yes. I just didn't know why. Many people don't want to hear that there was a reason for the fall. Instead they think I was crazy to be rollerblading in the first place, let alone down my steep driveway. At a check-up one year after my surgery, Dr. Isaacs told me I could do any activities I had been doing previously. He forgot to ask me what those activities were.

Seriously though, I am responsible for the activities I choose and for listening to my intuitive guidance regarding those activities. Because I am attuned to my oneness with Spirit, I also trust that I am guided when and when not to partake in activities *for my highest good*. (It doesn't feel right to be on the back of a motorcycle, so I listen to that feeling.)

If my rollerblading fall wasn't for some higher purpose, I believe I would have sensed the impending danger or "just happened" to not want to roller-blade that day. Intuition nudges us or not for a reason.

That sunny day I had enjoyed a six-hour drive home from Hilton Head, South Carolina with my convertible top down. I was on cloud nine, singing along with the songs on the radio, feeling grateful and saying affirmations. I was eager to get home and put on my rollerblades. I rollerbladed three times a week and had confidently and routinely rollerbladed down my steep driveway for six years.

This day, the result was different. In the middle of my cul-de-sac, my legs just flew out from under me. I was on my butt and in extreme pain. Curious, I looked around when I got up. Nope, not a rock or twig in sight. My feet just came out from under me. "Very strange," I thought. It didn't make sense, but I trusted there had to be reasons unknown to me. You may be thinking, "Lady, give it up! You could have just fallen for no reason."

But I don't believe in things happening for no reason. David Hawkins, M.D., PhD., speaks to this in his book, *Power vs. Force.* He says, "In a universe where everything is connected with everything else, there's no such thing as an accident. And nothing is outside of the universe. Since the power of causes is unseen and only the manifestation of effects is observable, there's an illusion of 'accidental' events."

To me, my "accident" was Spirit's way of aligning me with significant events. And, Spirit even went a step further in providing support for me; my neighbor "just happened" to be getting his mail and helped me into the house. "Thanks, Spirit, that I wasn't alone when I peeled myself off the asphalt."

It was more clear as time passed that there really were several crazy-ass (did I say that?) good reasons for the fall. First, falling on my butt got me to move a scheduled appointment with Dr. Isaacs up by two weeks. I waited a week after my fall to even call his office.

I thought I had cracked my coccyx and decided bed rest was the only treatment. Actually, I had no choice but to rest; I was so stiff and sore, and my buttocks were extremely black and blue. I stayed in bed for four days and did a lot of energy work on myself. I figured I attracted that fall to take the time out for healing and energy integration. Dr. Isaacs later confirmed there was nothing more he would have recommended.

Second, Dr. Isaacs knew I would be using the story of my recovery with my work and had agreed the year before to help. During my appointment, remembering his agreement, he asked how he could help. I said I first needed him to write my validation letter. He happily agreed and also, because of his intense schedule, gave me permission to remind him weekly via email until he got it done.

To my surprise, he needed no reminding. He called me one week later to tell me he had finished the letter. Because of the quick turn-around, I trusted Spirit was orchestrating something, giving him the necessary nudge and a window of opportunity in his busy schedule to get it done.

Then, a week after that, reason number three, I "just happened" to get an email about Dr. Christiane Northrup, a leading holistic OB-GYN and speaker. After reading that email, I felt guided to reach out to her about mentoring me. As a pioneer in stepping outside the box of traditional medicine, her wisdom is significant. We also shared another connection. She lives in my home state of Maine which I was planning to visit soon.

I followed my hunch and faxed a letter mentioning my impending visit to Maine and asked if she would be willing to meet with me. I shared my healing story and that my passion and life calling, like hers, is to inspire people to look outside the box of Western medicine and embrace mind, body, and spirit healing.

Timing is everything. I now "just happened" to have the validation letter from Dr. Isaacs, valuable information for her, as a doctor, to understand the seriousness of the scope of my injury. To give our meeting more momentum energetically, I put a photo of Dr. Northrup on my vision board.

I did not hear back for three weeks. So I faxed the letter again with a smiley face and a handwritten note mentioning my arrival in Maine in *two* days and I'd love to meet with her.

If something is in divine order, Spirit—the greater aspect of you, your
I AM— will jump through hoops to create it for you. Seeming obstacles will be circumvented. Always do what feels right and then allow Spirit, infinite Intelligence, to figure out *how* to make it happen.

184

The next day, one day before leaving for Maine, I got a call from Dr, Northrup's assistant, Diane. She told me they had been out of the office for three weeks and in spite of receiving numerous faxes and pieces of mail, "somehow" my fax ended up on top. Diane said, "Dr. Northrup is really busy trying to catch up from being gone." (I'm thinking she is about to tell me she doesn't have time to meet with me.) After a pause, Diane continued, "However, you're coming up tomorrow, is there any chance you can meet her for dinner?" I was also invited to join her after dinner for an energy healing program. I adjusted my plans and did just that.

The universe continued to orchestrate events. Dr. Northrup emailed my information to Christy Mack, co-founder and president of integrative medicine's Bravewell Collaborative. Through the Christy and John Mack Foundation, she and her husband funded the building of Duke University's Integrative Medical Center. And, one month later, at a local event I "just happened" to run into Larry Burk, M.D., co-founder Duke's Integrative Medical Center. Before we were done talking, he, without knowing of Dr. Northrup's suggestion, also suggested I contact Christy Mack and later provided me with her email address.

It was obvious to me Spirit was orchestrating something. We don't have to understand how Spirit orchestrates these events; we can just be grateful they happen.

That summer I was extremely busy and asked for a spiritual nudge for when to connect with Christy Mack. Four months passed, then, in November of 2007, upon returning from my Hawaiian dolphin trip, I got my strong feeling to follow up with Christy Mack. And I emailed her immediately. She replied two days later and was so supportive. She said she had forwarded my information to a dear friend whom I would recognize when he contacted me.

A few days later I had an email from Dr. Mehmet Oz. He was interested in my story and invited me to be on his XM radio show. He had called Dr. Isaacs to discuss my recovery. Dr. Isaacs had followed their talk by emailing him a digital MRI of my C2 neck vertebra showing spinal cord edema, which results in quadriplegia.

Ten days prior to the radio interview, my segment was postponed. My ego snuck in a bit and I began to question what I had said during my phone call with the producer that might have caused him to change his mind. I stopped that mind chatter and analyzing and, instead, went to my knowing that no matter what I said, if this interview was for the highest good of all, it would happen at the right and perfect time. Spirit had brought me this far and I trusted that I would get another nudge when the time was right to follow up.

So, I believe, I "just happened" to fall while roller-blading so I would get my doctor's validation letter *before* I had the nudge to contact Dr. Northrup. The information and credibility of the letter also grabbed Dr. Oz's attention. The Universe finds the path of least resistance or the easiest means to an end.

It has been four years since I fell and I have yet to re-connect with Dr. Oz. If it is meant to be, it will be. The timing of my fall and the subsequent events did allow Dr. Oz to personally connect with Dr. Isaacs. Dr, Oz's current schedule, which now includes *The Dr. Oz Show*, probably would prohibit him from doing that. Regardless, I don't need to analyze it (though, as a Virgo sign, it's tempting). My destiny path is unfolding and whatever is for the highest good of all will reveal itself in divine timing. The universe is aligning it all as I write.

I "just happened" to have another significant fall a year after my roller-blade spill. I met my daughter Brittany at a water park. I planned to enjoy the day with her and share in her fun, not do the water slides or rides. Before we even started, I tripped on the uneven cement walkway and fell forward, landing on my left shoulder, then rolling over to my right side. I had cuts and bruises on my shoulder, arms and knees. It was a hard enough fall, that three years later, I still have a quarter-size scar on my shoulder.

Brittany saw my fall and was very perplexed; we both wondered why I hadn't put my hands out to break my fall. I even said, "Who wouldn't instinctively reach out with their hands?" It certainly didn't make sense to me. But, I attracted it for some reason.

I set an intention to know what I needed to know from these falls, then, I let it go. A few months later, I got the answer during a healing session in which I was the recipient. The healing facilitator received clear guidance that the falls were recalibrating my energy field. I didn't understand it. But the goose bumps shot through me and every fiber of my being knew it to be true. It's one of those times I trusted what I didn't understand.

We attract all the scenarios we need for our destiny path's highest good and many times there are multiple reasons. I must admit, I prefer not to know all of the details of what else my soul has signed up for.

All Experiences and Feelings are Valuable

Many people judge difficult or challenging situation as "bad." Judgment, thoughts we have when we aren't accepting what is, creates resistance. Shifting from labeling experiences bad to seeing them as opportunities for growth or for a higher purpose allows healthy energy to flow.

Also, when you stuff negative feelings, your energy can't flow or vibrate properly and energetically gets blocked. You become mentally, emotionally and physically taxed and your stress levels increase. Like attracts like so this state of mind attracts problems and contributes toward depression, anxiety, and illness.

It is healthy to experience all of your feelings, the negative and positive. To spiritually honor your feelings recognize negative feelings as indicators of what needs to be released and then find a healthy and appropriate way to release them. If you are sitting at your desk at work, it probably isn't a good idea to release your feelings aloud, so try to find another way that honors yourself and others.

Crying, journaling, exercising, and coughing–or even doing the dishes or yard work with intention to shift–allow you to handle your feelings in a healthy way.

Crying is a natural way to release emotions, so please give yourself ample time to cry. If it isn't the right time or place to do so, make time when you are alone to allow those feelings to resurface and release them. If you skip over the opportunities to cry you will attract similar hurts until you eventually face and clear them.

A hot bath with two cups of Epsom salts will help you quiet your mind, relax your body and further heal your emotional pain. The hot water and detoxifying affect of the Epsom salts moves the energy, and helps you to cry.

I encourage you to memorize this intention and say it as needed, "I release and transmute to Love the root cause of this hurtful feeling and any vibrations that match it anywhere in my energy field." This "anywhere in my energy field" includes past lives and makes the most of transmuting this hurt. As saying it becomes a habit, you can even think it during an emotionally charged crisis which will put you in a stronger position to handle what's happening. This intention helps you transmute the root cause and, thus, you are less likely to attract that particular challenge again.

I got a chance to use this affirmation during a painful experience. While participating in family counseling it became obvious that my inner being was ready to clear some really old hurts because, during one of our sessions, all the comments were directed towards me. I felt like I was being emotionally beat up by my two children and ex-husband.

On one hand, I couldn't believe the counselor was allowing this; it went on for forty-five minutes. On the other hand, I could feel all this hurt rising up and I recognized that their hurtful words were forcing me to feel old, buried pain.

During my twenty-minute drive home, I cried so hard my whole body was tingling. By the time I got home, I was emotionally exhausted. I crawled into bed, still crying. Then, I began to wail profusely; the intense pain was unbearable.

I recognized that it wasn't their comments that caused my wailing, because their words wouldn't have hurt so much unless I had a corresponding vibration of that pain already in my energy field. But the comments did trigger me, once again, to face and release buried pain from many lifetimes. I decided that if I had to go through this pain, I wanted it to be as effective as possible. So, even as I wailed, I made an intention to clear the root cause and any matching vibration from any lifetime.

My dog, Ben, who slept only on the floor next to my bed, sensed my anguish. Hoisting himself up onto the side of my bed, Ben literally nosed his way *under* my covers and crawled in next to me.

I hated the intense pain I was feeling. I had a fleeting thought, "Spirit, if it's going to be this painful, let me go [transition]." It was that intense. My inner being recognized I had reached my limit. The pain soon relaxed. I calmed down after twenty minutes of wailing. I felt the short-lived but intense crying had a higher purpose—clearing lifetimes of pain. I reflected upon the bigger picture and accepted that the Universe orchestrated this whole scenario. With that understanding, I had no one to blame for my pain, not even the counselor who let the session escalate. She and my girls and ex-husband were all playing their parts perfectly to get my painful feelings to the surface so I could accept and release them. And I was able to be thankful that at least all this clearing allowed me to raise my vibration. I drifted off to sleep.

There may be times like mine when your pain feels like it's too much to bear. Hang in there and let yourself experience the pain as fully as possible. Go to your limit and, if needed, intend for the intensity to lighten up or call a friend or professional for support. Remember, your pain does have a higher purpose. Appreciate it when your feelings give you feedback. You attracted the situation and the emotions in order to see what needs to be released. It's all good.

Shifting Your Emotions

Remember, to create a different outcome, adjust your thoughts and say affirmations. They allow you to energetically move the blocks and reprogram your cellular memory.

For example, to release anger, affirm, "I release this anger and any vibration that matches it in my energy field." Then, because gratitude is a powerful shifting tool affirm, "Thank you, Spirit that I am flowing with positive feelings and experiences."

Also, consider coughing. The intention behind the action is powerful, so intend that the cough clears blocks. My clients experience significant shifting when they cough out the root cause of their frustration or pain. They not only feel lighter on the physical level but their coughing shifts the blocked energy, raising their vibration.

Journaling is another way to honor your feelings, more freely express yourself and release blocked emotions. People find they feel better after journaling. For issues that have significant emotional charge, consider burning your writings in a safe manner. This can assist your healing by symbolizing release and closure for painful memories.

Another simple way to release your bottled-up feelings from either recent or childhood issues is to release them into a small rock. A good place to start is by saying: "I intend and command that any discordant energy from any lifetime be released with ease and gentleness. Thank you, Spirit, for transmuting these energies to love." And, because everything is consciousness say, "Thank you rock for helping me." Then to the rock say (fill in the blanks with your different experiences), "I am angry because ___. I am angry because ___. I am angry because ___." Also, "I hated it when ___. I hated it when ___. I hated it when ___." Repeat until you feel complete. Then, to symbolize the release of these hurts, throw the rock into the woods, an ocean or a lake.

Another way to call back your power and energetically shift the emotional pain and cellular memory is to speak your truth aloud to yourself. For example, if you were ignored, disrespected, or abused as a child, ask yourself, "How can I speak now to my little-child self to soothe the pain of unworthiness and anger I took on?"

Envision your adult self holding your little-child self on your lap and lovingly talking to him or her. Tell him or her what he or she needed to hear at that time, and what would still feel good to hear—that which you want to own at a deeper level.

You might say, "Mom and Dad did the best they could even though we deserved more. They were perfectionists because that gave them control in their chaotic world." Or, "They hadn't dealt with their own painful childhoods and couldn't give us what we emotionally needed—what every child deserves. They were soothing their own pain with anger and burying themselves in work or alcohol." Continue to tell your little-child self: "Let's choose to see that painful time from a healthier perspective. Let's forgive them for not being what we needed."

In your mind's eye, with your little-child-self still on your lap, look straight into his or her eyes and continue. Say, "No matter how you were treated, you *are* worthy of love and of being treated respectfully. You *are* worthy of being heard even though they didn't hear you. It is now safe to speak your truth. You *are* brilliant and worthy of being successful. You *are* smart and creative and beautiful. We are both safe now and we have tools to continue healing. I believe in you. I love you. God loves you and me. We are one with God. We are whole!" Now, sit in stillness and allow yourself to be bathed in that truth.

Repetition changes your cellular memory. To continue changing the old programming, say "I am worthy (or, I am loved, respected) 100 times per day for 21 days consecutively. If you miss a day, start counting from day one again until you get to 21 days. Notice what feelings come up--tears, an inner voice that says, "No I'm not," or a bad feeling in the pit of your stomach. If you start to resist the feelings that show up and decide it is silly, just thank your ego for sharing and do it anyway.

Try any of these techniques that resonate with you to clear hurts. Doing them is liberating. You should feel lighter with every clearing you do. When done with a trusted energy healing facilitator you magnify the clearing because of the facilitator's consciousness.

Before doing a clearing technique, preferably each morning, call upon Archangel Michael, Jesus or other ascended masters or deities to protect you for your destiny path's highest good. Invoking them brings their energy presence to you.

Life is a journey. Honor your unfolding as being exactly right for you. Another learning curve is to refrain from judging yourself or comparing yourself to others as to how quickly you may or may not shift your programming. Your life is different from that of any other person and your accumulative past life experiences also affect your ability to shift. It may take you longer to let go of wounds or old programming than it takes others. I say it again. You are unfolding along *your* perfect path. Continue doing the best you can. You will know a particular block is cleared when thinking about that issue no longer pushes your buttons or sends negative vibes through you.

Your life experiences give you a never-ending opportunity to accept what is and to practice improving your ability to shift toward peace and wholeness. With practice, you will deal with hurts and feelings *as* they arise.

Facing your challenges head on and releasing the fears attached to them allows you to energetically raise your vibration. When you raise your vibration, you feel better and your life tends to move along more smoothly.

When a bump does show up, freedom is accepting what is and then making the best of it. Freedom is controlling how you look at any situation, how you react and how you feel. Freedom is in your hands. Yes, you are so powerful!

Purging negative programming, hurts from others, self-sabotaging talk and letting go of emotions that were not serving me have all been a necessary part of my journey. It hasn't always been fun or easy, but it has led to emotional freedom. Whenever those "perfect" learning experiences show up in your life, minor or life-altering, choose to call back your power and create the best outcome you can.

Respond to each negative feeling as a call to clear old cellular memories. Negative thoughts and feelings show up to remind you that those feelings are in your energy field and that you are allowing your situation to temporarily disconnect you from the wonderful stream of higher consciousness, the ever-available life force wanting to flow more powerfully through you. Let me clarify here. The essence of your being is never disconnected from Source but your human mind awareness can act and feel as though it is.

You alone are in charge of your life. Focus on the things over which you have total control, your beliefs, reactions and perspective.

It's all good. So, get ready, get set, go! Tap into the greatness of who you really are.

Chapter 16
Creating Your Financial Comeback

If a person gets his attitude toward money straight, it will help straighten out
almost every other area of his life.
– Billy Graham

There is a lot of energy around money. Many people feel powerful with it, others feel powerless without it, and still others, even with financial security, have a lot of fear around losing it. I like Billy Graham's quote; it talks about your *attitude*. No matter what your bank account or portfolio balances are, let's look at what you can start doing to align yourself with a financial comeback or to enjoy your wealth worry free. Join me in intending that by the end of this chapter you'll feel financially empowered.

More than any other time in history, humanity is now going through a time of great upheaval, actually, a time for personal and spiritual expansion. At this time you have access to the potential to expand your soul—to make the best of challenges or to sink into financial and emotional despair, forgetting your innate power to create change. The former requires looking within and understanding that your soul chose to be here during this time with a deep desire to look at your programming around money, release false beliefs and deepen your faith. The latter requires very little of you, just to give all your attention to what is. You are reading this book. You are probably ready for a change. Great. Let's get started.

If you want more money in your life, I invite you to accept that every financial challenge has a higher purpose. You may not like the challenge, you may not understand it, yet many people find comfort in reminding themselves they are part of, one with, a very profound universe, much of which is beyond your three-dimensional linear logic. From a soul perspective, your financial experiences are carefully orchestrated and are perfect situations for your destiny path. The journey of evolving helps you deepen your trust in this.

People come forth with certain financial life themes. Some souls set up this lifetime to experience financial success; others to heal the theme of lack consciousness which include income fluctuations, poverty, job loss, or bankruptcy. But, your soul even made a "bet" (for an undisclosed amount of heavenly currency) that you would eventually get the clarity and contrast needed to view your problems from a higher perspective, deepen your faith and move through your financial challenges.

It is a common reaction to feel like a victim when dealing with financial woes. What can be labeled from one perspective as a victim can be seen spiritually as a courageous person attracting the necessary challenges to launch an internal desire for change.

Strained financial conditions that create your desire for change can be the result of bad choices or of being part of something seemingly out of your control, for example, a company layoff or failed investment. At an energetic level, you still attracted those experiences, whether because of your personal vibration or the collective consciousness or a combination of them both.

Energetically, collective consciousness, the total vibration of humanity, radiates energy to everyone, affecting their experiences. We each are evolving to our next level of

196

awareness, so even highly conscious individuals are not fully protected from the collective consciousness energies that surround them. Though, the higher your personal vibration and the stronger your belief system, the easier it will be to surrender to what is and the less you will be negatively impacted by collective consciousness.

Bottom line, embracing your innate power gives you the tools to handle whatever shows up. No matter how they arrive, financial choices and experiences that have you "against the wall" are tests that hold the potential for monumental spiritual breakthroughs. That is the good news.

In his book, *Think and Grow Rich*, Napolean Hill reminds us that every adversity, every failure, every heartache carries with it the seed of an equal or greater benefit.

Instead of focusing on the problem, be open to the potential benefit or personal growth your challenge brings. When you accept what is and see your situation as temporary, you redirect your mind to thoughts of potential and move more easily to a resolution that is for your highest good.

No matter what you are facing, by diligently adhering to and believing in spiritual principles, you will release the energetic resistance which, as you know by now, is caused by worry, anger and fear accumulated over many lifetimes.

Realize that no matter where you are financially, it is temporary if you can successfully adjust your vibration. To raise your vibration, first accept what is and then change your thoughts and feelings to ones that feel good.

It is not your situation that is causing you to suffer; it is the thoughts you believe about that situation that make you suffer. Ask yourself, "Does this thought align to my goals or cause me to worry?" If it worries you then change that worrisome thought. As you change the fear-based thoughts to ones of acceptance and hopefulness, you move in the direction of financial stability, then to even greater prosperity.

Consider how one's vibration and programming plays a role in creating experiences. Many lottery winners have returned to their original financial state; the one to which their belief systems were a vibrational match. On the other hand, when self-made millionaires lose their money, they're quickly on their way back to prosperity through the use of their "millionaire mindset"—the positive expectant thoughts that they will attract success again. And they usually do within a relatively short period of time.

Why does one person have a millionaire mindset and another a poverty one? It is because of their beliefs, the ones with which they incarnated and further developed this lifetime. Beliefs are critical in determining one's level of success.

Recognizing False Beliefs

If one of your life lessons or life themes happens to be lack consciousness—not enough money—then to sufficiently shift this fear-based energy block and open yourself to financial freedom, look at your root beliefs around money. And for change to be permanent, the energy blocks need to be re-patterned at the cellular level where beliefs are encoded. This involves accepting and then changing the false beliefs, the "old tapes" that play in your head, regarding money.

These old tapes are often rooted in childhood. Ask yourself, "As a child, what did I hear or observe regarding money?" Did you hear: "We can't afford it?" "Money doesn't grow on trees." "Money is the root of all evil." Your parents were conditioned by these same statements during their upbringing. But, your parent's beliefs need not be yours.

Let's take a closer look at what your parents modeled. For deeper processing come back to this section with paper and pen. When you do, first meditate for 5-15 minutes to relax your mind. Then read through and answer the following questions.

Did your parents model financial success or failure? What limiting beliefs did they have? Did they barely get by? Was their financial condition one of hopefulness or victimization? Did they try to keep up with the Joneses? Did they make fun of people who had money? Did they think money was "dirty?" Did they think people with money were selfish? Were you told that getting ahead takes a lot of hard work or that nothing in life comes easily? Did they live with a glass ceiling regarding their income? Did they save excessively—avoiding nicer vacations and other pleasures even though they could afford it? Did they have a good balance between spending and saving and consider money an avenue for fun and pleasure? The answers to these questions shaped your beliefs.

Reflect on your parent's habits and attitudes about money. Your fears and habits may mirror both or more heavily one of your parents or you may have developed opposite beliefs to theirs in an attempt to feel good or improve your situation. Reflection allows you to see a correlation between your fears and spending habits and the beliefs you picked up from your parents.

Can you see a correlation with your parent's beliefs? If you're still not sure about what you believe or the lessons you incarnated with to heal, just look at your life; your experiences will tell you much. Where are you financially? Do you save regularly? Are you balanced in saving and spending? Is your income consistent or not? Is your income increasing each year or are you satisfied with the status quo? Do you believe that you are worthy of money, of goodness and ease? Are you pleased with your investment portfolio?

Every answer gives hints about your programming. Do not judge this new awareness as good or bad. It is just valuable feedback—an invitation to adjust your belief system. It is *all* good.

Childhood Conditioning

Extra money was scarce during my childhood. I was driven by my "lack conditioning" to work hard, save and invest. This conditioning—there is never enough money—followed me into my marriage. My husband and I had the money to live a more lavish lifestyle but we preferred to save. We kept our wardrobes and home accessories practical and chose not to buy a boat or build a swimming pool. I didn't realize it at the time, but I now feel the savings account compensated for my childhood insecurity.

However, another person may also grow up with limited finances but handle his spending in the exact opposite way. Perhaps, as a child, this other person also wasn't given the toys and sports equipment his friends were getting. So, he grew up vowing he'd work hard and always get what he wanted, a vow that, depending on his income, could lead to living paycheck to paycheck. Two people can grow up with similar financial situations and have it imprint them so differently.

A third person could spend her life not feeling worthy enough or smart enough because she grew up with a father telling her she'd never amount to anything. As a result, she would work extra hard to prove herself by spending money extravagantly, wanting success on the outside to hide the pain of "I'm not good enough" on the inside.

Whether we save money or choose to enjoy life's bounty are neither good nor bad, all are opportunities to see if there is a pattern and heal the associated fear. It is the "why" behind the action that affects your vibration, your health and your happiness.

In all three of the above examples, whether they were saving or spending, their money mindset was influenced by their childhood programming.

Life Themes

I realize that most of my life my desire to save a lot of money stemmed from a fear-based conditioning of financial lack. On the positive side, my savings gave me financial security during and after my marriage. Along my spiritual journey, I realized that two of my major life themes were unworthiness and lack mentality. So it makes sense that after my divorce, as I progressed spiritually, my soul was ready to address and move toward totally healing those false beliefs. In order to continue evolving, I needed to address and clear the fear-based beliefs that were present in my vibration.

You have many opportunities, lessons, to grow your soul; all intended, from a higher perspective, to raise your consciousness. A life theme is one of your soul-based lessons, but it is also a predominant one that your soul wants you to totally heal this lifetime. Interspersed with success in that area, your soul's vibration will continue to attract more experiences around that same theme until you fully clear the associated fear-based vibration. Vibrations like this are carried over from many lifetimes and can take years to clear.

My astrological birth chart points to the probability of fluctuations with my finances until midlife. With that information plus the financial fluctuations I've experienced, it's obvious to me that I incarnated with a life theme around money. I wish I hadn't. But I did. And arguing with what is doesn't get me anywhere. Choosing to accept it and clear it does.

Becoming Free

Are you wondering what you can do now to move through your challenges? Start with affirmations to improve your financial situation. But, remember, everything has a vibration and even though saying affirmations chips away at your false beliefs and re-programs your cellular memory, they aren't a cure-all. Your predominant vibration will determine what you attract. If you say affirmations daily yet always walk around feeling unworthy, focusing on what's missing in your life, and letting your false beliefs rule your vibration, then the vibration of those limiting thoughts is what you emit. And what will that vibration attract? Of course, like vibrations — more experiences of "lack."

I encourage you to look at the value of spending according to your vibration, not your affirmations. Learn to recognize any fear around money and pay attention to how often you're attracting challenging financial situations. Saying, "I'll buy this expensive outfit; new money will come," won't realize new money if your predominant vibration is one of fear and lack consciousness. You will be stuck with the frustrating balance on your credit card and think the law of attraction doesn't work.

Also, look at the emotional reasons for any over-spending. Are you trying to find happiness or worthiness from the outside? Buying things to fill a void are temporary fixes and block you from looking at the root emotional reason for overspending. I like this quote: *If you do not know your own intrinsic worth, no person or no thing can bring it to you.* Turn any overspending into an opportunity for soul growth. Spiritual life coaching and energy healing can help resolve the root causes responsible for your overspending.

To help avoid overspending, set a budget from empow-erment, not fear. Feeling good becomes your first re-sponsibility. You can reduce your entertainment spending based on fear and feel angry and frustrated — "I hate not going out to eat as often." Or, you can choose from empowerment — "It feels so good to pay cash for groceries and pay down my credit card bill." A positive, empowering attitude will make the process easier and help you attract what you want faster.

To get more of what you want, continue to review your predominant beliefs. Ask yourself what your first thought is when you consider purchasing a new outfit or the latest cell phone. Is it, "I can't afford this," "That costs too much," or "I never get to buy fun things for myself?" Those thoughts are lack thinking—there isn't enough money to go around. Vibrationally, those thoughts are contributing to your lack by energetically blocking the situations and synchronicities which would allow in more money.

To shift lack thinking, start by finding ways to reword your thoughts into positive, feel-good phrases. This may feel odd at first, considering you are exercising your mind muscles differently. For example, you can replace "I can't afford this" with "I prefer to use the money I would spend on this outfit toward a vacation or to pay a bill," "I will have that car as my abundance increases," or "Even though it feels good in the moment to splurge on this watch, it won't feel good when my credit card bill arrives." Rewording the limiting thoughts helps you stay more positive. Keep with it; you are reprogramming old, limiting belief systems.

If you were to take home a previously abused and neglected puppy from the animal shelter, you would expect it to need time to learn to trust you. His programming says humans are mean. Your old programming says there isn't enough money. Like the puppy, your thoughts need consistent, loving re-programming. In time, the new pro-gramming will replace the old, life will be easier and you and the puppy will feel friskier!

Deleting Old Programming

One of the powerful things about you is your ability to delete and reprogram your beliefs. There is no lack in our multi-dimensional universe. You experience lack in your life only when you default to your limited human-mind thinking and old programming instead of trusting your abundant spirit-mind thinking. Embrace the All-ness that you are and prepare for success and prosperity.

Intend to eliminate, with ease and gentleness, any thoughts that inhibit your financial success. Think of your false beliefs as computer files that are minimized, yet always running in the background, always energetically influencing your decisions and what you attract. Better yet, see your false beliefs as "viruses" in your financial files blocking your success. Decide right now that you no longer need the files that are full of "limiting belief viruses." Affirm that you are one with Spirit and deserve the fulfillment that is your birthright. When you are ready, and with eagerness for an easier and happier future, hit delete.

Affirmations Reprogram your Thinking

Affirmations get your energy moving in a positive direction and help reprogram your cellular memory; do them daily for best results. Affirm, "Thank you, Spirit, for clearing, cleansing and purifying me of any discordant and limiting beliefs." (I love how Spirit is always helping us clear in unexpected ways. Just now, right after I wrote the gratitude statement to Spirit, I had a hard, out-of-the-blue coughing spell. It's my inner being clearing a deeper layer of my limiting beliefs. Thanks, Spirit!)

To find your best affirmations, take your false beliefs and limiting comments and write down the opposite—this will be your positive affirmation. If you encoded into your cellular memory and automatically say "We can't afford that," affirm, "Money comes easily and abundantly." When choosing affirmations, choose ones that stretch your thinking yet still resonate in the realm of possibilities. For example, if you are affirming, "Thanks, Spirit, that I have attracted an unexpected million dollars within six months," and you can't really believe you could attract $1,000, then the underlying disbelief will block the energy from moving.

Allow yourself to set goals that stretch you yet resonate with your present vibration. As you experience success, expand your goals and rewrite your affirmations accordingly. Enjoy making up your own affirmations or use any of the ones below.

I AM one with the Divine and, with the Divine, all things are possible.

I AM accepting high integrity financial guidance, now.

I AM aligned to prosperity.

I AM worthy of financial security and abundance.

I AM sharing my abundance in a responsible, joyful way.

I AM thankful that I attract abundance flowing easily.

Gratitude, the Great Energy Shifter

If you want more money, appreciating what you do have or what is working elsewhere in your life aligns you with your desire. Accept your situation as temporary and have an attitude of gratitude. Quantum physics reminds us that the Universe doesn't recognize any difference between what is real and what is imagined so use this energy phenomenon to your advantage—intend that you are prosperous in all areas of your life. With your thoughts and feelings, live from your "already fulfilled" spiritual mind and not from your limited "I don't have enough money" human mind. Think of situations that you're grateful for and feel the essence of that gratitude in your body. The good feelings raise your vibration and momentum, allowing the Universe to orchestrate prosperity for you.

Another way to add momentum to increasing your finances is to improve your vibration around money: Bless the checks you write and receive, bless credit card or cash purchases of gas, clothing or groceries, and bless any cash in your wallet and the funds in your bank accounts or investment portfolios. Money passes through a lot of hands, often those of people whose own fear infuses the money with fear or worry too. Blessing your money also shifts this vibration.

I use Unity Church's offertory blessing for incoming or outgoing financial flow. I even offer my in-person clients to say the blessing with me when they pay. "Divine Love, flowing through me, blesses and multiplies all the good I am and have and all the good I give and receive."

The Universe is abundant. There is no shortage of anything you want—love, joy, health, and money. Yet, you have been trained to view your life only from the "distorted" view of the limited human mind—to see everything as physical matter and to believe that what you see is all there is—that there is not enough.

So when the fear of not having enough money shows up, call back your power. Remind yourself that fear is only created in the human mind. It isn't present in your infinite, invisible abundant spiritual mind. Fear is feedback that you are giving all of your power to what is visible—to the material world—and you have stepped outside of your true essence. Step into your true power. And yes, this is the journey, doing your best day to day, and allowing yourself to grow through challenges. While practicing this journey, embrace your One-ness with the invisible realm of Spirit. Embrace love, health and prosperity.

Get into the habit of thanking Spirit—the non-physical energy you are one with, your I AM—daily for lovingly co-creating with you. Then trust that whatever experience shows up, has a higher purpose, lesson or blessing.

One thing for sure, negative experiences help you clarify what you do want. Consider how each bad financial decision or purchase has given you valuable feedback. That feedback gives you more clarity and the clarity allows you to focus more on what you want.

A Major Investment Loss

I have practiced these principles continually since 2001. And I still attract setbacks. In other words, I still attract *opportunities* to release limited thinking, dissolve deeper layers of false beliefs and evolve to higher consciousness. Each setback helps me see where I am along the vibrational continuum of allowing in prosperity.

I chose an investment, recommended by my financial advisor, which had a 23-year track record of high returns. The monthly dividends supported me as I grew my holistic healing practice. However, after one year, my advisor called with the unexpected news of my investment's demise. I would have definitely preferred better news, but my response was different than he had expected.

I embrace that money is energy and we attract it through our vibrations and beliefs. I believe God, Spirit, is the ultimate source of my financial security and prosperity, not any specific dividends. But the dividends were an avenue for the flow to come through and I appreciate any and all avenues of flow.

On paper, this was a devastating blow to my financial security. I was a single woman stepping out in faith to develop my healing practice. Yet, whether I liked my situation or not, I understood the dynamics of the relationship between consciousness and manifesting. I knew the importance of accepting "what is." Arguing with what is would have been futile and would have had fear, anger, and blame screaming through me, blocking the very thing I needed—*another* avenue of financial flow. (Though if I had been angry it would have been important to feel it and release it in the healthiest way possible.)

I embrace that my power resides in how I perceive each setback, and not in the setback itself. My belief system allowed me to stay calm and I was confident in universal creative power. So I told my financial advisor the money would come another way. Even though he honored my spiritual perspective, he seemed surprised at my reaction and probably questioned my sanity. But I really believed the money would come another way. I just had to get out of my own way—which is the journey we all are on—and focus on the *feeling* that I was already financially prosperous.

I chose to ignore what my human mind was observing in my material world and, instead, I trusted the infinite possibilities available when I see through spirit mind. I expected Spirit to figure out the "how" and I just remained in a state of acceptance that, energetically, I was already abundant. I trusted Spirit would reveal plan B at the best possible timing for my highest good.

I did my part—I visualized how I would spend and invest the new money. I felt grateful daily as if I already was prosperous and focused on the many things I did have to be thankful for.

Patience paid off. An out-of-the-blue thought came to me to check some shares I owned in the company where my ex-husband was employed. I hadn't checked the price in over a year.

When we divorced it had been at $46 per share. Two years prior to the Spirit-inspired out-of-the-blue thought, it had dropped to $18. On the day I heeded my nudge and checked on it, it was $74 per share.

I called my ex-husband and said I wanted to sell my shares. I told him I thought the share price would go to $80. He said there wasn't any news to indicate that would happen. To the best of his knowledge, I'm sure that was true. Yet, Spirit saw the big picture and gave me that intuitive hint.

The stock value was over $79 when I sold it. I averaged $77 per share and after paying a 48% tax, I still netted $50,000 over what I had lost with my above-mentioned investment. Shortly thereafter, it dropped by $20 per share. Spirit, we are so cool!

How did I "just happen" to sell it at its high? Do you think it was a coincidence or my alignment with this intelligent Universe?

In hindsight, I realized I had ignored two financially savvy people who encouraged me not to make that investment. I went ahead with it because of its twenty-five-year healthy track record and I trusted my financial advisor. Yes, I missed the guidance, but because I trusted that God is my source, my spiritual GPS recalculated *my route* and guided me to the next best avenue for financial recovery.

Trusting the process and our co-creative abilities with Spirit opens up new and valuable windows of opportunities. If I hadn't stayed so calm or trusted universal law, if I had convinced myself that I "deserved" to be angry at my financial advisor and blame him for my loss, I would have blocked the divine timing and the inspired thought to check my stock.

Being Prepared for Blessings

Einstein said, "Intuition does not come to an un-prepared mind." When he discovered the theory of relativity, it came to him in a flash of intuition. But only after he had studied and pondered the great mysteries of physics for years. This preparation allowed him to observe things that would have gone unnoticed to the "unprepared mind."

Preparation—spiritually evolving—takes time and focus. In our busy world, it may seem hard to take time for this. But you may agree with me that investing in time and focus is a small price to pay for the eventual manifestation of your desires. You are a powerful creator and worthy of all you want to create.

When I broke my neck I had no health insurance. Spiritually, decisions are not right or wrong. The best decision for each person is the one with which they are most aligned, the one that feels the best. In seemingly wrong decisions, Spirit picks up the pieces wherever we are and guides us to the next best solution.

A few years prior to my biking incident, I had made a conscious decision not to have health insurance. I seldom used

Western medicine and decided I would pay out-of-pocket for the few tests and appointments I did have. I had the money for insurance premiums in savings but I chose to spend my money based on what *felt* the best and paying for what I didn't use didn't feel good.

I knew that insurance would definitely be of help with a catastrophic injury but I was unable to find a company that would carry me for that alone. Since I viewed life from a positive position and the law of attraction—like attracts like—I felt protected from attracting a catastrophic accident. But even so, when I made my decision, I said, "If I happen to attract a major accident, God is my Source and the money will come to cover it."

My decision was naïve—I had yet to understand that we also attract situations for soul purposes—like my broken neck.

I broke my neck, got my breath back and was lying on the ground waiting for EMS to show up. Guess what I was doing? I was giving over the impending hospital fees to Spirit. Of course, hindsight being 20/20, the thought did go through my mind that insurance would have been a very good idea. And, I understood the importance of not dwelling on that, not beating myself up for that "wrong" decision. So, I stayed in my power and several times a day thanked God for revealing the necessary money for me to pay off my hospital bill in less than a year. I was doing affirmations for physical healing and financial healing.

Two months after my injury, I paid my bills off in full with new money. The money that paid my bills "just happened" to be "in the ethers" with my name on it, but if I hadn't been actively affirming for money to pay my hospital bills, I would have overlooked it. Thankfully, Spirit orchestrated blessings. Thankfully, I heeded them.

The blessings came as part of my divorce settlement. It was my portion of my ex-husband's non-qualified 401K fund, money which I was not eligible to collect until six years after my divorce. I was aware of the account and so was my friend, Liz, who is a paralegal at the law firm that I had used in the divorce settlement. I knew some money was in that account, but it really was not my focus. I was focusing on healing from my spinal cord injury.

It is clear that since I wasn't paying attention to that account, Spirit worked through Liz. That is what Spirit does, finds the easiest and best path, the path of least resistance. Liz is married, the mother of two children and has a job of intense focus and responsibility. In spite of her hectic lifestyle and during the very busy month of December, Liz was prodded by Spirit and reminded me three times that month that we needed to take care of it. "It" wasn't a high priority of mine. Thanks, Liz, from the bottom of my heart responding to Spirit's call and making it a priority.

Non-insured patients usually are charged the full amount of the hospital fees, but insurance companies usually get 40-50% off. I believe in fairness and I liked the idea of also getting 50% off.

So, daily, two friends and I masterminded—affirming and visualizing together—for my whole body healing and a 50% discount on my hospital bill. I also affirmed that, no matter what, my bills were paid in full. God is my source. I trusted enough money would come to cover my bills, whatever they ended up being.

A friend coached me on how to confidently move right up through the ranks of management when calling the hospital and asking for the best discount they could approve. If one said that is all they could do, say 30% off, I asked to speak to their manager, until I received my blessing.

I started the last call with a sincere thank you for the hospital providing exceptional medical care. I shared my story and road to recovery. This person "just happened" to relate to my story and he even shared a story of his own about how his grandmother healed with energy healing too. I then asked if he could help me with my financial healing—with a 50% discount. He thought for a moment and then agreed.

I was smiling and thanking Spirit for this blessing. As an on-going thank you, I keep the hospital on my daily prayer list for their continued patient and financial success.

I'm grateful. Thank you, Spirit, for orchestrating this. Thanks to the hospital's financial blessing and thanks to Liz's perseverance in getting the 401K money, I was able, two months after my injury, to pay my bills in full with this "new" money. I even had $10,000 left over. You may comment, "If you had insurance you would have had your 401K money also." Maybe or maybe not, following up on that 401K wasn't a priority of mine and I hadn't dealt with it that year as it was. Since I was now vibrationally attracting a large sum of money, this became the avenue.

The bottom line—I'm thankful for that avenue of flow. I'm also thankful that faith can move mountains. Let me also mention that my injury came exactly six years after my divorce, the time at which I could receive the non-qualified 401K money.

Aligning to Your Prosperity

I invite you to use this affirmation, "Thank you, God that I am attracting all the resources I need for my destiny path's highest good," and then fine tune your vibration as you keep in mind the gold nuggets below.

Expect and energetically align to what you want but stay unattached to the outcome. Trust the outcome will be for the highest good of all, even if it is different than you had hoped. Being unattached to the outcome means having no resistance—in other words, not *needing* it to be a certain way. Yes, this takes practice.

Attachment to the end result is feedback that you are, intentionally or unintentionally, trying to control it. You may sincerely believe your way is the best solution for everyone. And it may be, but only from your perspective of what is obvious. There is also the big picture to take into consideration—the soul journey perspective. Trust that the greater intelligence of Spirit knows what is for the highest good of all.

Focus on what you want. Remember, you will attract what you focus on and align with unless there are blocks or soul reasons for you not to. So, monitor your thoughts and feelings. Ask yourself throughout your day: "Have I been looking at situations from the perspective of the glass half full or half empty?" "Have I been focusing on my problems or on the end result of what I really want?"

I focused on paying my hospital bill in full, not on how limited my savings account was or how many bills were piling up. The how is not our concern. Our only concern is to do our best to align with our goals.

Other ways to align with prosperity are to write "paid in full" on your credit card bill and print out a bank statement, white out the balance and replace it with a larger sum. Put pictures of items on your vision board that you will purchase as the money is revealed. Focus on an abundant savings account and the ability to always pay cash for your living expenses, your desires and the fun you want to have. And, always find something to be grateful for.

Visualize what you want and feel as if you already have it. The vibrations you emit attract people, situations and opportunities to you that will assist you in having more money. How would your life look with increased abundance? Picture yourself financially successful, with *all the details* of how that would look to you and feel the excitement and joy of having it!

Neither the universe nor your mind knows the difference between what is real and what is imagined. This is a vibrationally-based universe and you are attracting situations to you based on the vibrations—the feelings—that you project. You think a thought, that thought creates feelings, the feelings create a vibration and the Universe reacts to your vibration and takes action. It is totally irrelevant whether that vibration is the result of a real situation or an imagined one.

There is power in not giving your predicament so much negative energy; worry blocks the very thing you want. Part of being energetically focused is to ignore what is painfully showing up in your human-mind experience.

Change the channel to the energetic realm of Spirit where all possibilities exist. I clarify: those working with universal laws benefit from *ignoring* the predicament because they are doing the vibrational journey—accepting what is, giving their predicament over to Spirit, visualizing prosperity and finding a way to feel good. Those who don't work with universal laws and the energy consciousness of money do not benefit, the way I mean, from ignoring the predicament. I don't recommend ignoring high credit card balances and bills without reining in the spending. Until you can believe in and practice using the power of your mind daily and experience the positive results, I suggest financial counseling to raise awareness and help create a budget.

With that said, keep in mind that sometimes a dire problem is the wake-up call a spiritually aware beginner or advanced student needs in order to realize that *they* can't humanly do one more thing. They throw up their hands and "give it over to Spirit." Their inner essence celebrates because, even though it is an uncomfortable situation, the student finally releases resistance and reaches for help. Living from a spiritually aware perspective was not meant to be hard.

Life is easier when you call back your power and focus on what you do have control of—your thoughts. With your thoughts you shift your vibration. In this higher vibrational space, you are calmer and more open to hear intuitive spiritual guidance. You are aligned with Spirit who will orchestrate solutions for your highest good.

Be thankful throughout your day. Gratitude and Love are the two highest vibrations. In a challenging and painful situation it may be difficult to think loving thoughts. Yet, no matter what you are facing, you can always find something to be thankful for. Make it a point to look around and be thankful for what you see. Energetically, as you feel good about what you have, you attract even greater good for which to be thankful.

Gratitude is valuable. Be thankful for any amount of money you do have or have had. Be thankful for the payments you are making even if you can't pay your bills in full. Be thankful when you find items you need to buy and they are on sale. Remember, you are playing the vibration game—have fun with it. When you find coins on the street, play head games with yourself, be thankful for that unexpected abundance—consider it a windfall. Your happy vibration of gratitude will attract much, much more!

The universe handles the *how* as long as you stay in vibrational alignment with feeling good, accepting what is and focusing on what you want. My affirmation and meditation CD or mp3, *Remember Your Greatness*, will help you stay in alignment. My voice energetically magnifies the affirmations, shifting your old programming. You can find this on my website, http://suzettefoster.com/cd.php. For best results, to dissolve blocks in all areas of your life and reprogram cellular memories to positive ones, listen daily or as often as possible. At bedtime, go to sleep with the CD on repeat.

Aligning when People Disagree

A significant other with differing opinions or limiting beliefs can make it more challenging for you to stay on a positive roll, so practice, practice, practice not letting their limiting beliefs affect yours. Energetically *your* beliefs determine how you react and, thus, what shows up.

If you and your partner are in disagreement regarding an important financial decision, then, before discussing it further, position yourself energetically. For several days affirm, "Thank you, Spirit, for guiding this decision and revealing the best solution for the highest good of all." "Thank you, Spirit that we both learn and hear, in a way we can hear it, what is for our highest good." Then, visualize your preferred outcome daily.

Accept your present situation—what is—as temporary. Acceptance allows movement for financial flow. Fear, frustration, or worry is resistance and blocks the very thing you want. If fear pops up, intend to release the fear—chipping away at that fear-based thought. Even if one partner was negligent and put the family in a tight position, improve your attitude through forgiveness and gratitude.

Also, feel excitement and gratitude for your ability to work together in harmony to come up with a creative solution that feels good to you both (even if that is not yet true).

Spend a week or so getting aligned energetically and then ask to discuss the situation again. If what you want is in everyone's best interest, and you are now energetically aligned, then your partner will be more willing to agree or compromise. Be prepared for the possibility that what you want may not be for everyone's highest good. Accept that Spirit sees the big picture and is helping you make the best decision, even if it is not what you had planned.

Think Big

Focus constantly on what you really desire. For example, think bigger than just getting out of debt. Write statements such as "I am so grateful for my reserve account of X dollars." Or, "I am so excited and grateful that I was able to visit Paris. Thank you, Spirit."

Answer the following questions. The answers add prosperity consciousness to your vibration.

How big of a reserve account do you want?

What kind of organizations will you support with your money?

What kind of investments will you make?

What extras will you have? Cars? Jewelry? Trips?

Think as big as you can believe and always ask for "this or something better for the highest good of all."

Financial Freedom is an Inside Job First

Recognize that your choices, false beliefs, soul lessons and vibrations have put you in a position of energetic discord. New thoughts and choices—new vibrations—can get you back on track.

When you see a financial setback as an opportunity to let go of false beliefs and old ways of reacting, to surrender your situation to Spirit and to begin trusting in the abundant universe, you deepen your faith and the setback loses its steam. That is the journey of calling back your power.

Chapter 17
A Wealth of Health Naturally

The Doctor of the future will give no medicine, but will interest his patients in the care of the human frame, in diet, and in the cause and prevention of disease.
– Thomas Edison

Edison said those words 100 years ago. Even then he knew what much research now supports. Cardiac surgeon Dr. Mehmet Oz, a modern day teacher and visionary, was quoted saying that he has wondered what Western medicine doesn't yet know. Even though trained in Western medicine, Dr. Oz appreciates the importance of treating the whole person from the inside out and has said he feels the next big frontier is unlocking the doors to energy medicine.

Health and wellness can be achieved more easily and be less costly as more doctors and scientists are willing to open those previously locked doors and explore the unlimited potential of the body's energetic systems. But, for the time being, the "medicine ball" is in your court. You get to choose what feels best for you.

Holistic medicine is an art and science which emphasizes the need to look at the whole person, including analysis of physical, emotional, nutritional, environmental, social, spiritual and lifestyle factors.

Holistic medicine is gaining more popularity here in

the west, but Ayurveda, considered by many scholars to be the oldest holistic approach has been practiced in India for at least 5,000 years. The term Ayurveda is taken from the Sanskrit words *ayus*, meaning life or lifespan, and *veda*, meaning knowledge. Its main focus is to prevent or treat illness by maintaining balance in the body, mind, and consciousness.

Holistic modalities take into account the following ideas: your body is pure energy, moldable by your intentions; the parts affect the whole; and the mind is not separate from the body.

Let's look more closely at the first, your body is energy. This energy, which includes your attitudes, thoughts, and beliefs, also includes pathways or meridians that flow to all of the body's organs. Also, there are energetic vortexes in your body called chakras which have been scientifically measured and quantified; they emit sound and color. You can see your physical body (dense matter) because it is energy that vibrates at a very slow frequency.

Meridians and chakras are not found in autopsies because they are subtle energies (subtle matter) which vibrate at the speed of light. Subtle matter is as real as dense matter; its vibratory rate is simply faster. I offer balancing techniques, including one for balancing chakras on my website at www.Choose2Thrive.com/balancingtechniques.php

All energetic and spiritual healing modalities ultimately utilize the invisible flow of energy and the One Mind of a Higher Power. When treating your disease ener-getically, along with or without Western medicine, gift yourself with the commitment to improve your inner and outer environments. The body has an innate ability to heal itself when given the right environment. The right inner and outer environments involve balancing your subtle energy fields and ultimately balancing your life.

Health Becomes a Higher Priority as We Mature

People's priorities change as they age. Often, in their twenties, they are excited to be living on their own and beginning to make their way in the world with their first real job and a paycheck.

In their thirties people streamline their focus on success in the outer world, focusing even more on job status, money, a nice home, and family life. Then, in their forties, many people experience a midlife crisis; they sense a void in their lives. "All these things I've been chasing and achieving aren't enough; something is still missing."

That something is often a deeper awareness of themselves and the fulfilling discovery that true joy comes from within. So, in an attempt to find what is missing—because they have been taught to always look outside themselves for happiness—they buy that motorcycle or sports car or second home or have that affair. It's great to enjoy the abundance available to you, though it's a good idea to also check in with yourself to see if the real reason for the indulgences is to fill that void. If it is, be aware that it's a temporary fix.

Time allows us to awaken the deep wisdom within and most of us, in our forties and fifties, start reflecting on what is really important in life. And hurray for those of you who are between the ages of 20 and 40 and are already aware of where your real happiness resides. It is normal to adjust your priorities as you experience life. Studies show that people's health is at the top of the priority list in their fifties. It doesn't even make the list in earlier decades.

Many people are no longer taking their health for granted. Good health is about enjoying the time you do have, not spending precious time and money on surgeries, illness, low energy, depression, and pain.

Unfortunately, we have been trained to think we are destined to become dependent on prescription medicines in our fifties and sixties. I often hear people comment, "At my age, I'm lucky I'm not on any medication." It's as if taking prescription medicine is a normal part of aging. Please know it doesn't have to be. Nevertheless, it tends to be because we, as a society, have been taught to believe that surgery and medicine are the only answers to our health problems.

Finding the Root Cause of Your Disease

Let's compare how we handle our health problems with how we handle problems in business. Most of us have learned that the best way to deal with any business problem is to identify the cause, address it and solve the problem.

If a business was to just go for the temporary fix, for example, transferring money to a department that is continually overspending, without using their resources of time and money to understand and address the root cause of the overspending, the resulting budget shortfall would continue to haunt them. It would end up costing more money and hassle than the original investment to fix the problem.

A savvy businessperson reviews the situation and seeks out specialists to help identify the root cause and remedy the problem. This makes sense. To run a successful business you would expect no less.

So let's expect the same from traditional medicine. Most of traditional medicine does not focus on identifying the root cause; it focuses on identifying the disease. Then, medicine is prescribed to suppress the symptoms of the disease or the affected part is cut out or surgically repaired. Most doctors are not sufficiently trained to help you identify and rectify the root cause. This has become the acceptable approach.

Emotions and Healing

Emotions are created by your thoughts. And every emotion you've ever had is imprinted in your cellular memory. Basically, cells are informational fields of energy and these energetic imprints stay with you until you address the feelings causing them.

Every negative and fear-based emotion you've ever had accumulates and clogs up the pipeline that needs to be open for life force energy and healing. Clogged pipelines contribute to your tiredness and block your wellbeing, often resulting in a serious illness.

The reverse is true, too. Symptoms of illnesses go away and your health improves when you address the imprinted memories and beliefs and change your thoughts. It is beneficial to think of your health issues as simply the way in which your body gets your attention and as feedback to what emotional issues you need to address to create wellness.

If you're thinking that this can be extensive work, it can be, but most of my clients don't have to spend long hours going over the details of past hurts. They do name the feeling, for example, "abandonment," "resentment," or "unworthiness" and then we proceed with more life coaching and energy clearing. From a spiritual perspective, there is no right or wrong time to process your emotions; but to avoid feeling the pain will only leave you with a similar emotional upheaval or disease later on, even in another lifetime. You get to decide, freedom now or later.

Medicine and surgery make it easy for the patient to sidestep the necessary emotional work—the patient avoids the opportunity to heal the root cause of the illness or disease and to grow his soul.

Medications *suppress* blocked emotions, pushing them further down. Until people understand the big picture—that emotions contribute to their disease—they will cling to their hates, anger, and resentments and choose to ignore their emotions. They may not like their health problems, but most simply accept disease and illness as just part of life. What a medical myth.

Call back your power and begin to see your mind and body from the perspective of your amazing inner wisdom. View how healthy you are not from the *absence* of disease, but rather from the *presence* of optimal health and vitality.

Energy healing and life coaching teach you to *express* your emotions and toxins. When your emotional buttons get pushed, it is your divine essence saying, "Knock. Knock. This layer of anger is ready to be expressed." Let's admit it, it's not fun. It takes courage to endure and work through the temporary discomfort of emotional pain.

Spiritual growth and recovery from any disease is dependent on your willingness to endure the healing process which may shake your belief systems and expose raw emotions.

Think of disease as evidence that something is amiss in your mind—where all thinking begins. The value in holistic life coaching is that it helps you understand the correlation between your thinking and your health problem.

I invite folks to see that all health issues and injuries are wake-up calls to take care of themselves in a different way. Besides taking the time to face their emotions, some may need to get out of an unhealthy relationship or find a less stressful job. Others may need to slow down and commit to spending more joy-filled time with family and friends or to fulfilling that dream they've never given themselves time to pursue.

Also, everyone will benefit from eating a whole food diet, a practice that is integral to wellness. Improving their diet and doing detoxifying programs are crucial steps on the road to recovery.

Another consideration is guidance from a healing facilitator who can offer life coaching and energy healing. This maximizes the healing process as people heal emotionally, mentally, physically and spiritually.

Be the Star Student

See your health challenge as an opportunity to learn the lessons it is trying to teach you—see the wisdom your challenge brings and embrace it as a gift. You wouldn't consciously choose a major illness or life-threatening accident, yet I invite you to trust that, for some unknown reason, it has a higher purpose.

Affirm, "Thank you, Spirit, for revealing what I need to know and guiding me to the best practitioner and healing modality. Thank you, Spirit that I have the courage to see and let go of the root cause of my health issue. And thank you for results that will be for my highest good and for the highest good of all involved."

Holistic healing is an option that works best for clients who are ready to take a leading role in regaining their health. An experienced holistic practitioner can help you understand the lesson in your health challenge and transmute the associated blocks. If you have truly cleared the root cause and nutritionally feed your body at the cellular level, the healing will be permanent.

Better yet, don't force your body to "wake you up" through a major disease. Honor yourself now. Be proactive. Find a healing facilitator that can help you feel your best by clearing the blocks before they manifest into health problems. As you understand the importance of feeling your best each day, making the decision to improve and simplify your life becomes part of the formula. You and the quality of your life are worth it!

Remember, your body is pure energy. And physics tells us energy can neither be created nor destroyed, just altered. A healing facilitator, in tandem with the wisdom of your mind, body, and spirit, will help you re-pattern unhealthy energy fields to healthy ones.

In doing so, the pattern that created the emotional illness or disease is brought back into a pattern for health and well-being. In a balanced energy field, the body can heal itself and the symptoms will go away.

In this space of wholeness, many of my clients cancel scheduled surgery and, with the support of their doctor, get off prescription medicine. Even if you have had surgery or are on prescription drugs, it is still valuable to heal the emotional blocks associated with a past or present health problem.

Be willing to look outside the box and question the status quo. You will find plenty of highly respected research and innumerous reports of healing success regarding energy medicine, diet and emotional healing. Your body needs to be supported at the cellular and energetic level—the key to wholeness and well-being. You are worthy of the fabulous results you will experience when you invest in clearing your emotional blocks and limiting beliefs, a high quality whole food diet and, yes, a regular exercise program. Dust off those walking shoes!

Most major hospitals, as a bridge to holistic health, are offering Integrative Health Centers. As positive as this is, change often is slow. As you research your options you may choose an approach combining energy medicine with traditional medicine or solely one or the other—the right choice is the one that feels best to you. Enjoy the journey!

Traditional Medicine and Energy Medicine

Western doctors, without any real exposure to holistic modalities during medical school, do make use of the body's energy systems—their electromagnetic fields—through the use of EKGs, EEGs, and MEGs. EKGs measure the heart's electrical impulses and EEGs measure neural activities of the brain. MEG stands for Magneto encephalography, a procedure which involves holding a probe several inches from the head to read the fields of neural activity. MEGs show how the brain processes *fields of energy.*

Science has shown that these energy fields are interactive; each field and each thought affecting the field around it. A mammogram, used routinely, is not a photograph of a breast but an electronic image created by scanning the radiant energy characteristics of its tissues. The radiologist discerns healthy and diseased tissues by viewing the differentials in the energy spectra. Traditional medicine does make use of our energy fields, albeit only to the level of their comfort and training.

Evidence shows that energy healing not only works, but can give you phenomenal results—even where Western medicine has given up hope.

I give thanks for all that Western medicine does provide cutting-edge technology and exceptional medical care in several areas including pre-natal and crisis situations. Let's hold the vision that doctors are more receptive to the holistic view which they have yet to significantly study in medical school—the body as energy, the power of the mind, the debilitating effects of negative emotions and beliefs, and the value of whole food diets.

Praise to the doctors who are focusing on these areas. They have largely done so because of their own interest in holistic medicine. Unfortunately, it's seldom part of their formal education.

The health of our nation's people, our healthcare and our insurance programs are at a crisis point. It is time for quantum physics research, energy medicine, and whole food diets to be widely encouraged and more accessible.

Your power increases as you realize that a disease can't exist unless there is an environment to support it—inadequate diet, a stressful lifestyle, negative attitudes, and fear-driven beliefs and behaviors.

Wellness is supported by an environment which includes a nutrient-rich diet, a relaxed lifestyle, positive attitudes and love-inspired behaviors. Your body will heal itself with a healthy inner and outer environment. The good news is you get to choose the environment you want for your mind and body, even if its baby steps at first.

Our Bodies Can Heal Themselves

I am blessed that my passion and life calling is to help people call back their power—to choose to thrive. Calling back their power, for some, has meant getting off the chaotic roller coaster of life before illness came knocking at their door. For others, pain, depression, addiction, cancer or the need for surgery had already walked through the door before they called back their power and chose an easier, less costly and more permanent and effective way to heal.

You have already received a glimpse into the world of holistic healing through my healing experience. I hope, even if you don't fully understand it, that you are now more open to the wonder of it. It's not so black and white.

Your destiny and your beliefs play a critical role in your ability to heal. You will heal energetically unless it is your divine time to die and return to Source or it is part of your soul's purpose to continue experiencing your illness. That said, not everyone is ready to do the inner work and change their debilitating belief systems. Whether you choose to do the inner work or not, trust that it's all good—you are on your destiny path.

Some people get great healing results while others don't. There are many factors involved. No matter how hard people try to separate spirituality from science and healing, it cannot be done. They are all interrelated—everything is one with this mysterious, energetic Universe.

Remember the basics? Our life and experiences, including our health, center around the fact that we are spiritual and energetic beings. Albert Einstein, whose brilliant mind was ahead of his time said, "All religions, arts, and sciences are branches of the same tree."

228

God, Spirit will not do your soul work for you. A healing facilitator will not do your soul work for you. They play a significant role in the process, helping you align to your greatness and open the necessary doors but you are the real "healer." You determine whether you are willing to think outside the box and do the inner work. The degree to which you are willing to allow in Divine wisdom and God-force energy is equal to the degree to which you will heal your health problem.

Some people who seem very dedicated to their spiritual practice and address their buried emotions, still do not heal completely. This dedication is to be commended, yet the fact that they are not attracting the results they want is feedback that there are still discordant energy patterns blocking the full healing.

Remember, it is not what you say and do that attracts your experiences to you, it is what you vibrate. If a client doesn't heal completely, we just have to look deeper to reveal more discordant energy.

It could be, at the time that they can only shift their beliefs just so far. Perhaps they want to heal but are not quite able to totally believe that something as seemingly easy as energy healing can totally work.

Perhaps they are not able to entirely let go of the grip of their anger or the old programming of unworthiness. Some people, not totally trusting what they hear from their holistic practitioner, choose, instead, to give power to their stage 4 cancer or to the fact that their bones have actually disintegrated. They do not understand that none of those symptoms matter. Yes, you read that correctly. Symptoms are just feedback. The severity of your problem does not matter. You are still pure energy. Until you transition to Spirit, you are pure potential!

We were taught from childhood to give all of our power to our doctors, thinking they have all the answers.

Although they are very smart and dedicated, most doctors make their prognoses based on their belief that you are only a physical being. But, you are mind, body, and spirit. You are an energetic being and accepting the power of your mind and accepting that you are one with a Higher Power are critical in your process of returning to wholeness as quickly and easily as possible.

Consider how most patients react when their doctor tells them they will be in the intensive care unit for 7-10 days. Not aware of their innate power, patients accept that their recovery time will be 7-10 days and make plans accordingly. The doctor's decision is based on his training and the average recovery time of prior patients with the same condition. It is also based on the doctor's limited holistic perspective of the patient.

I use this example because it is what I was told when I broke my neck. With my deep-seated beliefs, including my awareness that I am more than a physical being, I refused to give any power to the severity of my injury or to the brilliant mind of my neurosurgeon. My doctor is the Director of Spine Surgery at Duke Medical Center. Who in their right mind wouldn't believe everything he was saying. Okay, I just raised my hand. Me. Because I knew and deeply believed what you have read within these pages, I chose to call back my power.

Seriously, it's easy to see how we have given our power away over the years, but today you can choose a more holistic and healthier approach to your healthcare. Enjoy reading client healing stories in the forthcoming chapters of folks who called back their power. As you continue to deepen your belief in your healing possibilities, you can create your reality from the full perspective of who you are—mind, body, and spirit.

Chapter 18
Body Fuel for Beautiful

Let thy food be thy medicine and thy medicine be thy food.
– Hippocrates (460-377 BC)

As you can see from Hippocrates quote, eating for health is not a new idea. People find it more challenging to eat healthily today because it is a tradition to socialize and celebrate around food—often it is highly processed food laden with fat, sugar and animal proteins. And most people don't want anyone messing with their traditions. And, if they aren't ready to make any changes in their food choices, many prefer not to know the facts. I understand that, food tastes good and is comforting; I have been there.

Eating the way we were brought up to eat and, more recently, eating what is easy, fast, and inexpensive contribute to the major health decline in America. It is time to take a serious look at the common denominator—an excess of low-nutrient food. If we understand the consequences of this nutrient-weak diet, we may be more motivated to change it.

If this ideology is of interest to you, I sincerely encourage you to read *The China Study* by T. Colin Campbell, Ph.D., and Thomas M. Campbell II. Dr. Campbell is a courageous man who puts your health and his integrity ahead of pleasing the establishment—the pharmaceutical, meat and dairy industries.

The China Study contains powerful research that validates the importance of a plant-based diet in preventing and reversing disease and illness.

Dr. Campbell in commenting about a plant-based diet says, "Heart disease, cancer, diabetes, stroke, hypertension, arthritis, cataracts, Alzheimer's disease, impotence and all sorts of other chronic diseases can be largely prevented. Additionally, impressive evidence now exists to show that advanced heart disease, relatively advanced cancers of certain types, diabetes and a few other degenerative diseases can be reversed by diet. Those in science or medicine who shut their minds to such an idea are being more than stubborn; they are being irresponsible. One of the more exciting benefits of good nutrition is the prevention of diseases that are thought to be due to genetic predisposition."

Research shows that 75% of health costs are due to chronic illness caused by diet and lifestyle. Changes made in diet and lifestyle will lead to healthier and more vibrant lives and a significant reduction in the cost of health care. *The China Study* shoots straight from the hip, addressing the direct correlation between diet and obesity, diabetes, cancer, heart disease and many other health issues.

Your Body is a Powerful Healing Machine.

Your body knows how to heal itself when given a healthy internal ecosystem combining emotional, physical, mental and spiritual well-being. To promote healing, the intelligence of your body will even try another avenue when one way is blocked. When all avenues are blocked, the body can no longer keep up and disease or illness sets in. Often, the longer you ignore the signs of stress, exhaustion, depression or low libido, the more serious is the disease or illness that shows up. Even with advanced stages of illness, unless it is your soul's divine time to die and go back to Spirit, generally, with energy healing and diet, you can reverse your health problems. Your body was built to thrive by an infinite intelligent creator, but it requires cooperation on your part.

Many people believe debilitating pain and disease are the unfortunate but inevitable byproducts of aging. This is a myth. The truth is that pain and disease are the result of a lifestyle that includes low-nutrient food choices.

Take osteoporosis, for example. First of all, you need to know that with the typical American diet, high in fish, meat, poultry, sugar, dairy, caffeine, alcohol and salt, your body's pH level becomes acidic.

Most whole foods such as fruits, vegetables, legumes, nuts and whole grains help the body maintain a healthy, slightly alkaline pH. Oranges and grapefruits are acidic fruits, but once they are digested they form an alkaline ash, which supports health.

So, back to osteoporosis. If your body becomes too acidic, it needs to neutralize that acidic condition. Using one of its brilliant backup systems, it rebalances itself by taking calcium from its calcium storehouse—the bones.

Unfortunately, over time, this process can affect bone density and the result is osteoporosis. Worse yet, if your system becomes heavily acidic and your body is still unable to stabilize the pH to the ideal slightly alkaline level—your immune system becomes weakened, you become exhausted, and illness and disease show up.

Research cited in studies, including the China Study, points to evidence that populations which eat a more alkaline diet and rarely eat dairy, do not have the number of cases of osteoporosis as does our Western population.

Hence, your bones grow weaker as you age because for years your body has been pulling calcium from them. There's a healthier way to correct this imbalance than taking prescription drugs; many people choose to raise their awareness and improve their diet. And think about this: dairy foods are consumed by people because they've been told dairy is a good source for calcium. It does have calcium. But dairy is also acidic so, with the typical American diet, every time you drink a glass of milk or eat cheese or yogurt your body has to rebalance your pH, taking more calcium from your bones.

Most people have a very strong belief that the calcium in milk is essential for healthy bones and teeth and that without it, any number of health risks can crop up. This belief comes from generations of dairy industry advertising promoting milk as nature's miracle food.

There are many foods that are very good sources of calcium. It is found in nuts, seeds, figs, oats, black-strap molasses, prunes, yeast, kale, collards, broccoli, cabbage, asparagus, and pretty much all other green leafy vegetables.

For example, sesame seeds have considerably more calcium than milk: just one cup of sesame seeds contains over 2,000 mg of calcium and just a slightly less amount of magnesium. Besides eating more salads and vegetables more often, a breakfast smoothie made by blending kale along with fruits and a handful of sesame seeds is good way to get calcium. Freezing your kale keeps it easily available for use in your smoothies.

Besides the obvious indulgence in low-nutritive foods—ones high in sugar and low in quality carbohydrates—the research speaks to the detrimental health effects from a regular diet of meat, chicken and fish, and dairy products, too. I know this is not what you want to hear. It's hard to hear that what you've always thought was healthy, isn't. Yet, ignoring the research won't make you healthy.

The China Study also gets real about the establishment's specifically, the pharmaceutical, meat and dairy industries'- resistance to this powerful information. Dr. Campbell has experienced firsthand how these industries report conflicting information seemingly to confuse the public. You're less likely to make changes when you are confused and frustrated.

To lessen the frustration, intend for your non-physical spiritual team to guide you to be healthy and to know the truth. Expect to find the information you need to achieve optimal health. Also, affirm that you will intuitively feel that which is for your highest good, then act upon your inner wisdom and pursue the avenues to which you are guided.

We are on the way to becoming one of the unhealthiest nations in the world. Americans are overweight and undernourished. How far would your car get if you watered down your fuel? How costly would it be to repair the engine if you used something that looked like and smelled like fuel but wasn't fuel?

To feed your body properly, you need *real* food that still has its vitamins and minerals intact. The typical American diet is "starving" us. And serious health issues such as obesity and diabetes which in the past were considered diseases of older adults are now showing up in young adults and children.

The good news is our health issues are giving us great feedback, letting us know it is time to reevaluate our lifestyles and priorities. And people are beginning to realize that dietary changes can make a positive impact on their health.

To permanently heal a health problem we need to address the root cause, not just treat the symptoms with prescription drugs and surgery.

I want to reiterate that most health problems can be healed with either a high-quality, whole food diet or by addressing associated stuffed emotions. Either way can heal your illness.

For best results from the mind, body, and spirit perspective, I recommend combining both. When you heal the emotional hurts, you are healing the emotional root cause and expanding your soul—the ultimate reason you are here on Earth. When you switch to a high-quality, whole food diet you will feel better, have more energy and help prevent future health issues. You deserve to experience the freedom of emotional health and physical health.

If it's not your time to look at these holistic avenues to health, please be aware that just treating the symptoms of an illness inevitably leads to further prescription or surgical treatments. If surgery removed an organ to control the symptoms, a new problem will appear elsewhere. Remember, your pain and health problems are feedback that your body is in a state of imbalance. The symptoms will show up again and often "knock harder" in order to get your attention.

Liver Cleanse—Cleaning the Body's Filter

I encourage you to take your health into your own hands. Besides improving your diet, another way to get excited about being in control of your health is to do a liver cleanse. I highly recommend *The Liver and Gallbladder Miracle Cleanse*. Andreas Moritz shares how "gallstones in the liver—yes, the liver—are the main impediment to acquiring and maintaining good health, youthfulness, and vitality. The liver has direct control over the growth and function of every cell in the body. Any kind of malfunction, deficiency, or abnormal growth pattern of a cell is largely due to poor liver performance."

By understanding how gallstones in the liver contribute to the occurrence or deterioration of nearly every kind of illness, and by taking the simple steps to remove the gallstones, you will put yourself in charge of restoring your health and vitality. Having a clean liver equates to having a new lease on life, so even if you don't have any obvious health problems, you regain your energy, libido and zest for life.

Moritz shares in his book that almost all health problems are a direct or indirect consequence of reduced bile availability caused by gallstones obstructing the flow of bile in the liver. To maintain a strong and healthy digestive system and feed body cells the right amount of nutrients, the liver has to produce 1-1.5 quarts of bile per day. Anything less than that is bound to cause problems with the digestion of food, elimination of waste and the body's continuous detoxification of the blood. Many people produce only about a cupful of bile or less per day.

In his years of holistic practice, Moritz's research and client data point to the typical American acid-producing diet as the cause of liver gallstones. He has observed that people with chronic illnesses often have several thousand gallstones congesting the bile ducts of the liver. As the gallstones are totally cleaned out, through several liver cleanses, most symptoms of discomfort or disease will begin to subside. Pain will dissipate, while energy and well-being will improve. He feels ridding stones from the liver bile ducts is one of the most important and powerful procedures you can apply to improve and regain your health.

Standard tests seldom reveal the occurrence of gallstones in the liver. Moritz explains that most doctors don't even know they develop there. Only some of the most advanced research universities, such as the prestigious Johns Hopkins University, describe and illustrate these liver stones in their literature or on their websites. They refer to them as "intrahepatic gallstones."

A liver cleanse is the only real proof of the presence of gallstones in the liver. Most gallstones are just congealed clumps of bile or organic matter that makes them practically invisible to ultrasonic technologies, CTs, and x-rays. The situation is different with regard to the gallbladder where up to 20% of all stones can be made up entirely of minerals, predominately calcium salts and bile pigments. Diagnostic tests can easily detect these hardened, relatively large stones in the gallbladder; they tend to miss the softer, non-calcified stones in the liver. A dilation of bile ducts caused by larger and denser stones in the liver may be detected more readily through an MRI. However, unless a doctor suspects liver trouble, he rarely checks for intrahepatic stones.

To assess liver health, conventional medicine relies heavily on blood tests. This may actually be misleading. Most people who have a health complaint have normal liver enzyme levels in the blood, despite suffering from liver congestion. The levels become elevated only where there is advanced liver cell destruction as in the case of, for example, hepatitis or liver inflammation. It takes years of chronic liver congestion before liver damage becomes apparent.

The body is only as healthy as are the blood and lymph. If blood and lymph contain large amounts of toxins—a signal that there is congestion in the liver—irritation, inflammation and infection, or damage to cells and tissues in the weakest parts of the body may result. If digestion, metabolism, and elimination of waste materials in the body are impaired as a result of poor liver performance, the immune system can't accomplish its healing work.

A biology teacher in high school, wanting to stress the power of a healthy liver, told his class, "The liver is the most important organ in your body. It performs over a thousand tasks daily and filters every drop of blood that flows through you. Don't tell your girl you love her with all your heart. Tell her you love her with all your liver."

If you are ready to make changes regarding your diet and your health, set an intention to nourish your body temple from the inside out. It will be beneficial to get support and ideas from a life coach, a healing facilitator, an herbalist or a whole food nutritionist. Enlist your friends to hold you accountable, too. Also, below, I will tell you about two more books I recommend. As you continually improve your diet, you and your body will be doing the happy dance!

Nutritional Supplements

Many people find it easier to transition to higher quality food choices when they first add high quality, whole food nutritional supplements to their diet. They feel better and have more energy. Many people find that with this boost in well-being they are more willing to look for nutrient-dense recipes and to shop for and prepare healthier meals.

With nutritional supplements, your body's cravings for sugar and fat often diminish and your body will make the transition to healthier eating easier. With more energy, you will also find yourself emotionally ready to address additional lifestyle changes.

Nutritional supplements vary greatly. Read labels and make sure the products you choose are whole foods with no additives or fillers. You do pay more for quality products but you get what you pay for—and you're worth it! Remember, preventative measures save you thousands of dollars in medical costs and lost time at work and play.

There are differing opinions regarding the need for supplementation. I eat a very healthy diet and I still supplement because our soil quality is so depleted of vital minerals and nutrients. Also, the nutrient value of food varies due to early harvesting and time spent in transporting and storage.

I suggest you start with quality products that will feed your body at the cellular level while improving your body's digestive system which includes assimilation and elimination. A healthy digestive system equates to a strong immune system. With my clients, I recommend the following basics: Super Food flakes, enzymes, probiotics and multivitamins. On my website at http://Choose2Thrive.com/basicsupplement.php you'll find more information about products that support vibrant health. Most people, just by adding these products to their diet, feel better and experience more energy; others experience increased sex drive, improved digestion, and a partial or complete releasing of painful symptoms.

Knowing that everything in the universe is energy, you won't be surprised to learn that every food or edible product has a vibration—a high, life-enhancing vibration or a low, life-depleting vibration or one somewhere in between.

For example, fresh vegetables have a higher vibration than canned; fresh juice has a higher vibration than soda; and free range, organic fed chickens vibrate higher than those injected with antibiotics and hormones and raised under unhealthy living conditions.

As you embark on your spiritual, emotional and physical health regime, you are raising your vibration and your body consciousness will make it easier for you to choose higher-vibrating foods.

Listen to Your Body's Wisdom

As I learned more about energy, I realized that eventually my body would no longer be a "vibrational match" to lower-vibratory food and drink, for example, my social drinking.

Since I like decisions to be easy and I knew my body consciousness would guide me, I told my body, "When it's time for me to stop drinking alcohol, please make sure I don't like margaritas." I loved my margaritas; my Aunt Roberta turned me on to them nearly twenty-five years earlier at a Mexican restaurant in Portland, Maine.

Margaritas were a favorite among my friends too. As a result, for parties and holiday gatherings, making them became my specialty.

I had no specific time in mind as to when my body would no longer want alcohol, yet, I knew it was inevitable. On my 46th birthday, in 2004, I invited a dozen of my girl friends to my home to celebrate our friendships. I made margaritas. During the stories, laughter, and silliness, I thoroughly enjoyed a few glasses of my favorite drink. As usual, when the party was over, I froze what remained.

In hindsight, my body let me fully enjoy my favorite drink one last time; I never desired another margarita after that evening. I gave away what I had frozen.

Even though it was obvious that my body was guiding me, I wasn't quite ready to give up the occasional glass of red wine. My body had a different idea, though.

A few months later, on two occasions, one week apart, I went out to dinner with friends and had a glass of red wine. The first time, I felt really tipsy after drinking only half a glass and the next day I had a horrific headache. I had a hangover; a "half-glass" hangover. The second time, the same thing happened—strong reactions to a half-glass of red wine. My body was making clear that it did not want any alcohol. With that level of body wisdom and support, it was easy to give up alcohol.

In 2008, to celebrate my daughter Bri and her two college roommates' 21st birthdays—they all turned 21 in January—their moms traveled to the University of North Carolina at Wilmington to join them and their friends for a night on the town.

One of the parents rented a limo; we were ready for a fun ladies' night out. My daughter, knowing I didn't drink, said, "Mom, you *are* going to drink for my 21st birthday, aren't you?" I replied, "No, babe. You know I don't drink anymore." She quickly suggested, "Just tell your body not to absorb it." She does listen. She was reminding me of what I had told her! Then, rethinking it, I said, "Sure, I'll have a few drinks and affirm I'm only absorbing what is for my highest good."

So, that night I bathed my taste buds with Bailey's Irish Cream and Butterscotch Schnapps. The ten of us celebrated life with so much fun and laughter while riding in the limo and dancing at different bars. Bri had to pull me away from the dance floor so we could move on to another bar. Being practical, I said, "Why leave here when we're having fun?"

We partied late into the night. I guess I didn't embarrass my daughter too much because when I told the group we should do this again in six months, she commented to do it every month. That night, actually it was four o'clock in the morning I remember thinking that monthly wasn't in the cards for me. Before falling asleep I affirmed that I would wake up feeling great and rejuvenated. And, I did, with no symptoms of a hangover.

Your body knows what it needs to move to its next level of health. It will be obvious. In the summer of 2008, I "just happened" to attend a vegan raw food class. We watched, learned and sampled.

Vegan raw food consists of fruits, vegetables, nuts, seeds, and legumes. Don't make a face yet. Raw food is "cooked" in a dehydrator, one with a temperature dial, at temperatures below 112 degrees Fahrenheit (feels warm to the touch) which keeps the nutrient value intact; at temperatures above 117 degrees all enzymes and many vitamins are destroyed. (Digestion and all other bodily and cellular functions need enzymes to do their work.) It was refreshing to eat food prepared this way—"spaghetti" was actually fresh organic zucchini shaved thin by a tool called a spiralizer. Savory flax seed and vegetable crackers—yummy—were dipped in hummus or onion dip, both made from wholesome ingredients including chick peas, cashews, onions and herbs.

We were also shown how a wide variety of fruits and vegetables could be combined to make sweet and tasty breakfast smoothies. I was intrigued and decided that I would integrate some of these recipes into my diet that year. I bought my Vita-Mix, a super-duper blender that can crush rocks. Well, almost!

At that time, my old habits were stronger than my new intentions. Two months passed and I still hadn't prepared food any differently. I finally read Alissa Cohen's raw food book, *Living on Live Food.* I had ordered it a month earlier and for "some reason" hadn't received it. It was now September and the book finally showed up in my mailbox.

I remember the day clearly; it was a Wednesday and, unusual for me, I was exhausted and decided to go to bed at nine o'clock. I convinced myself to read my new book for just a half hour. Much to my surprise, I read for three hours—until midnight. And during that time, a deeper awareness arose within me. The "I" of my infinite inner wisdom knew I would be eating 100% vegan raw the next day. The other I, Suzette, even asked, "Are you sure? I love my chocolate!"

My inner wisdom gave me the very clear guidance that I needed and has supported me every step of the way. It seems the Universe must have delayed my copy of *Living on Live Food* until I was ready to make the shift and got me tired enough to get to bed early to read.

It was the second day on my raw food diet when I met three friends for lunch to celebrate two of our birthdays. We met at one of our favorite restaurants, Parizade in downtown Durham, North Carolina. On earlier occasions, I had always ordered a salad and then would enjoy one of their decadent desserts. For birthday celebrations, the pastry chef arranges different desserts on one decorative plate for those at the table to share. We were presented with Black Velvet Praline Torte, Tiramisu and two other chocolate desserts. It all looked so beautiful. And, a new experience for me, I realized I could enjoy just the beauty of it. "I" didn't want even a bite! This was amazing because I love chocolate and desserts. My body *was* supporting me. It was an easy decision; it just felt right.

Totally unlike me, I went easily without chocolate for a month. I was then pleasantly surprised to learn I didn't have to give up chocolate. I discovered that I could use raw cacao to make delicious chocolate bars and mousse.

Regular cocoa is from cacao beans, yet is highly processed, stripping the cacao of its naturally high nutritional value. On the other hand, raw cacao is processed in a minimal way with low heat to preserve all its nutrients. Cacao, loaded with antioxidants, minerals and vitamins, is actually one of our planet's super foods. Oh, that was music to my ears!

The first half of *Living on Live Food* is inspiring information on nutrition, health, how to incorporate raw into your life, and menu planning, and also contains testimonials — all inviting you to partake of the health-enhancing benefits of vegan raw eating. Most of the testimonials and the Q & A address the many questions, concerns and possible road blocks of going raw.

The second half of the book has tasty, easy–to-follow recipes. I followed Alissa's suggestion to begin my raw regimen with her two-week program — a step-by-step menu guide complete with shopping lists and recipes. This allowed me discipline, focus and to step into this new way of eating with her help.

That was 2008, over three years ago, and eating raw has become a way of life for me. I thoroughly enjoy eating 99% vegan raw. My transition to raw was easier because I had already eliminated all meat, most dairy, caffeine, soda and alcohol from my diet and had participated in healthy detox programs on a regular basis. The detox programs help purge toxins which have been accumulating in the body for years and directly affecting the immune system, brain function, energy level, libido, and aging process.

At my website there is also information about a detox powder that "holds the toxins harmless" as they are moved safely out of your body. This is important to note. Too often, detox products flush the toxins back into the blood stream, wreaking even more havoc on your system.

As healthy as my old diet was, I require less sleep with raw eating. I still enjoy tasty desserts, just raw vegan choices. My favorites are chocolate mousse, chocolate chip cookies (made from cashew flour), carrot cake, and blueberry pie. They all have amazing flavors and textures and every one of them is made from wholesome raw ingredients with all nutrients remaining intact. With raw desserts, I can even enjoy pie for breakfast! I lost 10 pounds in the first two months of going raw—the only change in my routine was the vegan raw diet. Besides improving health, this diet has helped many people lose weight and keep it off, something they were unable to do with their previous attempts at dieting. If weight is a concern, just watch the intake of the nuts and other healthy fats like raw coconut.

Generally, I recommend people begin by simply adding some raw food to their day—either an extra salad, more fruit and cut-up pieces of raw carrots, cucumbers, peppers or zucchini. Incremental changes are powerful. If you feel guided, then read *Living on Live Food* or another book. You'll know if integrating raw cuisine is for you.

There is a wealth of research promoting a whole food diet, especially one that encourages less meat and dairy (ideally, no meat or dairy).

Another book I recommend is Chris Johnson's *On Target Living—Nutrition*. I heard Chris speak at a business function. His book is loaded with accurate, easy-to-understand information about whole foods. Chris raises your awareness while guiding you to integrate healthier foods into your present way of eating. His book includes exercises, recipes and a food-target pull-out guide to help you easily choose healthier carbs, proteins and fats. For your convenience, at www.CallingBackYourPower.com/URL there is a link to On Target Living and URLs for other people and products I mention.

Every *body* has different needs. Make small, consistent changes that feel comfortable to you. When your body knows it can trust you to take care of it, it will reward you by making further changes happen easily. For example, you will have less cravings for unhealthy foods, simply losing your taste for them. Making incremental dietary changes can be a great bridge to healthier habits. Experiment—you will find your own perfect way to health.

High quality whole foods are the high-octane fuel your precious body deserves.

Chapter 19
Heal Cancer Holistically

We are not victims of our genes, but masters of our fate, able to
create lives overflowing with peace, happiness and love.
– Bruce Lipton, PhD.

Your health is directly affected by your thoughts, emotions, and beliefs, making you one powerful person! When you truly embrace your power in regard to your health problems, no matter the severity, you can put yourself in a position of empowerment. You never again need to be at the mercy of a diagnosis.

Without this awareness, a cancer diagnosis can bring up fearful thoughts—the ones that normally race through people's minds—of chemo, pain, nausea, hair loss and the possibility of dying. Awareness can transmute fear and reveal healthy options.

I invite you to guide your body back to health through natural, life-affirming and health-enhancing avenues. As you read my client stories of cancer recovery, know that this is possible for anyone. Without the debilitating energy of fear, you can cure cancer from within. (Though, as mentioned earlier, there are no promises because of each client's personal factors.) Your health can be regained without surgery or without adding the excessive toxicity of chemotherapy and radiation to your system. As you look at all your options, you will know the avenue that feels best to you.

Doctors recognize the extreme toxicity of chemo-therapy and radiation. Yet, they still use these conventional treatments to kill the cancer cells at all costs. These toxic treatments cause terrible harm to the immune system, liver, heart, kidneys and brain.

Cancer suppresses the immune system and on-going prescribed treatments of toxins block the body's natural healing ability. In medical school, doctors learn a very drug-intensive style of medicine, treating the symptoms and not the cause. As a result, most doctors still think inside the box concerning cancer.

Be your own best health advocate; do not wait for traditional medicine to change. The available holistic research and results are astounding.

Every client's situation, background, limiting beliefs, fears, emotional blocks and diet are unique. The response we get during healing sessions depends not only on the client's ability to allow the energy in but on their willingness to change their belief systems and allow buried emotions to surface and clear.

Each person considering alternative treatment benefits from checking in on their fear level regarding stepping outside of the traditional medicine paradigm. There is a wealth of research from around the world on holistic healing results as well as what I can personally share from my own clients' results. As people learn to trust in the signs they are receiving from their infinite, intelligent guidance system, they expand their options and can choose the treatment that is for their highest good.

If you are interested, but unsure, in contemplating energy healing for cancer treatment then find a comfortable bridge between holistic healing and traditional treatment.

I encourage you to consult with your oncologist and get the furthest date out with which he is comfortable in setting for a recheck. Then, do energy healing and life coaching sessions one to three times a week, depending on the severity of the diagnosis.

If the cancer is stage III or IV and your doctor wants to see you again in two weeks, then I suggest you do three sessions a week and get on a vegan raw diet immediately. (Switching quickly to a vegan raw diet can cause detoxifying effects—flu-like symptoms and diarrhea. Detoxifying this quickly moves the toxins out quicker, which is good, but sometimes at a cost of being sick for the first few days. With energy healing, your body will adjust easier to the raw diet, generally with no ill effects.)

Then, before you have chemotherapy or radiation treatments, insist on being retested. Expect the results to show considerable improvement. With these improved results, let your doctor know what you are doing and then request more time to continue your energy healing regimen.

Most oncologists are not open to this natural and effective treatment and will encourage you to follow their protocol—surgery, chemotherapy or radiation—anyway. Trust your intuition here and ask God to guide you for your highest good. If you feel guided, seek out a second opinion or switch to an oncologist who is open to treating the whole body. Remember, you must feel comfortable that you and your doctor are in alignment regarding your treatment.

If your cancer is stage I or II, ask for six weeks before being rechecked. In that time or whatever amount of time your doctor is comfortable with, schedule as many energy healing sessions as you can afford. With the right approach, weekly sessions should be fine. Between our sessions, my clients have daily homework to continue clearing their blocks. Clients differ in their willingness to look at and let go of their blocks but with quality work between the client and practitioner, four weeks can be enough time to heal cancer. Again, your test results should show considerable improvement or, as in my client Amy's story below, hopefully your tests will show no cancer cells present at all.

The body, when given a healthy inner and outer environment, stays healthy or knows how to heal. Cancer is feedback that your body systems are unbalanced, unhealthy; or that you still have blocked emotions. Your immune system and inner healing mechanisms will naturally shift into healing mode as you choose health-enhancing ways to get your body back into balance. A holistic practitioner guides you to rebalance your body and environment by addressing stuffed emotions, diet and lifestyle.

Many people have never considered the fact that the body has the ability to heal naturally.

You see this healing process in nature. For example, in time the forest rebalances itself after a fire. You see this with your body, too. Most obvious are its simplest forms—when you heal from a cut, or get a fever to kill off a virus or bacteria, or you throw up to release toxins. And, of course, the human body responds beautifully to the power of the mind and to naturally grown foods and herbs—all things that are easily available.

As you consider other options besides chemotherapy and radiation, consider the spiritual perspective as well. Ask yourself, "Would my Divine Creator—infinite in its wisdom— create a body that couldn't rebalance and heal itself using what is healthy and easily available?"

Cancer Cells and Simple Sugars

Your body needs glucose, simple sugar, for energy; thus, sugar feeds every cell in your body. Your body can make the sugar it needs from sources such as protein and fat. For overall health it is best to avoid refined sugars. But it is even more important to avoid refined sugars if you have cancer. Cancer cells consume many times more sugar than normal cells. The excess of refined sugar in many folks' diets allows cancer cells to constantly grow.

When you eat a lot of refined sugar your body produces a lot of insulin. Insulin can accelerate cell growth, which is a good thing for healthy cells and not so good for cancer cells. By eating processed and refined sugars you are unnecessarily contributing to cancer cell growth.

Healing Cancer from the Inside Out

My client Amy told me during our first appointment that two years earlier she had been diagnosed with Hodgkin's disease. This is a type of lymphoma, a cancer that develops from the cells in the lymph system. At that time, even though her preference would have been alternative therapies, she was too sick to research any alternative options and chose traditional Western medicine's recommendation of chemotherapy for her treatment.

Now, two years later, after a suspicious ultrasound, Amy's doctor ordered a biopsy. The diagnosis was endometrial cancer, and she was referred to a reproductive oncology specialist; her appointment was scheduled for a month later.

In the interim she came to me for five sessions of energy and sound healing and life coaching. She also improved her already healthy diet with dietary supplements and practiced the positive imagery exercises and affirmations that I suggested. Amy was well aware of the body, mind and spirit perspective and, even though she didn't want to open that "can of worms," she knew the importance of looking at her emotional blocks. She was ready to acknowledge and feel her buried emotional hurts and disappointments.

Louise Hay's book *Heal Your Body* is a great resource for pinpointing the emotions associated with specific health issues. The book also gives an affirmation for each concern which you can use to reprogram your cellular memory.

Remember, everything is energy. Each of your thoughts and emotions has a specific vibration and each organ and body part has its own vibration, too. A fear-based or debilitating thought will energetically affect the body part which has the same vibration. I have found *Heal Your Body* to be a great place to start in helping clients address their undealt-with emotions; my clients are quite surprised when they discover that Hay's probable causes for their health issues are "right on."

I read Amy the probable causes related to cancer and also to endometriosis which affects the same lining that her cancer had affected. For cancer the probable causes were "Deep hurt; longstanding resentment; deep secret or grief eating away at the self; carrying hatreds, and 'What's the use?'" And for endometriosis the probable causes were "Insecurity, disappointment and frustration, replacing self-love with sugar, blamers."

Amy's cancer was in the second chakra. The concerns to address while clearing blocks associated with the second chakra can be one or several of the following: blame and guilt; money and sex; power and control; creativity; and ethics and honor in relationships.

Amy related to several of these. First, she admitted to having lived with disappointment and frustration regarding her relationship with her parents. As we probed into that relationship, Amy said she had never felt wanted: she was not abused but she had never felt safe with them. She had never received praise for doing things well and was never encouraged to try new things or to set goals.

At the time of our sessions, Amy was just getting by financially. Also, she had a creative streak but seldom acted on it to bring an idea to completion—her creativity, a healthy outlet for blocked energy, was not being honored. And for years, she had nursed an aching heart because she was unable to be with her true love. She felt powerless in several areas of her life.

The life coaching part of our sessions helped her acknowledge and name these hurts. She worked at seeing her parents from a different perspective. Even though they weren't able to meet her emotional needs, they were doing the best they were emotionally equipped to do—considering their own upbringing and undealt-with emotions.

Once Amy and I set an intention for healing and she was willing to face and release her painful emotions, I energetically directed Divine Light and healing energy to her, thanking Spirit that she was receiving for her highest good. I focused on who she really was—a spiritual being who, on a higher dimension, was already whole, healthy and perfect. I gave no attention to the cancer that was expressing through her three- dimensional physical body. As I held that unwavering belief in consciousness in oneness with the spiritual doctors and ascended masters who worked with me, her blocked energy dissolved. Her symptoms went away.

While processing and releasing the emotions that had been dammed up for years, Amy let out heaving sobs. Her heavy crying spells were emotionally tiring, and yet so freeing. Throughout the healing process, she released a great deal of emotional pain.

At her appointment with the reproductive oncologist she requested a second biopsy which came back with "no ab-normal cells"—in other words, no cancer. Her work had paid off. Not trusting the result, the oncologist scheduled a D and C to check the tissue and, again, no cancer cells were found. An ultrasound one year later also confirmed the presence of healthy cells.

You do not catch cancer; you set up an environment for it emotionally and physically. Our job is to re-establish a healthy environment. When you no longer feed the cancer cells emotionally or with poor dietary choices, the body can do what it is designed to do—heal itself. Great job, Amy!

Stage IV Cancer—Healing at any Stage

79-year-old Chuck is another client who is a great example of how the body can respond, seemly, against all odds, when we approach wellness from the mind, body and spirit perspective. He had stage IV lung cancer that had metastasized to his lymph nodes and adrenals. The doctors stopped his radiation treatments after two weeks because they interfered with his breathing. Also, during that time, he had a heart attack. Due to his breathing issues and to the severity of his heart disease, he left a prestigious cancer treatment center; there were no traditional cancer treatment options available to him. He was growing extremely weak and then his family contacted me.

Our first appointment was a family meeting during which I shared with them my energy healing, life coaching and spiritual approach. I honestly shared with Chuck, "All is in Divine order; trust that whatever happens is for your highest good. If it's your time to return to God, then—as part of your destiny path—you will." I continued, "Regardless of how much time you have left on earth, our sessions help clear the emotional blocks you have been holding on to all of your life. This is the work your soul came here to do—to clear those blocks. As a result you will spiritually and energetically move to a higher vibration. And, if it's not your time to transition, the repatterning of your energy field will cause the cancer symptoms to go away and you'll enjoy more of life!"

One of his daughters had told me that Chuck had always stuffed his emotional pain. At our first private session, he learned that everything is energy and unexpressed negative feelings create blocked energy and that blocked energy greatly contributes toward cancer (or any disease).

It was obvious to me that his angels and spiritual guides were assisting him because he immediately felt safe and was willing to get the emotional baggage he had carried all his life off his chest. He quickly admitted that as a young boy and then continually throughout his 23-year military career and his 20-year business career, he had held on to major feelings of anger and resentment.

I sensed that these emotions, because of their intensity and longevity, were two life themes that he came here to heal; by addressing them he would be doing his soul work and with sufficient shifting he'd return to health.

He briefly told me of the key players in his life that had disappointed him. I helped him see these people and his anger and resentment toward them from the perspective of their unresolved pain being projected onto him. I helped him release taking it so personal. He resonated with this and could feel the emotional shift—he was doing the emotional journey, he was dissolving the blocks.

With prayer I energetically set the intention for the healing. Then we would talk as I directed energy into his chest area. Blocks associated with anger and resentment reside there—affecting the lungs, heart and breasts, and he "just happened" to have lung and heart issues.

To make things even worse he was exposed to Agent Orange in each of two Vietnam tours. Thanks, Chuck, for being such a committed military man. In 1976 he quit a twenty five-year habit of smoking 2-3 packs of cigarettes a day.

He had been a non-smoker for thirty-two years when he was diagnosed with lung cancer. As damaging as cancer is, the body is pure energy and the damage can generally be reversed.

Because I'm here to help my clients embrace all aspects of their life journey, I find it best to address health issues spiritually, emotionally and physically through the healing of

God-force energy, emotional purging and feeding the body at the cellular level with high quality nutrition.

The more severe the diagnosis, the more strict I recommend the diet to be; as close to vegan-raw as possible. Again, the energy healings reduce or eliminate any discomfort normally experienced with a drastic change in diet. Chuck wasn't happy about changing his way of eating, but he was a trooper. Sugar feeds cancer cells and because his cancer was Stage IV, it was critical for him to eliminate sugar, including most fruits. I assured him that we would add some of his favorite fruits back in as he felt better.

He had 2 or 3 sessions a week. He immediately had more energy and could walk further before tiring. With each successive session, he was feeling better.

Within 3½ weeks, during his waking hours, he was off the oxygen mist he had used continuously. His doctor felt more comfortable having him sleep with it, so he did.

Also, the severe arthritis in his hands went away and he got off his blood pressure medicine. Though we didn't directly focus on his hands or blood pressure, they improved because those areas are also related to the energy center of the heart and lung area. And, energy healing balances the whole body, not just where we focus.

My intention with my clients is always for their highest good and to allow the energy, with its own divine consciousness, to balance the client as needed. In oneness with Spirit, we dissolve the energetic and physical density that is present.

Chuck's doctors couldn't believe how great he looked and how wonderful he felt. Unfortunately, most doctors observing results like Chuck's never delve into the how behind the healing, but, fortunately, they accept that something good is happening and often say, "Just keep doing what you are doing."

Chuck had dearly wanted to attend his Marine Corp Combat Engineer Association reunion, four busy days of socializing and Marine Corp events held in California. Before we started working together he was too weak and knew he couldn't travel cross-country. His doctors had felt it was an impossible dream, too far out of reach for him and so he had let go of that hope. With our sessions his health improved considerably and he got some great news—his doctors approved the trip!

Following his trip to California, his family and I noticed something had shifted; he no longer focused on his daily health routine and didn't care to meet with me as suggested. He started regressing.

Upon my probing into what had changed, he finally answered, "I don't believe a 79-year-old man can heal from cancer." I responded: "Weren't you 79 when you got your great healing results and went to California?" He realized I had a good point. Yet, his *belief* and *will* certainly had shifted. And, remember, your thoughts are energy and either allow or block the flow of life force through your body. He continued regressing and a few weeks later transitioned back to God with the love of his family at his side.

Even though Chuck died, his sessions allowed for great soul growth. Having done significant work at the end of his life—releasing his anger and resentment—he literally went back to God at a much higher consciousness and as a much freer soul. Spiritually, transitioning—dying a physical death—is actually the ultimate healing. He shed the physical shell, the temple that housed his soul; and his soul went back to pure Love and Light—vibrant and whole once again.

The healing sessions also allowed him to live past the date that, upon his death, would secure full pension benefits for his wife of fifty years. To ensure that his wife received benefits from the Survivor Benefit Program, Chuck had to meet two criteria: contribute for 360 months and live past October 1, 2008. Chuck narrowly met both of these conditions;

he contributed for 361 months and he died on November 18, 2008.

He also lived long enough to see Congress pass a law that presumed that several very serious medical conditions suffered by Vietnam veterans were caused by exposure to Agent Orange. Lung cancer was one of these conditions. Once the proper paper work was filed, the veteran would be granted up to 100% disability. Chuck was able to apply for this benefit a few weeks before his death.

What relief he must have felt—these benefits would leave his wife financially secure. His financial worries were behind him and he attended his Marine Corp reunion, two milestones that brought joy to his heart and comfort to his soul.

From the onset, I had encouraged his family to pray for his highest good. We can not know the highest good for another person and desperately praying for Chuck to live may not have been for his soul's highest good.

I was so proud of Chuck. He stepped outside his comfort zone and did his emotional work. As he noticed the improvement he was making, I asked him if he would have considered energy healing several months earlier—before traditional medicine could no longer help him. Good naturedly, he admitted, "No, not at all." Thankfully, he was open to energy healing when he had no other options.

Integrating Cancer Treatment with Visualization

For those whose who are comfortable using the power of the mind along with traditional or alternative cancer treatment, the following example demonstrates the impact that visualization has on healing. It is from the research of Stephanie Matthews-Simonton, O. Carl Simonton, MD., and James L. Creighton, authors of *Getting Well Again*. They welcome you to peruse their website. For your convenience www.CallingBackYourPower.com/URL is a webpage with the URLs for this website and the others I mention.

"A 61-year-old man we'll call Frank was diagnosed as having an almost always fatal form of throat cancer and told he had less than a 5% chance of surviving. His weight had dropped from 130 to 98 pounds. He was extremely weak, could barely swallow his own saliva, and was having trouble breathing. Indeed, his doctors had debated whether to give him radiation therapy at all because there was a distinct possibility the treatment would only add to his discomfort without significantly increasing his chances for survival. They decided to proceed anyway.

"Then, to Frank's great good fortune, Dr. O. Carl Simonton, a radiation oncologist and medical director of the Cancer Counseling and Research Center in Dallas, Texas, was asked to participate in his treatment. Simonton suggested that Frank himself could influence the course of his own disease. Simonton then taught Frank a number of relaxation and mental-imagery techniques he and his colleagues had developed. From that point on, and for 3 times a day, Frank pictured the radiation he received as consisting of millions of tiny bullets of energy bombarding his cells. He also visualized his cancer cells as weaker and more confused than his normal cells, and thus unable to repair the damage they suffered. Then he visualized his body's white blood cells, the soldiers of the immune system, swarming over the dead and dying cancer cells, and carrying them to his liver and kidneys to be flushed our of his body.

"The results were dramatic and far exceeded what usually happened in such cases when patients were treated solely with radiation. The radiation treatments worked like magic. Frank experienced almost none of the negative side effects of damage to skin and mucous membranes that normally accompanied such therapy. He regained his lost weight and his strength, and in a mere two months all signs of his cancer had vanished. Simonton believes Frank's remarkable recovery was due in large part to his daily regimen of visualization exercises.

"In a follow-up study, Simonton and his colleagues taught their mental-imagery techniques to 159 patients with cancers considered medically incurable. The expected survival time for such a patient is 12 months. Four years later 63 of the patients were still alive. Of those, 14 showed no evidence of disease, the cancers were regressing in 12, and in 17 the disease was stable. The average survival time of the group as a whole was 24.4 months, over twice as long as the national norm." (Comment from Suzette: These numbers are great feedback as to what is possible. Yet they vary greatly due to the degree each individual was able to take a serious role in his own healing and the level of his beliefs regarding the power of the mind.)

Psychologist Jeanne Achterberg, director of research and rehabilitation science at the University of Texas Health Science Center in Dallas, Texas, is one of the scientists who helped develop the imagery (visualization) techniques that Simonton uses.

In the June 1988 issue of the ASPR Newsletter, p. 20, Achterberg states that she found the physiological effects produced through the use of imagery to be not only powerful, but also to be extremely specific. For example, the term white blood cell actually refers to a number of different kinds of cells. In one study, Achterberg decided to see if she could train individuals to increase the number of only one particular type of white blood cell in their body. To do this she taught one group of college students how to image a cell known as a neutronphil, the major constituent of the white blood cell population. She trained a second group to image T-cells, a more specialized kind of white blood cell. At the end of the study the group that learned the neutrophil imagery had a significant increase in the number of neutrophils in their body, but no change in the number of T-cells. The group that learned to image T-cells had a significant increase in the number of T-cells, but the number of neutrophils in their body remained the same.

She says that belief is also critical to a person's health. She feels that even a person with a common cold should recruit as many images (what she calls neural holograms) as possible, such as images of well-being and harmony, and images of specific immune function being activated. She feels we must also exorcise any beliefs and images that have negative consequences for our health.

Children and Cancer

No one likes to suffer or watch others suffer, especially children. People can get quite angry at God as they watch a loving person or child suffer. I invite you to feel your pain and try to see suffering from a higher perspective.

I like Ekhart Tolle's spiritual explanation of suffering in *A New Earth*. "Suffering has a noble purpose: the evolution of consciousness and the burning up of the ego. As long as you resist suffering, it is a slow process because the resistance creates more ego to burn up. When you accept suffering, however, there is an acceleration of that process which is brought about by the fact that you suffer consciously. You can accept suffering for yourself, or you can accept it for someone else, such as your child or parent. In the midst of conscious suffering, there is already the transmutation. The fire of suffering becomes the light of consciousness."

Remember, from a spiritual perspective everything has a higher purpose—even a child with a life-threatening illness. With compassion and love, I invite the parents of a child with cancer to reflect on what they could possibly learn from this experience.

On a soul level, the dynamics are often different for a child with cancer than an adult. An adult, through lifestyle choices and undealt-with emotions, has set up the environment to be at risk for cancer. A child usually chooses at the soul level to come forth willing to experience the pain and setbacks of cancer in order to help his family and himself learn valuable life and soul lessons.

People find that understanding suffering and death from a soul perspective helps them process the pain. If a child dies from cancer please consider that, on a soul level, each family member chose to be part of a deep grieving experience. This can pertain to anyone that loses a loved one; yet having your child die can energetically break your heart wide open. And why would a soul need to grieve so deeply? If the parents had lived many lifetimes in a culture or in life situations which prevented them from expressing their grief, the blocked energy of grief would be in their energy field. And each lifetime we choose scenarios that help clear lifetimes of blocked energy. That child's soul, in contemplating another incarnation, may have wanted to help the souls of the parents clear their blocked grief and, therefore, chose, in this incarnation, to have a shorter life.

Whether a child survives the cancer or transitions because of it, there are other lessons one or both parents may have chosen, from the soul perspective, to learn from their trials. For example, they may have needed to learn how to open their hearts more and express painful feelings and emotionally align with each other through a very difficult experience. Or, they may have needed this experience to re-prioritize and appreciate life.

When the family can see their experiences from a higher perspective, it helps them cope from a position of understanding instead of sinking into despair. It seems to help lessen the pain's grip.

Genes—Not the Role You Think They Have in Cancer and Disease

It is all around us; I still hear doctors, renowned experts, on television news programs or health related programs make claims about cancer that look at it from a limited physical aspect and without considering the new research regarding nutrition and genes. This has got to be confusing for the general public. I heard one expert make a claim about lung cancer in those who had never smoked. She commented, that predominately, it's just the genetic cards you were dealt. And if you have lungs you can get cancer.

Ouch, that's hard to hear. But you can relax. You are much more blessed than traditional medicine recognizes. We can respect brilliant scientists and doctors and, at the same time, accept that their opinions are based on their training in Newtonian physics: to focus only on physical matter and that genes control life.

Time and awareness changes each of us, as it did cell biologist Bruce Lipton, PhD. Today he is an internationally recognized authority in bridging science and spirit. In his book *Biology of Belief*, Dr. Lipton tells about his and others' research with the science of epigentics which literally means "control above genes." This research shatters conventional belief that genes control who we are. Dr. Lipton shares, "Epigenetics shows that genes, DNA, do not control our biology. Instead, DNA is controlled by signals from outside the cell. Environmental influences including nutrition, stress and emotions can modify genes without changing their basic blueprint."

This research shows that we can no longer view the human body as a bio-chemical machine controlled by genes. But rather incorporates the role of the mind and cell environment in defining the cell's and thus, the body's state of health.

Dr. Lipton realized, "The premise that genes control life is a major flaw in biology's central dogma. This premise, accepted by traditional medicine, ignores the fact that genes cannot turn themselves on or off; something in the environment has to trigger gene activity." Doctors are letting you off the hook by blaming your genes or the disease.

This breakthrough in biology is vital information regarding all healing for it recognizes that as you change your perception and beliefs you change the messages you send to your cells. This also validates, from a scientific viewpoint, what I have shared—an unhealthy, out-of-balance environment allows disease to take hold. And since you have the power to improve your inner and outer environments you have the power to return to health through non-invasive, health-enhancing avenues.

Breathe in all that power; let it permeate every cell. You are the best health advocate you have. As long as the you are willing to look outside the box for treatment options, be open to what you may not understand, let go of old hurts and make the sometimes necessary radical changes to your diet and lifestyle, you can expect significant improvement— hopefully, a 100% recovery.

If there are loved ones in your life who aren't willing to try holistic healing and you fear they may be in danger of imminent debilitation or death, as difficult as it is, it is important to love them unconditionally with *their* beliefs and comfort levels. Pray that they are open to what they need for their highest good. Then, lovingly get out of the way. You and I grow spiritually when we do not force our will on anyone else, as "right" as it appears to be to us.

If you are facing a cancer diagnosis, while researching your options I recommend you to grant yourself some daily quiet time for affirmations and meditation. You could affirm several times a day, "Thanks, God, that I am getting through this process with ease and gentleness and have loving support from family and friends. I am guided to the best information, treatment, and experiences for my highest good. Reveal to me what this cancer has to teach me."

You may be blessed with love and support of family and friends, great insurance coverage and a savings account. Still, practicing affirmations and meditation will put you into energetic alignment which will then magnify those blessings for your highest good. You'll "just happen" to be given a special book and "something" inside you will say, "I want to read that!" Or, someone will recommend a great doctor or wellness facilitator who *feels* right for you. Or friends will seem to come out of the woodwork and jump through hoops to help you in a myriad of ways—reminding you of what is great in your life.

As they follow their guidance and move forward, people begin to see their stressful world from a new perspective and reprioritize their life. They may trust an inner knowing that it is time to leave their stressful job or marriage, or to follow a dream they had put on the back burner. They realize the silliness of holding on to grudges and they recognize the importance of being grateful for all the goodness that surrounds them.

Usually, new perspectives are the natural result of a cancer diagnosis—the diagnosis can bless you with the force to reevaluate and improve your life. When you can accept any diagnosis as a wake-up call and see it from the onset as a gift, you will be accepting "what is" and allowing the blessings to flow unencumbered.

Stand tall. Heal thyself! You are one amazing person!

Chapter 20
Inspirational Stories of Healing

*Health is a state of complete physical, mental, and social well-being
and not merely the absence of disease and infirmity.*
– World Health Organization

All healing is divinely orchestrated and happens in divine order. Many clients get healing results as they address their emotional blocks and change their diet. On occasion, one can get healing results without these specific changes, possibly to widen his scope of spirituality and deepen his belief in the unseen. A friend's nephew had one such healing.

I visited my girlfriend Valerie and her mom and sisters during a vacation in Maine. I met them at her Mom's lake cottage and Valerie and I drove to nearby Gulf Hagus, the part of the Appalachian trail which is nicknamed the Grand Canyon of Maine, to enjoy a beautiful day hike. After our hike, we returned to the lake cottage, had dinner with Valerie's relatives and then settled in for an evening of relaxing conversation.

We were not consciously aware of it, but Spirit was arranging an eye-opening experience for Valerie's nephew, Jason. He hadn't visited his Grandmother in nine months and the night he finally came to visit "just happened" to be the night I was there. As planned, I started running healing energy on his Mom's aching wrist.

Jason was curious; he had never heard of energy healing. He jokingly said, "I should have you heal my leg." I asked him what was wrong with it. He explained that as the result of a motorcycle accident he had no feeling in the seven inches below his knee and when he touched one spot on his calf, a piercing pain would shoot up his leg. Also, he was unable to rest his buttocks on his heels in a squatting position.

I said, "I have two hands. Come on over. I can place one hand on your Mom's wrist and one hand on your knee." I set my intention and allowed the energy to start flowing through my hands.

I shared with Jason how his body and everything else is energy, moldable by our thoughts and beliefs, and that this energy session along with his and my intentions for healing could bring his body back into balance.

Jason experienced an 80% improvement after forty-five minutes. When he touched his calf there was no shooting pain. He could squat fully so his heels now touched his buttocks, and the numbness below his knee was almost gone. I told him if he wanted a 100% healing, to come back first thing in the morning. He did, this time with his fiancé, and we did another forty-five minute healing session. Jason regained full feeling below his knee. He felt great.

Jason is an example of someone who didn't have to work with his beliefs and emotions to receive a significant healing. I feel Spirit orchestrated this for his highest good, whatever that may be.

Healing From Addiction

The universe can orchestrate a meeting with those who need help in any place, for example, at a nail salon. I enjoy getting a pedicure once a month yet I have no set schedule. One particular day, I had an impulse to go for a pedicure. The timing in my day felt right so I went.

I settled into the massage chair, immersed my feet into

the hot water and relaxed. I noticed a man who was getting a manicure; this is not typical, but my thought was "good for him." I noticed as he walked to the bathroom that he was hunched over and walking very slowly. I said to Spirit, "If it is in our highest good for me to offer my work, have him look directly at me on his way back to his chair." He did and I said hello.

After some chatting, our conversation turned to his back pain. I said to him, "If you are open to what you may not understand, the energy sessions I offer could help you." I suggested he peruse my website to see if he resonated with my work.

I'll call this client Barry. He called me three weeks later and asked if I had ever helped an addict; he was smoking $400-500 of crack-cocaine a day. Barry continued to explain that he had called three of the six drug rehab centers his doctor had recommended when he noticed the paper on which he had written my name and phone number lying in the middle of his living room floor. Unaware that he was probably being nudged by Spirit, he called me.

In response to his question, I said, "No, I've never worked with an addict but your body is just like everyone else's. It is pure energy. And, yes, I can help."

I arranged time in my schedule to see him that day. Barry told me he had been a crack addict for 20 years. His use had become excessive during the previous five years after he inherited a sizable monthly income from his father's estate. He had spent $15,000 on crack in the previous month; one binge alone cost $2500.

Due to his addiction, his nervous system was fried; he jerked his head and body continuously and smacked his lips often. His mind and body were extremely unstable. My intuition told me to see Barry twice a day for the first three days, then daily for the next seven. After that we met two to three times a week for six weeks and then weekly.

Barry's healing is one of my favorite examples of the human body's ability to rebalance even though he previously knew nothing about energy healing. Once the sessions commenced, he gave up crack cocaine and alcohol and, a few days later, cigarettes. He had *no* withdrawal symptoms. This is significant; most people can't even give up coffee without experiencing headaches.

Here is his testimonial and following it is my update:

"Suzette Foster saved my life. For six months in 2008 my smoking crack had progressed from out-of-control proportions to a 500-dollar-a-day habit, burning through financial savings. In fear of dying, I called Suzette whom I had coincidentally met a couple of weeks earlier. Even though I had seriously wanted to quit many times, this time I felt something shift throughout my body, a feeling I had never experienced with any other detox treatment.

"Amazing changes happened immediately; on day one, I completely stopped using drugs and alcohol! Realize that for 20+ years I had steadily smoked crack, cocaine and meth. I also smoked cigarettes, drank beer and vodka and then coffee to try and maintain the appearance of a normal life. I was very sick emotionally and physically. I was burning the candle at both ends. Until 5 years ago, I held down a job. During my years of drug addiction I have attended multiple drug treatment programs and have failed to even put a dent in my using. I was obviously ignoring the dangers and taking great risks with my life.

"Then, 3 days after starting sessions with Suzette, I cut out nicotine completely. My shift proved significant when my drug dealer showed up at my house two days into this treatment with great looking cocaine. I even smelled it. I could *feel* the difference of my new conviction; I told him no, and meant it. I had no second thoughts. The release of my addiction, amazingly, felt complete. To understand the importance of this, know that in the past, even after a 4-month in-house treatment program, I would go right back to using.

"A step further and three weeks into treatment with my life really looking up, I had the mental and physiological strength to also cut out all caffeinated beverages. I had a few setbacks with coffee but overall did well.

"Today, 6 weeks later, I remain free of all four of those destructive substances. My life has changed dramatically and I feel great! I hadn't heard of energy healing before, but it definitely works. Today I feel safe from drugs, I am getting to know myself, and I am confidently planning a future without the influence of these harmful drugs. Experts and former drug users like me know that an addict generally cannot stop by himself. Sadly, so many end up dying. Suzette Foster provided a life-saving option, allowing me to see my life with respect to my body, soul journey, and the Universe. Change felt easy and complete."

It was certainly exciting to be part of Barry's amazing turnaround. Two weeks into his sessions, his nervous system was responding; his tics and mouth smacking were barely noticeable.

To transition Barry into eating more nutritiously, I encouraged him to take supplements and make fruit and vegetable smoothies for breakfast—which he did sporadically. To help him integrate into the real world, I encouraged him to set goals and create a budget to track his spending. I suggested that he volunteer weekly and take a class at the community college.

Barry was feeling great and even though he saw the value in those suggestions, cleaning and organizing his home became his priority along with meeting new friends. And he wanted to date.

I encouraged him to meet people and do group activities through meet.up.com but I advised against dating. I shared with him the importance of significantly healing emotionally before adding the dynamics of a relationship to the mix. Against my advice, Barry convinced himself that dating without becoming intimate would be a happy medium.

Two months into our weekly sessions and also against my recommendation, Barry stopped the sessions. He felt healthy and didn't want to be "dependent" on them. He stayed clean another two months; a noteworthy four months of not using.

He was traveling out of state and realized his girlfriend was avoiding telephone or email contact with him. Barry and I talked by phone that week and I encouraged him to have a distance healing to strengthen emotionally. He was unhappy about his situation but felt strong enough to handle it and refused any help. On his way home, Barry called from the airport and told me he was hoping he would find an email message from his girlfriend to give him closure. He arrived home at midnight. There was no email. There was no phone message. He felt abandoned. He couldn't handle the disappointment. Instead of calling me, he called his dealer.

Barry called me the next day after his binge and admitted he had smoked $1000 worth of crack. He came in for an emergency appointment.

Due to the way he holds his body as he smokes, he arrived totally hunched over and experiencing a lot of back pain. I was certainly disappointed, yet I knew that healing any illness is a process. I focused on the positive. He had at least given his brain, internal organs and nervous system four drug free months. And I know that each stretch of being clean gets an addict closer to eventually staying clean.

This was his last session I had with me. Barry lived in a different state than his family and had kept the severity of his drug use and our sessions from them. Because of this setback, a friend contacted his family who arranged for him to attend a long-term program.

I am happy to report that, after a few more setbacks, Barry has managed to stay clean for over two years. He has moved back to his hometown and is now enjoying family relationships from a healthier perspective.

This is a beautiful story of how our bodies can return to health differently than we've ever been taught or thought possible.

Body, Heal Thyself

With support, the body knows how to heal itself whether the problem is minor or serious. One client came monthly for life coaching and energy healing to deepen her ability to call back her power. Toward the end of one session, she mentioned that a skin tag under her left arm was very sore as it rubbed against her clothing.

She had a dermatologist appointment the following week to have it removed. I directed energy to that area for the remaining fifteen minutes. She could feel heat and soon the discomfort went away. (Heat or coolness is often felt during energy healing.)

She later called with an update. The skin tag had turned black over the next two days and then fell off. She got to cancel her appointment with the doctor.

The human body, with the right environment, can heal itself. Yet, when people are faced with serious health issues, programming can get in the way.

The willingness to shift old programming and make changes differs from person to person but ultimately affects one's receptivity to healing energy and life coaching.

Part of the healing facilitator's role is to help clients see that they are energetic beings with infinite innate wisdom and powerful potential. But their beliefs about their inner power have been honed by the experiences of many lifetimes; consequently, many still believe they must look for answers outside of themselves.

I've learned to respect and honor the fact that my clients are shifting their beliefs in their perfect timing—not mine. So, until their beliefs sufficiently change, they may not experience the complete healing available from the energy sessions.

Distance Healing

Energetic healing has no boundaries. Much of the healing work I do is with clients who live in other parts of the country. Healing is possible even though the client and healing facilitator are in two different locations, sometimes continents apart. In the non-physical world of Spirit, healing is not limited by time or space.

Try not to overanalyze this. Until you see the body as energy, distance healing may seem strange or impossible. It may be hard to wrap your head around the idea of distance healing because you have been taught to view your world from the limited perspective of the third dimension—which is only one aspect of your multi-dimensionality.

Distance healing taps into the non-physical, infinite consciousness that pervades all things; as does prayer. There are a number of scientific studies that have demonstrated the effects of the healing power of prayer. Both prayer and distance healing are intentional connections with the powerful organizing intelligence many of us call God, Spirit or the Universe.

If distance healing feels "too out there" for you, read the following client stories or my website testimonials with an open mind. If it is still confusing, just put this concept on a shelf. You'll revisit it if and when it feels right.

Some clients get dramatic shifting of their pain or health condition during the 5-15 minute phone conversation to schedule their appointment. They are connecting to my field of consciousness and getting results even with no conscious intention on my part to do healing at that time. I invite you to be open to the amazing being that you are, even if this confuses you.

Distance Healings—While Hiking the Appalachian Trail

My friend Dave hiked the entire 2175 miles of the Appalachian Trail in 2006. This is an extreme physical and mental challenge and only 20% of those setting out to hike the entire trail actually do it. We decided, prior to his leaving, that I would be his personal medic throughout his 6-month excursion.

During that time period he requested three distance healing sessions, and later he told me that each one was a Godsend. When he needed healing, he called and we agreed on the night I would do the distance healing. He would lie in his tent in the wilderness, set an intention to receive the energy I was directing and drift off to sleep.

One session was directed at an old metatarsal injury, one that had given him regular pain for three years. He dealt with this pain for a few weeks until debilitating pain shot through his leg each time his foot hit the ground. He decided it was time to do a distance healing.

Another session dealt with the excruciating knee pain he endured while hiking all day. The knees take a beating with hiking on rocky and hilly terrain ten hours a day, week after week. Dave had seen young and old hikers alike have to quit due to knee problems. Each time, after receiving the healing sessions at bedtime, he awoke feeling great. He was back to normal with no pain.

About two months into his trek, he developed a water sac under the skin of his right knee. Even though it was sore, he was more concerned with its continuous swelling.

He decided, after several days of this, to ask me to do another healing instead of interrupting his trip to go to a hospital to get the fluid drained. The morning after the scheduled healing, the fluid-filled sac persisted. He jokingly told his hiking buddy, "I guess Suzette's touch doesn't work all the time."

He of little faith—I called him that day and apologized;

I had forgotten to do his distance healing. And true to the realm of energy healing, once I did, the large water sac was gone the next morning.

It is now five years later and none of these issues have returned. What makes this even more remarkable is that he is now an ultra runner. Running 50 miles and biking 100 miles a week, for training, he has also run 14 marathons and two 100-mile and two 50-mile endurance races in the last 18 months. You go, Dave!

Whether it is an injury, pain, depression, disease or illness, energy healing and life coaching will help the body to rebalance itself. The symptoms usually go away.

The distance between the healing facilitator and client is irrelevant. A distance healing can be just as effective as an in-person session. I am the same consciousness and have the same intention—that my clients receive for their highest good—whether they are participating distantly or at in-person session. But the client has to believe that distance healing is effective to receive the directed energy fully. Clients get more consistent results when they are meditating or lying down while receiving the distance healing energy. Their stillness allows for deeper integration of the energy that is being transferred.

Avoiding Surgery and Shifting Pain and Disease

My mom, who lives in Maine, is a great example of the success one can have after limited beliefs are released. She participates in my twice monthly life-coaching tele-classes and distance healings, and she reviews her class notes and says her prayers and affirmations each morning and evening. She has even, on her own, experienced the feeling of heat radiating down her spine while she visualized green healing energy flowing there. I was thrilled that she was getting her own feedback—experiencing her body as energy.

Mom was doing the inner journey needed for spiritual expansion. She released layers of blocked energy caused by her emotionally painful experiences with those who had belittled her and disrespected or abandoned her—all feeding her lifelong issue of unworthiness. She gave a voice to her distressing childhood memories and learned to accept and honor the emotions that were rooted in those experiences. She understood that stuffed emotions blocked her from feeling better.

Mom was shifting and clearing layers of emotional blocks; yet, she experienced back pain that would come and go—feedback that there were more layers of emotions or false beliefs to clear. She didn't think she was blocking anything, yet old programming runs deep and her old programming continued to unconsciously hover in the shadows of her belief system.

I complimented her on her daily discipline of prayer, affirmations and deep emotional work. I reminded her that accepting her experiences and healing them was part of her soul journey. I reminded her that people first process information in their head. Introspection and releasing blocks allowed her to get ah-has and move from knowing these teachings in her head to owning them in her heart—to being them, to living them.

She was learning and embracing this new way of being. She was doing her best, but, it was not enough to completely shift the pain. On a subconscious level, it appeared, she didn't feel worthy of receiving a complete healing. But remember, exactly as it was unfolding, this was her divine path. As her healing facilitator, I could not do her soul work for her. As powerful as divine intelligence is, Spirit would not do her soul work for her either.

The back pain became more severe, enough to stop her from her weekly volunteering and attending church. Our healing sessions totally relieved the pain but it would return.

As I've mentioned before, until a client does a sufficient amount of corresponding emotional work, their healing is a combination of their partial clearing and the facilitator's consciousness.

I have always told my mom to call me whenever she needed a session. Not wanting to bother me, she seldom did. One evening, I called to say hi. She was in excruciating pain and admitted feeling she was on the verge of having a nervous breakdown, which she'd had once before in the distant past. I asked her if she'd like me to send her some energy. She agreed to anything that could help.

There we sat, she in Maine and me in North Carolina, as I set the healing intentions and allowed the Divine to work through us for her highest good. In fifteen minutes she felt 100% better—the physical pain and the impending feeling of a nervous breakdown were totally gone. This is what the body is capable of.

Though, later that week, my mother experienced the return of some pain. She believed in me and my work and saw firsthand what I had accomplished in healing my own body. But, I recognized that at some level she didn't totally believe it could happen for her. I reminded her that we are both pure energy and if I can heal from my injury then she can heal from her pain. I told her that the only difference between us is our emotional blocks because they are caused by our unique beliefs and our stuffed emotions.

She couldn't think of any emotions she was still blocking. Yet, something in her belief system had to be blocking her healing. Clearing all the layers of stuffed emotional pain and opening up to new perspectives can take time; healing is a layer-by-layer process.

Her pain continued to worsen. She was diagnosed with Lumbar Spinal Stenosis, which according to www.spinalstenosis.org is the most common indication for surgery for people over 60 years of age. It is a narrowing of the spinal canal and as the space in the canal is reduced, pressure is put on the nerves.

This causes pain to radiate from the lower back to the buttocks and down the legs. Her severe pain was caused by what is called a disc protrusion. The disc, the cushion between the vertebrae, is strained beyond its limits and the jelly-like substance of the disc bulges out and puts pressure on the spinal nerve.

In Mom's case, two discs had ruptured and dried out, pinching the nerve. And, without the cushioning of the discs, the vertebrae were rubbing bone against bone. Excruciating pain now traveled from her lower back to both legs. When she wasn't in severe pain, her back and legs still ached. She couldn't sit comfortably nor find a comfortable position in bed; pillows propped to support her back or placed between her legs didn't help; neither heat nor cold helped; and neither did taking a strong narcotic pain medication four times a day for two months.

She was in too much pain to drive and became mostly homebound. She slept a lot and didn't feel like reading or watching television; nothing interested her. She hired a housekeeper because she couldn't do anything around the house. That was just not like my mom; she was always a caregiver to others and kept her home clean and attractive.

For months we had been unable to identify another block in her belief system. The doctor said she did not need surgery but if she chose to have it, it could relieve the pain in her legs but would not help her back pain.

Then, one day while we were talking, a subconscious belief of hers became obvious to me. She had looked at her MRI in the doctor's office, and, in a self-convincing strong tone, she told me she saw, right there in black and white, how degenerated the vertebrae were. The bones were rubbing against each other.

Giving all this "reality" her power, she emphatically

said, "I saw the bone rubbing on bone. You and I can't fix it." That statement revealed to me the grip of her belief system — that she was only a physical body and energy healing couldn't fix the "bone rubbing on bone." It was a powerful grip indeed.

I wanted my mom to go through as little pain or surgery as possible. I want that for all my clients. And, that said, I've also come to honor that all of us as humans are doing the best we can with our old programming, beliefs and emotional hurts.

Yet, I guess I had more to learn and my mother was my teacher. I had an a-ha moment when I heard her statement. I said, "Mom, bone and discs appear to be hard matter but they, like everything in the universe, are pure energy. Your old programming can't allow the belief that they can be repaired energetically. And, I finally get what your block is. You have an unconscious belief that there's too much damage and your body needs surgery."

This was the block we were looking for. And, it also told me where she was at. I have learned not to argue with what is and honored her by saying, "I totally support the path that feels best to you. Surgery seems to be your answer." I could feel in my heart that I sincerely meant those words. I could feel that my reaction to her comment was also feedback as to how far I have come along my path in accepting others' choices, in spite of what I know is possible. I love Mom unconditionally and I was able to want for her what *she* wanted.

My client experiences taught me not to want a healing for someone else more than they can allow it for themselves. I immediately released the desire I had had for her — a non-surgical outcome. I also accepted that all of our work up to that point had the value it was meant to have. (As I've awakened along my spiritual journey, I've learned to accept that every experience is just that, an experience. I've learned not to judge them as good or bad but to accept them.) I knew I would do whatever she needed, including traveling back to Maine after her surgery to help nurture her back to health—just as she had done for me.

Her surgery was scheduled for two months later. She continued doing her daily prayers and affirmations and remained open to the coaching and healing she received during my tele-classes.

Two weeks after my a-ha moment her pain started diminishing. She continued to feel better. I said, "Mom, this is feedback that you are shifting the blocks." I asked her what was different in her thinking. She said, "I finally get it. If you can do it, so can I! I now feel I am worthy of healing!"

She said she found herself reminiscing about how she helped me during my recovery and about what I had accomplished—relearning how to walk, feed myself, button my blouses and write with a pen. She remembered, as part of my therapy, how I had worked at picking up playing cards, pennies or dried lentils off the table. She had witnessed how I had used my mind before I tried to move my hands or my body. She knew my mind and attitude had played a huge part in my recovery. She was now able to do that for herself.

She said that the words to the Serenity Prayer, which she had repeated for years, now had a deeper meaning for her: God, grant me the serenity to accept the things I cannot change, the courage to change the things I can, and the wisdom to know the difference. An inner shift took place as she went from thinking about what she knew in her head to owning and feeling it in her heart.

She continued to heal, Mom got off all medicine, including the anxiety prescription she had taken for twenty years. She also felt a significant shift toward being more positive.

She happily cancelled her scheduled surgery.

Everything we had discussed seemed to be magically downloading. She owned this wisdom deep in her heart and soul. It has been a year and she continues to be pain free with only a few tinges of discomfort when she overtaxes her back. What a blessing!

Disease, illness and pain show up to give you feedback and an opportunity to shift your limiting beliefs, old habits and unsupportive environment. You can also grow your soul by improving your reactions and being more compassionate when others are dealing with pain and disease. I grew when I accepted that my mother's path included a belief in the need for surgery. I grew when I learned to not make it about me, to not take her decision personally and to love her unconditionally.

She must have been close to grasping these teachings when she shared her limiting comments and got the opportunity to love her unconditionally. On a soul journey level, she was also my teacher. Once I got my lesson, our combined fields of consciousness made it easier for her to get her ah-ha. It was not a coincidence that she downloaded these truths after I accepted her situation. We all influence each other's lives so much more than we think we do.

It is important to recognize that the discs between the vertebra and the pinched nerves didn't improve until my mom changed her belief system and chose more positive thoughts to focus on. From that new belief system, her energy field started to repattern itself and rebalance, first on the energetic level and then on the physical. Note, on occasion, symptoms can go away as a result of changes on the energetic level even though there are is no physical changes. It is possible that an MRI could still show a certain physical problem, even though the client functions normally with no pain. This is another testament to the truth that we are more than a physical body.

As you have seen here, my mother and I needed to change our thoughts before a complete healing could occur. My mother had chipped away at the blocks enough to finally break through the brick wall. We dealt with the cause of the pain—the emotional blocks and her limited beliefs. When we addressed the cause, not the symptoms of her pain, her energy was repatterned to health and the symptoms went away.

When you understand how powerfully creative, and destructive, your thoughts and beliefs can be, you can become more conscious of them and move more easily toward wholeness. My client stories illustrate the inherent power already within you. You are pure energy and repatterning your energy field is a life-affirming, health enhancing avenue to claiming your greatness.

Chapter 21
A New Beginning

The spiritual journey is individual, highly personal. It can't be organized or regulated. It isn't true that everyone should follow one path. Listen to your own truth.
– Ram Dass

We've made it to this point together. I've given you a lot to ponder. And as Ram Dass says, listen to your own truth. Honor what resonates with you and incorporate it into your life. We're in this together and I am passionate about helping you step into the Light—the truth of your Being— and live a more fulfilling and happy life. For starters, I have added to my daily intention list "Blessings for the highest good of all to the readers of *Calling Back Your Power*."

I've said it often in this book, Spirit, we are so cool! I'm happy and excited about you tapping into the energy of more possibilities. At your perfect timing, take this information, utilize it for your highest good and have fun changing your life with it.

I appreciate your willingness to look at life differently, to go a little deeper inside yourself and to remember who you really are. Your true nature is pure energy, pure Spirit and pure potential. And, I appreciate you for being a positive force improving collective consciousness. You are very, very important. Thanks for being you!

Part of being you is enjoying the freedom that is your birthright. You will enjoy more of that freedom as you make feeling good and raising your vibration daily priorities. Your life, in its divine perfection, will still have challenges but for shorter periods of time because you will be more able to transmute or avoid them altogether.

And at those times when you temporarily forget who you really are and find yourself engaging in the chaos and focusing too much on "what is," be gentle on yourself; you are in the process of evolving.

You are reprogramming what you have been taught — to look outside of yourself for the answers and that you are a limited human being. With your renewed passion for a better life you are more apt to notice those feelings that create resistance to your joy, health and success.

Give yourself permission to feel the anger, resentment, blame or whatever else is arising. And realize you dissolve resistance when you can sit with and feel those horrific feelings, allowing them to come up and be cleared out of your energy field.

You also dissolve resistance each time you accept what is and trust the outcome has a higher purpose. Your power is in becoming a divine *observer* of what is and focusing on all the things you are grateful for.

As you change your perspective and beliefs, and improve your thoughts you raise your vibration which makes you a stronger magnet to attract blessings and solutions.

A quote by Albert Einstein speaks to this. "Everything is energy and that's all there is to it. Match the frequency of the reality you want and you cannot help but get that reality. It can be no other way. This is not philosophy. This is physics."

Our souls chose to experience this time of major individual, collective and planetary expansion. Universal energy and time are speeding up and the result is a quickening of the evolution of our consciousness.

Shifts of this magnitude include chaotic times. We may not like them, but we get through them more easily when we see them for what they are—opportunities that can move us to higher awareness. Let any suffering during these trying times be the impetus to transform what no longer serves you and to remind you of who you really are.

Challenges are not fun, but please find comfort in knowing that your soul chose this experience of expansion with its eyes wide open. Your journey is to stay in alignment with joy and gratitude—with Spirit—to the best of your ability. And remember, Spirit has your back and loves to do what it does so well, figure out how to move you through the challenge.

Spirit, transformative divine consciousness, is already within you. I invite you to see God, Spirit as a Presence always being expressed in and through you. Your daily journey is one of remembering the Allness of who you are. You don't have to become anything. Simply embrace this Presence and allow your awareness of it to be awakened more fully. It is yours to nourish as you deepen your belief in it. And as you do, you will naturally experience more peace and happiness.

Let your desire for more love, peace, joy, health, prosperity and soul expansion be the really good reason to jolt yourself out of any limited thinking and conditions and back into an empowering, life-enhancing way of seeing your world. Let your desires propel you forward to a better life. I'm excited because I know you can make the best of this journey.

Congratulations on your commitment to invest your time and deepen your awareness through the energy and wisdom in this book.

To keep the momentum going, it is my pleasure to offer you a parting gift. I invite you to go to my website and download the recording of one of my twice-monthly classes.

Included in this hour of teaching are the energetic shifting qualities of my voice and three Oneness Blessings—laser-like beams of divine Love—to help dissolve fears and limited thinking. You'll find this mp3 at www.suzettefoster.com/gift-mp3.php. After you sign in, please remember to check for another email to actually opt in. The next email will include your mp3. Periodically, I will send notices of other free offers.

I would love to hear from you. Please let your stories inspire others by sharing them on my facebook page, Calling Back Your Power, or at my blog at www.CallingBackYourPower.com

This is the end of this book; the beginning of our tomorrows. My hope is that it has inspired you to dance, with beloved courage, into a new way of Being.

No matter how much or how little you have engaged with your inner power in the past, may you now see your world and experiences from a deeper and more powerful view and trust that you are much more than you might think you are.

May you trust there is a Light at the end of the tunnel. May you remember you are worthy of all that is and it is your birthright to be love, peace, joy and prosperity.

Namaste, dear one. *The divine in me honors the divine in you.*

Continue Your Momentum:

Join Suzette's Tele-Classes/Distance Healings
for a continuation of personal and spiritual transformation
http://suzettefoster.com/sound_healing.php

Signup for Suzette's Monthly Newsletter and
twice weekly Power Reminders at
www.SuzetteFoster.com or www.Choose2Thrive.com

Meet Suzette Online

Blog: CallingBackYourPower.com

Suzette is pleased to share a portion of
the proceeds of this book with:

Habitat for Humanity
and
Saving Grace Animal Rescue

ABOUT THE AUTHOR

The Universe is so cool! Suzette was born with the name Suzette Faith Foster. And now, she fosters people's faith. She feels blessed that her passion is her life's calling–to inspire people to remember who they really are. Besides this book, Cds and mp3s, she shares enthusiastically through life coaching, speaking, tele-classes and facilitating energy healings.

Suzette is a certified Reiki Master, wellness consultant and ordained minister. She has studied with renowned sound healers Tom Kenyon and Jonathan Goldman. Suzette's great appreciation for Mother Earth and the environment has led me to work with the Humpback Whales and Hawaiian Spinner Dolphins. As a mother of two young-adult daughters, she also enjoys yoga, biking, hiking and dancing.